I0119385

Behring Sea Tribunal of Arbitration

Case Presented on the Part of the Government of Her Britannic Majesty to the Tribunal of Arbitration

Volume 1

Behring Sea Tribunal of Arbitration

Case Presented on the Part of the Government of Her Britannic Majesty to the Tribunal of Arbitration
Volume 1

ISBN/EAN: 9783337389840

Printed in Europe, USA, Canada, Australia, Japan

Cover: Foto ©Suzi / pixelio.de

More available books at **www.hansebooks.com**

BEHRING SEA ARBITRATION.

APPENDIX

TO

CASE OF HER MAJESTY'S GOVERNMENT.

VOL. I.

GENERAL TABLE OF CONTENTS.

BEHRING SEA ARBITRATION.

Appendix to Case of Her Majesty's Government.

Vol. I.

UKASE OF SEPTEMBER 4, 1821.

Edict of His Imperial Majesty, Autocrat of All the Russias.

THE directing Senate maketh known unto all men :
Whereas in an Edict of His Imperial Majesty issued to the directing Senate on the 4th day of September, and signed by His Majesty's own hand, it is thus expressed :—

"Observing, from Reports submitted to us, that the trade of our subjects on the Aleutian Islands and on the north-west coast of America, appertaining unto Russia, is subject, because of secret and illicit traffic, to oppression and impediments; and finding that the principal cause of these difficulties is the want of rules establishing the boundaries for navigation along these coasts, and the order of naval communication, as well in those places as on the whole of the eastern coast of Siberia and the Kurile Islands, we have deemed it necessary to determine these communications by specific Regulations, which are hereto attached.

"In forwarding these Regulations to the directing Senate, we command that the same be published for universal information, and that the proper measures be taken to carry them into execution."

(Signed)   COUNT D. GURIEFF,
Minister of Finances.

It is therefore decreed by the directing Senate that His Imperial Majesty's Edict be published for the information of all men, and that the same be obeyed by all whom it may concern.

[The original is signed by the directing Senate.]
Printed at St. Petersburgh. In the Senate, the 7th September, 1821.
[On the original is written, in the handwriting of His Imperial Majesty, thus :]
Be it accordingly.

(Signed)   ALEXANDER.

Kamennoy Ostroff, September 4, 1821.

Rules established for the Limits of Navigation and Order of Communication along the Coast of the Eastern Siberia, the North-West Coast of America, and the Aleutian, Kurile, and other Islands.

§ 1. THE pursuits of commerce, whaling, and fishery, and of all other industry on all islands, posts, and gulfs, including the whole of the north-west coast of America, beginning from Behring Straits to the 51° of northern latitude, also from the Aleutian Islands to the eastern coast of Siberia, as well as along the Kurile Islands from Behring Straits to the south cape of the Island of Urup, viz., to the 45° 50′ north latitude, is exclusively granted to Russian subjects.

§ 2. It is therefore prohibited to all foreign vessels not only to land on the coasts and islands belonging to Russia as stated above, but, also, to approach them within less than

100 Italian miles. The transgressor's vessel is subject to confiscation along with the whole cargo.

§ 3. An exception to this rule is to be made in favour of vessels carried thither by heavy gales, or real want of provisions, and unable to make any other shore but such as belongs to Russia; in these cases they are obliged to produce convincing proofs of actual reason for such an exception. Ships of friendly Governments, merely on discoveries, are likewise exempt from the foregoing Rule 28. In this case, however, they must be previously provided with passports from the Russian Minister of the Navy.

§ 4. Foreign merchant-ships which, for reasons stated in the foregoing rule, touch at any of the above-mentioned coasts, are obliged to endeavour to choose a place where Russians are settled, and to act as hereafter stated.

§ 5. On the arrival of a foreign merchant-ship, wind and weather permitting, a pilot will meet her to appoint an anchoring place appropriated for the purpose. The captain who, notwithstanding this, anchors elsewhere without being able to assign a reason to the Commander of the place, shall pay a fine of 100 dollars.

§ 6. All rowing-boats of foreign merchant-vessels are obliged to land at one place appointed for them, where, in the day-time, a white flag is hung out, and at night a lantern, and where a clerk is to attend continually to prevent importing and exporting any articles or goods. Whoever lands at any other place, even without an intent of smuggling, shall pay a fine of 50 dollars, and if a person be discovered bringing any articles ashore, a fine of 500 dollars is to be exacted and the goods to be confiscated.

§ 7. The commanders of said vessels being in want of provisions, stores, &c., for the continuation of their voyage, are bound to apply to the Commander of the place, who will appoint where these may be obtained, after which they may, without difficulty, send their boats there to procure all they want. Whoever deviates from this rule shall pay a fine of 100 dollars.

§ 8. If it be unavoidable, for the purpose of repairing or careening a foreign merchant-ship, that she discharge the whole cargo, the master is obliged to ask the permission of the Commander of the place. In this case the captain shall deliver to the Commander an exact list of the nature and quality of the goods discharged. Every one who omits to report any part of the cargo will be suspected of smuggling, and shall pay a fine of 1,000 dollars.

§ 9. All expenses incurred by these vessels during their stay in the Russian territories must be paid in cash or bills of exchange. In case, however, the captains of these ships have no money on board, and nobody gives security for their bonds, the Commander can, at their request, allow the sale of such articles, stores, or goods, required merely for defraying the above-stated expenses. These sales, however, can be made only to the Company, and through the medium of the Commander, but must not exceed the expenses of the ships, under penalty of the cargo being seized and a fine paid of 1,000 dollars.

§ 10. As soon as said foreign merchant-vessels are ready for their cargoes, stores, provisions, &c., they must immediately proceed to take them in, and after an examination, if they have loaded all the above-stated articles, and a written certificate of their not having left anything behind, they are to set sail. Such vessels as have not been unloaded are likewise subjected to sail without the least delay as soon as they are able to proceed to sea.

§ 11. It is prohibited to all commanders of the said foreign vessels, commissioners and others, whosoever they may be, to receive any articles, stores, or goods in those places where they will have landed, except in the case as per § 7, under penalty of seizure of their ship and cargo.

§ 12. It is prohibited to these foreign ships to receive on board, without special permission of the Commanders, any of the people in the service of the Company, or of the foreigners living in the Company's Settlements. Ships proved to have the intention of carrying off any person belonging to the Colony shall be seized.

§ 13. Every purchase, sale, or barter is prohibited betwixt a foreign merchant-ship and people in the service of the Company. This prohibition extends equally to those who are on shore and to those employed in the Company's ships. Any ship acting against this rule shall pay five times the value of the articles, stores, or goods constituting this prohibited traffic.

§ 14. It is likewise interdicted to foreign ships to carry on any traffic or barter with the natives of the islands, and of the north-west coast of America, in the whole extent here above mentioned. A ship convicted of this trade shall be confiscated.

§ 15. All articles, stores, and goods found on shore in ports and harbours belonging to Russian subjects (carrying on prohibited traffic) or to foreign vessels are to be seized.

§ 16. The foreign merchant-ships lying in harbour or in the roads dare, under no pretence, send out their boats to vessels at sea, or to those already come in, until they have been spoken to and visited, according to the existing customs. Whenever a foreign vessel hoists a yellow flag to announce an infectious disease being on board, or the symptoms of the same, or any other danger of which she wishes to be freed, every communication is interdicted until said flag is taken down. From this Rule, however, are excepted persons appointed for the purpose and whose boats be under the colours of the Russian-American Company. Any vessel acting contrary to this Regulation shall pay a fine of 500 dollars.

§ 17. No ballast may be thrown overboard but in such places as are appointed by the Commanders. The transgressor is liable to a fine of 500 dollars.

§ 18. To all foreign merchant-ships, during their stay in anchoring-places, harbours, or roads, it is prohibited to have their guns loaded either with balls or cartridges, under the risk of paying a fine of 50 dollars for each gun.

§ 19. No foreign merchant-ship in port, or in the roads, or riding at anchor, may fire guns or muskets without previously informing the Commander of the place or Settlement, unless it be for pilots, signalizing the same by the firing of one, two, or three guns, and hoisting her colours, as is customary in similar wants. In acting contrary thereto she is subjected to a fine of 100 dollars for each shot.

§ 20. On the arrival of a foreign ship in the harbour, or in the roads, a boat will immediately be sent to meet her, and to deliver to the captain a printed copy of these Regulations, for which he must give receipt in a book destined for the purpose. He is further obliged to state in the book, as per annexed form, all information required of foreign vessels. All ships refusing to comply with these Regulations dare not approach the harbour, roads, or any anchoring-place.

Destination of the Vessel.	Place where the Vessel comes from.	Cargo.	Number of Guns.	Number of Crew.	Name of the Captain.	Name of the Owner.	What Nation.	Name and Burthen of the Vessel.

§ 21. The captain of a foreign merchant-ship coming to an anchor in the port or in the roads is obliged, on his arrival, to give a statement of the health of the ship's crew, and should, after this, a contagious illness be discovered on board of his vessel, he must immediately inform the Commander of the place thereof. The vessel, according to circumstances, will be either sent off or put under quarantine in a place appropriated for the purpose, where the crew may be cured without putting the inhabitants in danger of infection. Should the captain of such a ship conceal the circumstance, the same will be confiscated with her whole cargo.

§ 22. The master of a vessel, at the request of the Commander of a place, is obliged to produce a list of the whole crew and all the passengers, and should he omit any, he shall pay a fine of 100 dollars for every one left out.

§ 23. The captains are bound to keep their crew in strict order and proper behaviour on the coasts, and in the ports, and likewise prevent their trading or bartering with the Company's people. They are answerable for the conduct of their sailors and other inferiors. Illicit trade carried on by sailors subjects the vessel to the same penalty as if done by the captain himself, because it were easy for the captains to carry on smuggling without punishment, and justify themselves by throwing the fault on the sailors. Therefore, every article found upon sailors which they could not hide in their pockets or under their clothes to screen from their superiors, sold or bought on shore, will be considered as contraband from the ship, and is subject to the prescribed fine.

§ 24. Foreign men-of-war shall likewise comply with the above-stated Regulations for the merchant-ships, to maintain the rights and benefit of the Company. In case of opposition, complaints will be made to their Governments.

§ 25. In case a ship of the Russian Imperial Navy, or the one belonging to the Russian American Company, meet a foreign vessel on the above-stated coasts, in harbours or roads, within the before-mentioned limits, and the Commander find grounds, by the present Regulation, that the ship be liable to seizure, he is to act as follows:—

§ 26. The Commander of a Russian vessel suspecting a foreign vessel to be liable to confiscation must inquire and search the same, and finding her guilty, take possession of her. Should the foreign vessel resist, he is to employ first persuasion, then threats, and at last force, endeavouring, however, at all events, to do this with as much reserve as possible. If the foreign vessel employ force against force, then he shall consider the same as an evident enemy, and force her to surrender according to the naval laws.

§ 27. After getting everything in order and safety on board the foreign vessel, the Commander of the Russian ship, or the officer sent by him, shall demand the journal of the captured vessel, and on the spot shall note down in the same that on such a day, mouth, and year, at such an hour, and in such a place, he met such and such a foreign vessel, and shall give a brief account of the circumstance, pursuit, and, finally, of the seizure. After signing the same he shall desire the captain of the captured vessel to confirm the same in his own handwriting. Should he, however, refuse to sign the same, the Russian officer is to repeat his summons in presence of all the officers, and if on this it be again refused, and nobody will sign in lieu of the captain, he is then to add this circumstance, signed by himself. After this arrangement, the journal, list of the crew, passports, invoices, accounts, and all further papers respecting the views and pursuits of the voyage of the vessel, shall be put up in one parcel, as well as all private papers, viz., the journals of the officers, letters, &c., and sealed with the seals of the Russian officer, and those of the captain and first officer of the foreign vessel. This packet shall remain sealed with the Commander of the Russian vessel until their arrival at the port of St. Peter and Paul, where it shall be deposited in the Court as mentioned in § 33. Besides this, everything else must be sealed by the Russian officer and the foreign captain that is not requisite for the continuation of the voyage to the port of St. Peter and Paul, excepting the effects for immediate and sole use of the ship's crew, which shall not be withheld from them.

§ 28. Having thus fixed all means of precaution, the officer sent to arrest the foreign vessel shall make instantly his report to his Chief, and await his orders.

§ 29. Thus, should by any cause stated in the 2nd, 11th, 12th, and 21st sections of these Regulations, a foreign vessel be subjected to confiscation in any port near the Settlement of the Russian-American Company, the Commander of that Settlement is obliged either to ask the assistance of the Russian man-of-war, if there be any, and the Commander of which, on receipt of a written request, is obliged to arrest the vessel, and use all the precautions prescribed in the foregoing Article, or, if there be no Russian man-of-war in the harbour or its neighbourhood, and the Commander of the Settlement find that he and his people can arrest the vessel by themselves, he then is to act according to the 26th, 27th, and 28th sections, and putting ashore the captain, and every means of getting the vessel away, he must endeavour as soon as possible to give information of this event either to the Governor of the Colonies of the Russian-American Company or the Commander of the Imperial man-of-war, if it be known where she lie.

§ 30. When, in consequence of such a report, the Governor of the Colonies shall send the Company's vessel, or a Government vessel arriving, then the Commander of the place shall deliver up the vessel seized, and all belonging to her, and shall report respecting his reasons for confiscating the vessel.

§ 31. The Commander of the vessel, taking charge of the seizure per inventory, shall examine immediately into all circumstances mentioned, and compare it with the accounts of the Commander of the Settlement, who will give every elucidation required.

§ 32. All vessels detained by Russian men-of-war are ordered by these Regulations to be brought to the port of St. Peter and Paul, where the sentence is to be passed on them by a Court established for adjudging such cases.

§ 33. This Court, under the presidency of the Commander of Kamtchatka, shall consist of the three senior officers under him, and of the Commissioner of the Russian-American Company.

§ 34. As soon as a Russian vessel, bringing into the port of St. Peter and Paul a foreign vessel arrested by her, has come to an anchor in the place assigned her, the commander of her is immediately to repair to the Commander of Kamtchatka, stating briefly what vessel he had brought in, the number of the crew, and the sick, specifying their diseases, and reporting likewise whether the vessel has sufficient victuals, and what goods, guns, and other arms, powder, &c., are on board.

§ 35. The Commander of Kamtchatka, on receiving this report, will order two officers and a sufficient number of men on board the captured vessel.

§ 36. These two officers, together with the officers who brought in the detained ship, when on board, are to summon the master and two of his mates or men in command next to him, inspect all the seals put on the vessel, and then, taking them off, begin immediately to make an accurate list of all the effects belonging to the vessel.

§ 37. This list is to be signed by all the officers on both sides who were present in drawing it up. The Commander of Kamtchatka is to use all possible endeavours to secure from embezzlement or damage all effects belonging to the detained vessel.

§ 38. The crew of the vessel is then to be sent ashore to such place as shall be appointed by the Commander of Kamtchatka, and remain there until the close of the investigation.

§ 39. The Commander of the Russian vessel is obliged, in the course of two days after his arrival at the port of St. Peter and Paul, to make a minute representation to the Commander of Kamtchatka of all that shall have happened at the detention of the foreign vessel brought in by him, and to deliver said vessel, together with the sealed paquet containing her papers, expressed in § 27.

§ 40. If the Russian vessel that brought into the port of St. Peter and Paul a foreign vessel cannot for reasons remain there until the close of the investigation, but be obliged to proceed to sea in a very short time, the Commander, in order not to detain her, shall use all possible dispatch by bringing forward the investigation of such points as may require the presence of the Russian vessel.

§ 41. Having settled everything on board the arrested vessel and landed the crew, the Court immediately shall open the session, and endeavour to ascertain as soon as possible the solution of the inquiry, whether the vessel be lawfully arrested or not.

§ 42. In order to ascertain this, the following proofs shall be substantiated:—

1. That the vessel was met with within the boundaries prescribed in § 2 of these Regulations, and that her having been within such limits was not occasioned by reasons stated in § 3.

2. That the vessel is a lawful prize by virtue of the §§ 2, 11, 12, 14, and 21 of these Regulations, and the §   of the Instructions to the Commander of the Russian man-of-war.

§ 43. In order to decide either case, the Court is to inspect all documents presented, and tracing on one part all proofs of guilt, and on the other all doubts which might clear the foreign vessel, summon the commanding officer of the Russian vessel to give all additional information deemed needful, and completing thus all circumstances condemning the foreign vessel, the Court shall draw up a clear statement of the reason of her condemnation.

§ 44. Should the Court, in making out said statement, find that the foreign vessel has been arrested without sufficient cause, said Court on passing sentence is to determine the damage suffered by such detention, and to furnish both parties with a certified copy of this Resolution.

§ 45. In the course of two days, both parties shall declare whether they are satisfied with the decision of the Court or not, and in the latter case (should it happen) assign it in writing.

§ 46. Should both parties be satisfied with the decision of the Court, then the Commander of Kamtchatka is to release immediately the detained vessel, returning everything to the master according to the inventory, along with the adjudged damages, exacting them from whomsoever is to pay the same.

§ 47. If, on the contrary, the Court receive on the third day a repeal to its decision, it is bound to take that repeal into immediate consideration, and finding it just, to change its decision, if not, to confirm the same, and make it known to the parties a second time. After this no representations shall be admitted, and both parties shall be summoned before the Court, which shall allow them to make their protest in writing, and will then state all the reasons why the sentence passed should be carried into execution.

§ 48. If the Court find by the indictment that the vessel has been lawfully detained, then the master of the foreign vessel, or the two eldest in command under him, shall be summoned, and the reasons of their detention made known to them, giving them a certified copy of the condemnation.

§ 49. The Court is to receive within three days, and no later, the representations of the master, and if he do not present the same within the time limited, the Court summoning him, with two of his crew, notifies that his silence is received as a mark of compliance, and that the condemnation is just.

§ 50. In this case the Court comes to its final decision, which, on the following day, is communicated to the whole crew of the foreign vessel, who shall sign, all and every one, that such sentence has been made known to them, after which the Commander of Kamtchatka is to carry the sentence of the Court into execution, as will be explained hereafter.

§ 51. Should, however, the master deliver within the time limited his protest, then the Court, examining it with all possible impartiality, shall call for all further explanations, and, having inserted the whole into the journal of the Court, shall pass a final sentence, and pronounce it, as stated in § 47.

§ 52. If, by sentence of the Court, the arrested vessel be released, and adjudged to receive damages for her detention, and if the vessel has been arrested by any of the Company's officers, and the damages are not above 5,000 roubles, the Commander of Kamtchatka shall demand immediate payment of said sum from the office of the Russian-American Company, but if the damages exceed that sum, he is to notify it to the Company's office, and give to the foreign master a certificate; but the money cannot be paid by the Company otherwise than after the inspection and Resolution of its Court of Directors. If, on the other hand, the foreign vessel has been detained unlawfully by a Russian man-of-war, the Commander of Kamtchatka is to pay the adjudged damages (not exceeding the sum of 5,000 roubles) out of any Government sum, and to report, in order to incash it from the guilty, but if the damages should exceed the sum of 5,000 roubles, the Commander of Kamtchatka is to furnish a certificate for the receipt of the money after the regulation and confirmation of the Russian Government.

§ 53. The reimbursement of such damages as may have been incurred by unlawful detention shall be exacted from the Commander and all the officers of the man-of-war, who, having been called by the Commander to a council, shall have given their opinion that such a ship ought to be detained.

§ 54. As soon as a foreign ship is sentenced to be confiscated, the Commander of Kamtchatka is to make due arrangements for transporting the crew to Ochotsk, and from thence to any of the ports in the Baltic, in order to enable every one of them to reach his own country. With the confiscated ship and cargo, he is to act as with a prize, taken in time of war.

§ 55. After this the Commander of Kamtchatka shall order a Committee to value the vessel and her cargo. This Committee is to be composed of one member appointed by the Commander of Kamtchatka, one by the Commander of the man-of-war, and a third by the Russian-American Company.

§ 56. These Commissioners are to make up a specified list and valuation according to the following rules:—

1. All provisions, rigging, iron, powder, and arms shall be put down at such prices as they cost Government there.

2. All merchandize which might be used in Kamtchatka and the Company's Colonies, and which are carried there at times from Russia, shall be valued at their prices then existing.

3. All goods which are not imported into these places from Russia, but are wanted there, shall be valued like goods brought from Russia, being the nearest to them, and in proportion to their wants.

4. All goods not in use at Kamtchatka or the Colonies shall be sent to Irkutsk and sold at public auction by the proper authorities.

§ 57. The said Commissioners shall present their valuation to the Commander of Kamtchatka for his approbation, who, in case of not finding the same exact, shall return it, with his remarks, and shall appoint other officers to inspect such articles as may appear unfairly valued.

§ 58. If the Commissioners hereafter continue in their opinion, and the Commander of Kamtchatka find it impossible to agree thereto, he shall provisionally consent and leave the final decision to Government.

§ 59. According to this valuation the Commander of Kamtchatka shall mark, for the use of Government, all those articles which he thinks are wanted; the remainder is left at the disposal of the officers of the ship or of the Russian-American Company. The seized vessel shall be valued by the Court, and the valuation sent immediately to the Minister of the Navy, with a report whether such a vessel is wanted for Government service or not.

§ 60. The whole sum of valuation of the confiscated vessel and cargo is to be divided in the following manner. The expenses necessary to forward the ship's crew to one of the ports in the Baltic are to be deducted, and the remaining sum divided, if the vessel has been taken by the Russian-American Company's officers, and carried to the port of St. Peter and Paul by a ship of said Company, without the interference of a man-of-war, into five parts, of which one goes to the Government, and the remaining four-fifths to the American Company. If the vessel be taken in any of the Company's Settlements by the Company's officers, but brought to the port of St. Peter and Paul by a man-of-war, after deducting one-fifth for Government, two-fifths are to belong to the crew of the man-of-war, and the remaining two-fifths to the Russian-American Company, and finally, if such foreign vessel be detained by men-of-war only without the assistance of the Company's officers, then, after deducting one-fifth for Government, the remainder is left to the officers of the men-of-war.

But if a vessel be taken by the conjoint forces of a man-of-war and a Company's vessel, then the prize shall be divided between them in proportion to their strength, regulating the same according to the number of guns.

§ 61. The sum coming to the officers of the man-of-war shall be divided according to the Rules for dividing prizes in time of war. In all cases, officers who had a share in seizing foreign vessels convicted of the intention of infringing the privileges most graciously granted to the Russian-American Company, may expect to receive tokens of His Imperial Majesty's approbation, especially when, after deducting the expenses for conveying the crew, their part in the prize-money should prove but trifling.

§ 62. If a foreign vessel detained by a Russian being under the command of a Russian officer should be cast away before reaching the port of St. Peter and Paul, the following principle shall be observed:—

If the foreign vessel alone be lost, and the Russian accompanying her arrive at the port of St. Peter and Paul, then the Court acts according to the foregoing Rules to determine whether that vessel was lawfully seized. In this case Government takes upon itself the expenses of conveying to a port of the Baltic such of the ship's crew as were saved. But if such a vessel should not be proved to have been detained lawfully, then, independent of those expenses, the ship shall be valued, and such valuation forwarded to Government for the payment of what may be deemed just; at the same time investigation shall be made on the loss of the vessel, and the officer that had the command (if saved) is to be tried according to the Maritime Rules and Regulations.

§ 63. The Commander of Kamtchatka is bound to make a special report to the Governor-General of Siberia respecting every circumstance happening to foreign vessels, annexing copies of all documents, journals, and sentences of the Court, and of all papers relating thereunto.

The original is signed:
COUNT D. GURIEFF,
Minister of Finances.

UKASE OF SEPTEMBER 13, 1821, GRANTING PRIVILEGES TO THE RUSSIAN-AMERICAN COMPANY FOR TWENTY YEARS.

" The Ukase of His Imperial Majesty the Autocrat of All the Russias is hereby published by the Ruling Senate.

(Translation.)

"BY His Imperial Majesty's Ukase, bearing his signature, and communicated to the Ruling Senate on the 13th day of September, of the year 1821, it is decreed :—

"' The Russian-American Company, under our protection, availing itself of the privileges conferred on it by Imperial Decree in the year 1799, has completely fulfilled what we expected of it, by its success in navigation, by what it has done to develop the trade of the Empire, to the benefit of all, and by securing considerable profits to those who are directly interested in it. In consideration whereof, being desirous of prolonging its existence and establishing it yet more firmly, we hereby renew the privileges granted to it, with the necessary additions and modifications, for a period of twenty years from this date, and having sanctioned the new Regulations drawn up for it, hand this over to the Ruling Senate, commanding them to prepare the necessary document setting forth these privileges, to lay it before us for our signature, and to take the proper further steps in the matter.'

" Privileges granted to the Russian-American Company for twenty years from this date.

" 1. The Company founded for the exercise of industries on the mainland of North-western America, and on the Aleutian and Kurile Islands, shall be, as heretofore, under the protection of His Imperial Majesty.

" 2. It shall have the privilege of carrying on, to the exclusion of all other Russians, and of the subjects of foreign States, all industries connected with the capture of wild animals and all fishing industries, on the shores of North-western America which have from time immemorial belonged to Russia, commencing from the northern point of the Island of Vancouver, under 51° north latitude, to Behring Straits and beyond them, and on all the islands which belong to that coast, as well as on the others situated between it and the eastern shore of Siberia, and also on those of the Kurile Islands where the Company has carried on industries, as far as the southern extremity of the Island of Urup under 45° 50'.

" 3. It shall have the exclusive enjoyment of everything in that region which it has hitherto discovered, or which it may in future discover, either on the surface of the earth or in the earth.

" 4. The Company make discoveries within the limits defined above, and it is authorized to annex such newly-discovered places to the Russian dominions, provided they have not been occupied by any other European nation, or by citizens of the United States, and have not become dependencies of such foreign nation ; but the Company may not found permanent settlements in such places unless authorized to do so by the Emperor.

" 5. Within the limits defined in section 2, the Company is authorized to found new settlements, and to construct works of defence at any point, should such be necessary, at its own discretion, and to enlarge and improve existing settlements or works of defence ; it is permitted to send ships with men and merchandize to those places without hindrance.

" 6. In order to insure to the Company the enjoyment of the exclusive rights granted to it, and to prevent for the future any interference or damage to it arising from the action of Russian subjects or of foreigners, Regulations are now drawn up regarding the manner in which those persons are to be dealt with who, either voluntarily or under stress of circumstances, come to the places defined in section 2 of these privileges, in spite of the fact that they are prohibited from coming to them. These Regulations must be strictly observed both by the Company and by those authorities whom they may concern.

" 7. The Company is authorized to communicate by sea with all neighbouring nations, and to trade with them, with the consent of their Governments, except in the case of the Chinese Empire, the shores of which the Company's ships are never to approach.

" In regard to other nations, the Company's ships shall not have trade or other relations with them against the wish of their Governments.

" 8. All Courts of Law shall recognize the Administration of the Company as established for the management of its affairs, and all writs from Courts in matters concerning the Company shall be addressed to that Administration, and not to any one of the members of the Company.

" 9. In handing over so large an extent of territory to be administered by the Company, the Emperor grants to the latter the following advantages, in order to enable it the better to carry out the objects of the Government, by encouraging the Company's officials in all its factories and dependencies both inland and on the sea-coast, its managers, book-keepers, cashiers, and their deputies, supercargoes, shipping clerks, and others :—

D

"(1.) The Chief Manager, on appointment to the office, shall, if he be a military officer or belong to the Civil Service, enjoy the precedence defined by the Ukase of the 21st March, 1810, concerning officials appointed to the Siberian Governments.

"(2.) With regard to Government officials whose services are applied for temporarily in accordance with the Ukase of the 9th April, 1802, they are to be considered as being on active service so far as all rewards are concerned; they shall, however, receive promotion in official rank according to their seniority and merit at the post which they actually occupy. They shall continue to draw half their pay and allowances, in accordance with the terms of the same Ukase.

"(3.) Retired Government officials, on entering the service of the Company, shall retain their general official rank, and shall be considered to be on active service. This right is extended also to those who have served the Company in any capacity subsequently to the grant of the privileges by the Emperor in 1799. Those persons who belong to (social) classes having the right to enter the Government service, but who have not served, and have no official rank, shall, after serving the Company for two years, obtain the rank of Collegiate Registrar, on application being made on their behalf by the Administration of the Company, and shall be promoted to the higher official ranks by length of service, according to the General Rules; on retirement they shall retain their rank only if they have held it for at least five years, and if the Administration bears testimony to their abilities and value.

"(4.) Persons in the employment of the Company who belong to (social) classes which have not the right to enter the Government service, shall not, until they are taken out of those classes, be on the same footing as those referred to in (3). But if they hold the appointment of Manager of a station, they shall, during the time that they occupy the post, enjoy the privileges of the ninth official class, that is, of Titular Counsellor; with regard to persons holding appointments as book-keepers, cashiers, their assistants, supercargoes, &c., the Administration is authorized to place them in any official class between the fourteenth and ninth according to their abilities and value; but none of these officials shall, on vacating their posts and leaving the service of the Company, retain the precedence of their official class, unless they have been taken out of the (social) class to which they originally belonged, and have fulfilled all the conditions prescribed by the General Regulations on the subject, and unless they have served the Company for at least twelve years and are certified, on their retirement, to be deserving and capable.

"10. In accordance with the Ukases of the Ruling Senate, dated the 16th February, 1801, 6th April, 1805, and 20th March, 1808, the Company may take into its employ, in any Government of the Russian Empire, for service at sea, or for the exercise of industries, or to serve in its factories, persons with or without means, being free and of good reputation, and furnished with ordinary passports, or workmen's passports; and the authorities of the Governments shall be instructed to give to all such persons engaged by the Company passports to run for periods from one year to seven years, as the Company may wish; and the Company shall pay the dues and fees on behalf of such persons to the proper authorities.

"11. If any persons in the employment of the Company, on the expiration of the periods of service agreed upon with them, wish to remain in its service in America, or if they owe money to the Company, the latter shall not be obliged to send them back to Russia, but new passports shall be granted to them, on the application of the Company; such applications must, however, be accompanied by proofs in writing that the persons concerned consent to remain in America for one of the reasons specified above. The documents must be signed by them, or, if they cannot write, by some other person at their request and before two witnesses.

"12. All persons in the employment of the Company are bound to obey implicitly the orders of their superiors, and are answerable to the Company for all losses caused by their fault. The Courts will compel all such persons to give an account of their proceedings, and, on the application of the Administration of the Company, will, without loss of time, subject them to a legal inquiry. Such persons may, however, appeal to the Ruling Senate, such appeal to be lodged within six months from the date on which they have been informed of the decision arrived at.

"13. No Court or Governor of a town shall, under any circumstances, compel any station or agency established by the Company to make any payment, unless explanations have previously been called for from such station or agency, or unless it has been authorized to make the payment by the Administration of the Company, to which all such demands should be addressed.

"14. If a shareholder of the Company owes money to the Government, or to private persons, and his estate, apart from his share in the Company, is not sufficient to cover the debt, the debtor's capital which is in the hands of the Company under the Regulations drawn up for it shall become, to the extent of the debt, the property of the Government, or of his creditors, together with all profits not yet distributed belonging to his share of the Company's capital; and the Company shall accordingly transfer the capital to the Government, or to the creditors, in accordance with the notice given by the Government, or with the decree of a Court of Justice assigning the amount of the debt, as the case may be.

"15. The Company's shares may, in accordance with the decision of the Committee of Ministers of the 19th September, 1814, be mortgaged to the Government to the extent of half their value. If the property of the owner of the shares is attached, and he is unable to pay off the mortgage, the shares shall be sold by public auction. Any surplus there may be after the amount for which the shares were mortgaged is paid shall be handed to the owner; if less than the amount of the mortgage is realized, the Government have the option of keeping the shares; otherwise the Company will at once pay the amount of the mortgage to the Government, and take over the shares.

"16. If a dispute, in connection with the business or accounts of the Company, arises between the Company and one of its shareholders of so serious a character that it cannot be speedily arranged in an amicable manner, such dispute shall be inquired into and settled by a general meeting of the shareholders who have a right to vote; the shareholder with whom the dispute has arisen shall be present. The decision of the meeting shall be carried out without delay; but, if the shareholder considers himself aggrieved, he may appeal to the Ruling Senate, such appeal to be lodged within six months from the day on which he has been informed of the decision.

"17. The Emperor is pleased to allow the Russian-American Company to take on board its ships which are sent round the world from Cronstadt, or dispatched from Okhotsk to the Russian Colonies, cargoes of Russian or foreign products on which duty has been paid, and when they return from those Colonies with cargoes of furs and other colonial products, to unload them without hindrance, on notice being given of such cargoes at Cronstadt by the Administration of the Company to the custom-house, and at Okhotsk by its agent to the local authorities. No duty is to be paid on either of these classes of merchandize when taken from one Russian port to another, except when, in the case of furs, a special internal duty is fixed by law.

"18. Although it is forbidden by Imperial Ukases to cut wood in any forest belonging to the State without the permission of the Department of Forests, nevertheless, in view of the distance of the Okhotsk territory, where the Company requires wood for repairing its ships, and sometimes for building new ones, it is authorized to cut wood for those purposes in any part of that territory without making payment for the same, provided that information is given, without delay, to the Forest Department of the territory, both of the place chosen for cutting the wood, and of the amount and quality of the wood cut.

"19. In case communications by sea between the Colonies and European Russia are interrupted, the Company may obtain from the Government Artillery Stores at Irkutsk from 40 to 80 poods of gunpowder a-year, and from the mines at Nertshinsk up to 200 poods of lead a-year, to be used for shooting game, for signalling at sea, and in unforeseen contingencies. The proper price must be paid in ready money.

"20. In order to enable the Company to carry on its operations without interruption or molestation, the privilege of exemption from the quartering of troops is granted in the case of all buildings used for factories by the Company.

"In conclusion, all civil and military authorities, and all Courts of Justice, are ordered not only not to interfere with the enjoyment by the Company of the privileges hereby granted to it, but also, if necessary, to guard it from losses or damage, and to give all the protection and assistance they can to the Administration of the Company, and to the stations and agencies belonging to it."

Regulations of the Russian-American Company.*

General Provisions.

§ 1. [Description of the Company.]
§ 2. [Origin of the Company. Number of shares.]
§ 3. [Persons allowed to hold shares.]
§ 4. [Form of shares.]
§ 5. [Limited liability.]
§ 6. [Transfers of shares.]
§ 7. [Division of profits.]

The Administration of the Company and the Meetings of the Shareholders.

§ 8. [Persons having a voice in the management.]
§ 9. [Manner of voting.]
§ 10. [Cases of absence of shareholders from meetings.]
§ 11. [Notice of meetings.]

Council of the Company.

§ 12. [Authority of Council.]
§ 13. [Composition of Council.]
§ 14. [Election of Council.]
§ 15. [Retirement of members of Council.]
§ 16. [Retiring members eligible for re-election.]

* The portions in brackets are abstracts.

§ 17. [Important and secret political or commercial matters to be dealt with by the Council and Administration jointly.]

§ 18. [The Directors may ask that such matters may be dealt with by the Council and Administration jointly.]

§ 19. [Members of Council to observe secrecy.]

§ 20. [Directors have voices at meetings of Council.]

§ 21. [Decisions of joint meetings of Council and Administration.]

§ 22. [Quorum of joint meetings of Council and Administration.]

§ 23. [Procedure in cases where a joint meeting of the Council and Administration cannot arrive at a decision.]

The Administration.

§ 24. [Description of Administration.]

§ 25. [Administration consists of not more than four Directors.]

§ 26. [Directors are chosen by ballot.]

§ 27. [Only persons holding at least ten shares may vote at election of Directors.]

§ 28. [Oath to be taken by Directors.]

§ 29. [Retirement of Directors.]

§ 30. [Powers of Directors.]

§ 31. [Objects to be aimed at by the Administration.]

§ 32. [The founding of new stations.]

§ 33. [Seal of the Administration.]

§ 34. [Each station to have a seal.]

Of the Company's Responsibilities.

I.—In relation to the Government.

§ 35. [The Company will use its best endeavours to prove that it deserves the confidence reposed in it by the Emperor.]

§ 36. [The Company will keep the Government informed of its proceedings.]

II.—In relation to Russian Subjects residing in the Territory administered by the Company.

§ 37. [The Company will provide for the religious wants of the territory by seeing that there are always enough priests for its requirements.]

§ 38. [Great caution will be exercised in the choice of persons to serve under the Company.]

§ 39. [The Company will do all in its power to provide for the bodily welfare of its servants.]

§ 40. [Russian births and deaths are to be announced to the proper authorities in Russia.]

§ 41. [The position of "creoles," i.e., the offspring of Russian fathers and native mothers.]

§ 42. [Native races inhabiting the Company's territory.]

§ 43. [Position of the natives of the islands.]

§ 44. [The natives of the islands are subject to Russian law.]

§ 45. [They shall not pay taxes.]

§ 46. [The Company to furnish statistics of the number of islanders, births, deaths, &c.]

§ 47. [The natives of the islands are to be ruled by their own Chiefs under Russian overseers.]

§ 48. [Position of the Chiefs and overseers.]

§ 49. [The natives of the islands are to be provided with land by the Company.]

§ 50. [Persons guilty of oppressing them are to be punished.]

§ 51. [The islanders are to assist the Company in fishing and hunting.]

§ 52. [The Chiefs will provide the requisite number of natives for this purpose.]

§ 53. [Conditions of service of the islanders.]

§ 54. [Re-engagement of the islanders who have served their time.]

§ 55. [Conditions under which native women and children may be employed.]

§ 56. [The islanders may fish and hunt on their own account under certain conditions.]

III.—In relation to the Natives inhabiting the Shores of America where the Company has Colonies.

§ 57. [Attitude to be observed by the Company towards the natives of the Continent of America.]

§ 58. [The natives are not to pay any kind of taxes, and are to be well treated.]

§ 59. [Position of natives of the continent who may wish to reside in the Russian settlements.]

IV.—*In relation to neighbouring States and their Subjects.*

§ 60. In return for the confidence reposed in the Company by the Government in granting to it so vast an extent of territory on the frontier of the Empire, the Company is bound to abstain from any action which might cause an interruption of friendly relations with neighbouring States. The Company must be careful to observe all the rules laid down by foreign Powers for the guidance of their subjects in their relations with foreigners, as well as all the provisions of the Treaties in force between Russia and foreign countries, especially those relating to the Chinese Empire.

§ 61. Questions concerning the relations with foreign Powers which are beyond the competence of the Colonial Administration are to be referred to the Minister of Finance, who will communicate the decision of the Government.

§ 62. For the guidance of the Company in the matter of the steps to be taken in regard to foreign ships entering the colonial waters, in exceptional cases, or in contravention of the privileges granted to it by the Emperor, special rules have been drawn up, entitled : " Regulations on the subject of the Limits of Navigation and Communication by Sea along the Shores of Eastern Siberia, North-western America, and the Aleutian and Kurile Islands."

Of the Supervision of the Company's Proceedings by the Government.

I.—*Of the Supervision of the Company's Proceedings by the Department of the Minister of Finance.*

§ 63. [The relations of the Company with the Government are under the supervision of the Finance Department.]

§ 64. [The Minister of Finance will see that the Company keeps strictly within the terms of its privileges.]

§ 65. [In case of necessity the Minister of Finance will take steps for the protection of the Company from any danger that may threaten it.]

II.—*Of the Supervision of the Proceedings of the Company's Servants in Siberia and in the Company's Colonies.*

§ 66. [Action to be taken by the authorities in Siberia in case of irregularities on the part of the Company's servants at stations in Siberia.]

§ 67. [In order to control the proceedings of the Company's servants in the Colonies, the Government stipulates that the Chief Manager shall be a naval officer, and that the sanction of the Emperor shall be necessary to his appointment.]

§ 68. [Points on which the Government wishes to be kept informed.]

§ 69. [Action to be taken by Commanders of ships of war if any one complains to them of ill-treatment.]

§ 70. A ship of war, after visiting, not only the Company's settlements, but also, and more particularly, the channels which foreign merchant-vessels are likely to frequent for the purpose of illicit trading with the natives, will return to winter whenever the Government orders it; but if the Chief Manager of the Colonies considers it necessary for a ship of war to winter in the Colonies, the Commander will receive orders accordingly.

The Commanders of ships of war will receive orders to capture all foreign ships found in Russian waters.

[The Naval Regulation prohibiting the officers and crews of men-of-war from engaging in trade will be strictly enforced.]

(Signed)   COUNT D. GURIEFF,
Minister of Finance.

No. 3.

EXTRACT FROM THE "QUARTERLY REVIEW" OF JANUARY 1822.

A Voyage of Discovery into the South Sea and Behring Straits, for the purpose of exploring a North-East Passage, undertaken in the years 1815–18, at the Expense of his Highness the Chancellor of the Empire, Count Romanzoff, in the ship "Rurick," under the Command of the Lieutenant in the Russian Imperial Navy Otto von Kotzebue. 3 vols. London. 1821.

SINCE the general peace of Europe, and more particularly within the last three years, the Russian Government has been anxiously and eagerly employed in prosecuting discoveries in every part of the globe. In the Southern Ocean her ships have penetrated the fields of ice as far as the 70th parallel of latitude, and discovered, it is said, islands which had escaped the searching eye of Cook ; they boast of having rounded the Sandwich-land of that celebrated navigator, and of having ascertained that the Southern Shetland, which was supposed to be a continent connected with it, consists only of numerous groups of small islands. They have sent land expeditions into the unknown regions of Tartary, behind Thibet, and into the interior of the north-western side of North America. Men of science have been commissioned to explore the northern boundaries of Siberia, and to determine points, on that extensive coast, hitherto of doubtful position. In February 1821 Baron Wrangel, an officer of great merit, and of considerable science, left his head-quarters on the Nishney Kolyma, to settle, by astronomical observations, the position of Shalatzkoi-Noss, or the North-east Cape of Asia, which he found to lie in latitude 70° 5' north, considerably lower than it is usually placed on the maps. Having arranged this point, he undertook the hazardous enterprise of crossing the ice of the Polar Sea on sledges drawn by dogs in search of the land said to have been discovered in 1762 to the northward of the Kolyma. He travelled directly north 80 miles without perceiving anything but a field of interminable ice, the surface of which had now become so broken and uneven as to prevent a further prosecution of his journey. He had gone far enough, however, to ascertain that no such land could ever have been discovered. The idle speculation, therefore, of the junction of Asia with North America, which we always rejected as chimerical, may now be considered as finally set at rest. Indeed, the simple narrative of the voyage performed by Deshnew in the year 1648, from the mouth of the Kolyma to the Gulf of Anadyr, never for a moment left a doubt on our minds of its authenticity.

The reader will recollect our recent statement of that enterprising pedestrian, Captain Cochrane, having reached the Altai Mountains, on the frontier of China. Further accounts from this extraordinary traveller have since reached us ; they are dated from the mouth of the Kolyma, and from Okotsk, the former in March, the latter in June, 1821. He had proceeded to the neighbourhood of the North-east Cape of Asia, which he places half a degree more to the northward than Baron Wrangel ; but either he had no instrument sufficiently accurate to ascertain its latitude with precision, or, as we have some reason to believe, he states it only from computation ; for it does not clearly appear from his letter to us that he was actually on that part of the coast, though, from another letter addressed to the President of the Royal Society of London, it might be conjectured that his information was obtained from observation on the spot. "No land," he says, "is considered to exist to the northward of it. The east side of the Noss is composed of bold and perpendicular bluffs, while the west side exhibits gradual declivities ; the whole most sterile, but presenting an awfully magnificent appearance." From the Kolyma to Okotsk he had, he says, a "dangerous, difficult, and fatiguing journey of 3,000 versts," a great part of which he performed, on foot, in seventy days. After such an adventurous expedition from St. Petersburgh to the north-eastern extremity of Siberia, we regret to find that the shores of Kamtchatka are likely to be the boundary of his arduous and perilous enterprise. After gratefully noticing the generosity and consideration which he everywhere experienced at the hands of the Russian Government and of individuals, he adds : "that Government has an expedition in Behring Straits, whose object is to trace the Continent of America to the northward and eastward. I had the same thing previously in view, but it would be vanity and presumption in me to attempt a task of the kind, while their means are so much superior, and those who are employed on it *authorized* travellers. Thus circumstanced, it can create no surprise that an humble individual like myself should submit to make a sacrifice of private gratification and every prospect of success to a sense of the impropriety of proceeding farther at present, and of the indelicacy which would result from such a step ; but, should the commander of the expedition, from any circumstances, desist from the further prosecution of his discoveries, *I shall, in that case, continue my journey eastward*," the meaning of all which will, we think, be perfectly intelligible from what we are about to state.

The expedition noticed by Captain Cochrane consisted of two ship corvettes which left Spithead in the year 1819, at the same time that the expedition alluded to in our first paragraph proceeded to the Southern Hemisphere. In July 1820 they reached Behring Strait, and were supposed to have passed it in that year ; they returned, however, in the winter to some of the Russian settlements on the coast of America, and, as now appears from Captain Cochrane's letter to us, were again in that neighbourhood in June 1821; of their ulterior proceedings no intelligence had reached St. Petersburgh at the period of the latest accounts from that capital. If they should have succeeded in doubling Icy Cape, it is just possible that they may fall in with Captain Parry, provided they are lucky enough to escape the fate of Sir Hugh Willoughby and his unfortunate associates; of such a catastrophe we are by no means sure that they do not run a very considerable risk, from the slight and insufficient manner in which they were fitted out, being, in fact, destitute of every necessary for passing a winter in the Frozen Ocean, and, as we happen to know, in want even of the common implements for encountering the ice; with some of the latter, however, they were supplied from the Dockyard of Portsmouth, on application to the British Government.

We should not be disposed to detract from the merit which, in this instance, would be justly due to the Russian Government, if we could persuade ourselves that the extension of geographical knowledge, for its own sake and the benefit of mankind, was the prime object of this expedition; but when we couple it with the cautious language of Captain Cochrane, and the sudden and unexpected check thrown in the way of his further progress, after reaching the shores of Behring Strait, and also with a contemporaneous Ukase of a most extraordinary nature (if we may credit what appears in the public journals), we cannot but entertain some suspicion that His Imperial Majesty, in his northern expeditions, has been governed by other motives than those of merely advancing the cause of science and discovery.

In this curious manifesto (for such, in effect, it is) the Maritime Powers of Europe and America are given to understand that His Imperial Majesty of Russia has assumed possession of all that portion of the north-west coast of America which lies between the 51st degree of latitude and the Icy Cape, or extreme north; and, moreover, that he interdicts the approach of ships of every other nation to any part of this line nearer than 100 miles. Whether this wholesale usurpation of 2,000 miles of sea-coast, to the greater part of which Russia can have no possible claim, will be tacitly passed over by England, Spain, and the United States, the three Powers most interested in it, we pretend not to know; but we can scarcely be mistaken in predicting that His Imperial Majesty will discover, at no distant period, that he has assumed an authority, and asserted a principle, which he will hardly be permitted to exercise; and that there is an ancient common law of nations which will not, and cannot, be abrogated by the *sic volo* of a Power of yesterday. It has apparently escaped the recollection of His Imperial Majesty's advisers that if his example were to be followed by the maritime nations of Europe, his own ports would be hermetically sealed, and an end put at once to the assumption of long-appropriated coasts by Russia.

With respect to the legality of taking possession of an unoccupied territory, to the exclusion of the original discoverer, some doubts, we understand, are still entertained among jurists. It is time, we think, to come to a decision one way or another on a point of so much importance.

Let us examine, however, what claim Russia can reasonably set up to the territory in question. To the two shores of Behring Strait, we admit, she would have an undoubted claim, on the score of priority of discovery, that on the side of Asia having been coasted by Deshnew in 1648, and that of America visited by Behring in 1741, as far down as the latitude 59', and the peaked mountain, since generally known by the name of Cape Fairweather; to the southward of this point, however, Russia has not the slightest claim. The Spaniards visited the northern parts of this coast in 1774, when Don Juan Perez, in the corvette "Santiago," traced it from latitude 53° 53' to a promontory in latitude 55°, to which he gave the name of Santa Margarita, being the north-west extremity of Queen Charlotte's Island of our charts; and on his return touched at Nootka, about which we were once on the point of going to war.

In the following year the "Santiago" and "Felicidad," under the orders of Don Juan Bruno Heceta and Don Juan de la Bodega y Quadra, proceeded along the north-west coast, and descried in latitude 56° 8' high mountains covered with snow, which they named Jacinto, and also a lofty cape, in latitude 61° 2', to which they gave the name of Engano. Holding a northerly course, they reached latitude 57° 58', and then returned.

Three years after these Spanish voyages Cook reconnoitred this coast more closely, and proceeded as high up as the Icy Cape. It was subsequently visited by several English ships for the purposes of trade, and though every portion of it was explored with the greatest accuracy by that most excellent and persevering navigator, Vancouver, as far as the head of Cook's Inlet, in latitude 61° 15', yet, on the ground of priority of discovery, it is sufficiently clear that England has no claim to territorial possession. On this principle, it would jointly belong to Russia and Spain; but on the same principle, Russia would be completely excluded from any portion of it to the southward of 59°. She has, however, been tacitly permitted to form an establishment named Sitka at the head of Norfolk Sound in latitude 57°; and this, apparently, must have tempted her to presume that no opposition would be offered to an extension of territory down to the 51st degree of latitude, which includes all the detailed discoveries of Cook and Vancouver, *i.e.*, New Hanover, New Cornwall, New Norfolk on the main, and the Islands of King George, Queen Charlotte, and Prince of Wales upon the coast.

There is, however, one trifling circumstance of which we are persuaded His Imperial Majesty was ignorant when he issued his sweeping Ukase, namely, that the whole country, from latitude 56° 30' to the boundary of the United States in latitude 48°, or thereabouts, is now, and has long been, in the actual possession of the British North-west Company. The communication with this vast territory is by the Peace River, which, crossing the Rocky Mountains from the westward in latitude 56° north and longitude 121° west, falls into the Polar Sea by the Mackenzie River. The country behind them to the westward has been named by the settlers New Caledonia, and is in extent, from north to south, about 500 miles, and from east to west 300 miles. It is described as very beautiful, abounding in fine forests, rivers, and magnificent lakes, one of which is not less than 300 miles in circumference, surrounded by picturesque mountains, clothed to their very summits with timber trees of the largest dimensions. From this lake a river falls to the westward into the Pacific, either into Port Essington or Observatory Inlet, where Vancouver discovered the mouths of two rivers, one in latitude 54° 15', the other in 54° 59'. In the summer season it swarms with salmon, from which the natives derive a considerable part of their subsistence. The North-west Company have a post on its borders in latitude 54° 30' north, longitude 125° west, distant about 180 miles from the "Observatory Inlet" of Vancouver, the head of which lies in latitude 55° 15' north, longitude 129° 44' west, where by this time the United Company of the North-west and Hudson's Bay have, in all probability, formed an establishment, and thus opened a direct communication between the Atlantic and the Pacific, the whole way by water, with the exception of a very few miles across the high lands which divide the sources of the rivers and give them opposite directions.

Thus, then, it is obvious that, as we have actual possession of the 6 degrees of coast usurped by Russia in her recent manifesto, her claim to this part is perfectly nugatory. Indeed, as we before observed, the assumption must have been made in utter ignorance of the fact, which is the less surprising, as this part of the world remains as yet a complete blank on our best and latest charts.

It is not easy to conjecture the precise object of Russia in this intended extension of territory on the Continent of North America, unless it be to push along the northern coast as far as Mackenzie's River, which, running at the feet of the Rocky Mountains to the east, would, with the Pacific on the west, afford two excellent barriers to a territory of at least 70,000 square miles, or one-half nearly of all that part of North America in which the fur animals are found, and thus put the Russ-American Company in possession of an almost exclusive monopoly of the trade, as it is well known that, in a few years, the fur-bearing animals will all be destroyed on the eastern side of the Rocky Mountains. In any other view of the subject, it is utterly incomprehensible that the possession of one-tenth part of the habitable globe should not satisfy the ambition, if ambition could ever be satisfied, of one man.

But whatever the object of the Russian Government may be in its expeditions and its Edicts, that of the voyage we are about to notice was purely the promotion of physical science and geographical discovery. We have more than once had occasion to mention, in terms of admiration, the liberal support which an exalted individual of the Russian Empire has always been ready to give to every national scheme for enlarging the sphere of human knowledge: by this munificent patron the present expedition was fitted out. That it failed in the main point was no fault of him who planned it. The commander was recommended by Captain Krusenstern, than whom Russia cannot boast an officer more accomplished in every part of his profession; and if, on his return, he met, as we have heard, with a cool reception in the Imperial circles of St. Petersburgh, it only proves that, amidst an affectation of disappointment, they were not very sorry for the failure of a private enterprise which afforded an opportunity of attempting the same thing as a national measure; for the two ships we have mentioned above were dispatched almost immediately after the return of Lieutenant Kotzebue.

It had been the intention of Count Romanzoff to equip an expedition to explore the North-west Passage by Hudson's Bay or Davis' Strait: but on finding that preparations were making in England to attempt it by that route, he determined on prosecuting the discovery from the eastward. For this purpose he caused a ship of 180 tons to be built of fir at Abo, to which he gave the name of "Rurick." Her establishment consisted of Lieutenant Kotzebue, Lieutenant Schischmareff, two mates, M. A. von Chamisso, of Berlin, naturalist, Dr. Eschholz, surgeon, M. Choris, painter, and twenty men; and, to the credit of the commander, it may be mentioned that, over a navigation of three years in very opposite climates, and in so small a vessel, he lost one man only, who left the Baltic in a consumption.

The "Rurick" sailed from Plymouth in October 1815, and on the 28th March had reached that solitary spot in the midst of the Great Pacific which bears the name of Zeapy, but which is better known as Easter Island. Some of the natives swam off to the "Rurick" with yams, taro roots, and bananas, which they gave in exchange for bits of iron hoops. As the boats approached the shore they began to assemble in great numbers, and though unarmed, and apparently desirous of the strangers landing, they were thought to exhibit a terrific and hostile appearance, having painted their faces red, white, and black, and making all manner of violent gestures, accompanied with a most horrible noise, this was soon ascertained to be the case, and the boats were repelled from the shore by volleys of stones. This conduct, so contrary to their former practice, was afterwards fully explained to Lieutenant Kotzebue when at the Sandwich Islands.

An American, who commanded a schooner called the "Nancy," from New London, having discovered a vast multitude of seals on the little uninhabited island of Massafuero, o the west of Juan Fernandez, thought it would be an excellent speculation to establish a Colony there in order to carry on the fishery. For this purpose, having but just sufficient hands to navigate his ship, and there being no anchorage off the island, the wretch (base and brutal beyond the ordinary degree of such characters) proceeded to Easter Island, and landing at Cook's Bay, succeeded in seizing and carrying off twelve men and ten women, to people his new Colony. For the first three days they were confined in irons; when fairly out of sight of land, however, they were released, and the first use made by the males of their liberty was to jump overboard, choosing rather to perish in the waves than to be carried away they knew not whither, or for what purpose. The women, who were with difficulty restrained from following them, were taken to Massafuera; what became of them afterwards Lieutenant Kotzebue does not inform us, and we fear to guess.

On the 16th April they descried a small island, probably the Dog Island of Schouten, but which, differing 22 miles in latitude from that given by him, Kotzebue is pleased to call Doubtful Island; and on the 19th they discovered another small island, covered with majestic cocoa-nut trees, to which he gave the name of Romanzoff. It had no inhabitants, but boats and deserted huts were visible on the shore. This new discovery so delighted our young navigator that, inconsiderable as he felt it to be, "I would not," he says, "have resigned the pure and heartfelt joy which it gave me for the treasures of the world."

On the 22nd they fell in with another island, in 14° 41' south longitude, 144° 59' 20" west, which was also considered as a new discovery. The truth, however, is that they all belong to those groups whose numbers are not yet ascertained, but which are known by the name of King George's and Palliser's Islands, discovered by Cook, to which also belong what he is pleased to call Rurick's Chain and Krusenstern's Island. The sea, in fact, is here covered with innumerable low rocky islets, formed by the coral animals, the discovery of any individual one of which scarcely seems to merit a distinct claim to notice.

On the 19th May they crossed the chain of Mulgrave's Islands, in 8° 45' 52" north, and on the 21st discovered a group of low coral islands, lying in about 11° north and longitude 190°, and separated by a channel which, considering it as a new discovery, they named Kutusoff and Suwaroff; "and I felt myself inexpressibly happy," says Kotzebue, "in being the first who had erected an eternal monument in the South Sea to these two men, who had so highly deserved of their country." Our navigator is somewhat enthusiastic in his language, but we have little doubt that his "new discovery" forms a part of the group long known as Wallis' Islands on the charts.

On the 19th June they reached Avatscha Bay, in Kamtchatka, which they left on the 15th July; on the 20th they descried Behring Islands, and on the 27th were close in with St. Lawrence Island, where they had some communication with the natives, who resembled the people whom Cook found on the shores of Norton Sound and the Aleutian Islands, and were living in tents made of the ribs of whale, and covered with the skin of the morse. Their mode of salutation was somewhat like that of the Esquimaux of Baffin's Bay; "each of them," says Kotzebue, "embraced me, rubbed his nose hard against mine, and ended his caresses by spitting on his hands, and wiping them several times over my face."

On the 30th July they were on the American shore, between Cape Prince of Wales and Garozdeff's Island, which being found to consist of four instead of three, as laid down on Cook's chart, induced Kotzebue to conjecture that the fourth must have subsequently risen out of the sea, "otherwise," says he, "Cook or Clarke would have seen it;" the more probable supposition is that the fog prevented them. At all events, he looked on it as a new discovery, and named it after Ratmaroff, who had been Krusenstern's First Lieutenant on his voyage to Japan. To the northward of Cape Prince of Wales is a long tract of low land, covered with luxuriant verdure, and apparently well inhabited. On landing they found only dogs in the houses, the people having fled; these houses were not merely temporary abodes, but had mud walls; the interior was cleanly and convenient, and divided into a number of apartments by boarded partitions; the floors, raised 3 feet from the ground, were also of wood, which is supplied by the vast quantity of drift brought by the north-east current from the mouths of the rivers of America to the southward of Behring Straits, and thrown on the shores of the straits.

Our navigators soon discovered that they were on an island about 7 miles long, and a mile across in the widest part; beyond it was a deep inlet, running eastward into the continent. On entering this bay, two boats were observed, of the same kind as those made use of in the Aleutian Islands. The appearance of the people in them was extremely filthy and disgusting; their countenances had an expression of fierceness, and all endeavours to induce them to land were unavailing. To this bay, which was not examined, Kotzebue gave the name of his Lieutenant, Schischmareff, and to the island that of Vice-Admiral Saritscheff.

In proceeding northerly they met with two light boats, the people in which were extremely savage, making hideous grimaces, uttering the most piercing cries, and threatening to hurl their lances. Pointing muskets at them had no effect, which convinced the Russians that they were wholly unacquainted with fire-arms. The land continued low, and trended more to the eastward, when, on the 1st August, the entrance into a broad inlet was discovered, into which the current ran very rapidly. As the interior of this great inlet is the undoubted discovery of Kotzebue, though the opening in the land was before known, it may be proper that the account of it should be given in his own words:—

F

"I cannot describe the strange sensation which I now experienced at the idea that I perhaps stood at the entrance of the so long sought north-east passage, and that fate had chosen me to be the discoverer. I felt my heart oppressed, and at the same time an impatience which would not let me rest, and was still increased by the perfect calm. To satisfy myself, at least by going on shore, and clearly observing from some eminence the direction of the coast, I had two boats got ready, at which our naturalists were highly delighted. We set out by 2 o'clock in the afternoon; the depth regularly decreased; half-a-mile from shore we had still 5 fathoms. We landed without difficulty near a hill, which I immediately ascended; from the summit I could nowhere perceive land in the strait; the high mountains to the north either formed islands or were a coast by themselves, for that the two coasts could not be connected together was evident, even from the great difference between this very low and that remarkably high land. From the eminence on which I stood I had a very extensive view into the country, which stretched out in a large plain, here and there interrupted by marshes, small lakes, and a river, which flowed, with numerous windings, and the mouth of which was not far from us. As far as the eye could reach everything was green; here and there were flowers in blossom, and no snow was seen but on the tops of the mountains at a great distance; yet one had to dig but half a foot deep to find nothing but frost and ice under this verdant carpet. It was my intention to continue my survey of the coast in the boats, but a number of 'haydares' coming to us along the coast to the east withheld me. Five of them, each of them with eight or ten men, all armed with lances and bows, soon landed near us. At the head of each boat was a fox-skin on a high pole, with which they beckoned to us, uttering at the same time the loudest cries. I ordered my crew to be prepared for defence, and went myself, with our gentlemen, to meet the Americans, who on seeing us approach sat down like Turks in a large circle on the ground, by which they meant to manifest their friendly intentions; two Chiefs had seated themselves apart from the rest. We entered this circle well armed, and perceived that they had left most of their arms in their boats, but had long knives concealed in their sleeves. Distrust, curiosity, and astonishment were painted on their countenances; they spoke very much, but unfortunately we did not understand a word. To give them a proof of my friendly sentiments I distributed tobacco; the two Chiefs received a double portion, and they were all evidently delighted at this valuable present. Those who had received tobacco first were cunning enough secretly to change their places, in the hopes of receiving a second portion. They prize tobacco highly, and are as fond of chewing as of smoking it. It was a curious sight to see this savage horde sitting in a circle smoking out of white stone pipes with wooden tubes. It is very remarkable that the use of tobacco should already have penetrated into these parts, which no European has ever visited. The Americans receive this, as well as other European goods, from the Tschukutskoi. To the two Chiefs I gave knives and scissors; the latter, with which they seemed to be quite unacquainted, gave them particular pleasure when they remarked that they could cut their hair with them, and immediately they went from hand to hand round the whole circle, each trying their sharpness on his hair. It was probably the first time in their lives that these Americans had seen Europeans, and we reciprocally regarded each other. They are of a middle size, robust make, and healthy appearance; their motions are lively, and they seemed much inclined to sportiveness. Their countenances, which have an expression of wantonness, but not of stupidity, are ugly and dirty, characterized by small eyes and very high cheek-bones; they have holes on each side of the mouth in which they wear morse bones, ornamented with blue glass beads, which gives them a most frightful appearance. Their hair hangs down long, but is cut quite short on the crown of the head. Their head and ears are also adorned with beads. Their dresses, which are made of skins, are of the same cut as the Parka in Kamtchatka, only that there it reaches to the feet, and here hardly covers the knee; besides this, they wear pantaloons and small half-boots of seal-skin."—(Vol. i, p. 207.)

The latitude of the ship's anchorage was 66° 42' 30", longitude 164° 12' 50". Nothing but sea was seen to the eastward, and a strong current ran to the north-east, from which circumstances our navigators still cherished a hope of discovering through this inlet a passage into the Frozen Ocean. With this view they spent thirteen days in examining the shores of the inlet, but the only passage out of it was on the south-eastern shore, apparently communicating with Norton Sound, and a channel on the western side opening probably into Schischmareff Bay.

We do not, however, exactly comprehend M. Kotzebue, where he says, "I certainly hope that this sound may lead to important discoveries next year, and though a north-east passage may not with certainty be depended on, yet I believe I shall be able to penetrate much farther to the east, as the land has very deep indentures." Does this mean "farther to the east" within the sound, or to the northward of the sound? If the former, it is quite clear that the examination in that direction was not satisfactory to himself; and knowing, as we do, what mistakes have occurred by the overlapping of points of land when seen only at a distance, we confess that we are not quite satisfied with the examination of the north-east coast to the eastern extremity, when, as appears by the chart, the approach was seldom nearer than 10 miles. Our hope, however, of a clear passage does not lie in Kotzebue's inlet.

On a promontory which juts into the south-eastern part of the bay, the party who had landed made "a singular discovery":—

"We had climbed much about during our stay without discovering that we were on real icebergs. The doctor, who had extended his excursions, found part of the bank broken down, and saw to his astonishment that the interior of the mountain consisted of pure ice. At this news we all went, provided with shovels and crows, to examine this phenomenon more closely, and soon arrived at a place where the back rises almost perpendicularly out of the sea to the height of 100 feet, and then runs off, rising still higher. We saw masses of the purest ice of the height of 100 feet, which are under a cover of moss and grass, and could not have been produced but by some terrible revolution. The place which, by some accident, had fallen in, and is now exposed to the sun and air, melts away, and a good deal of water flows into the sea. An indisputable proof that what we saw was real ice is the quantity of mammoth's teeth and bones which were exposed to view by the melting, and among which I myself found a very fine tooth. We could not assign any reason for a strong smell, like that of burnt horn, which we perceived in this place. The covering of these mountains, on which the most luxuriant grass grows to a certain height, is only half-a-foot thick, and consists of a mixture of clay, sand, and earth, below which the ice gradually melts away, the green cover sinks with it, and continues to grow, and thus it may be foreseen that in a long series of years the mountain will vanish, and a green valley be formed in its stead. By a good observation we found the latitude of the tongue of land 66° 15' 36" north."—(Vol. i, p. 219.)

This result of "a terrible revolution" is considered by M. Chamisso, the naturalist, "to be similar to the ground ice, covered with vegetation, at the mouth of the Lena, out of which the mammoth, the skeleton of which is now in St. Petersburgh, was thawed." He makes the height of it to be "80 feet at most," and "the length of the profile, in which the ice is exposed to sight, about a musket-shot."

We have little doubt that both Kotzebue and Chamisso are mistaken with regard to the formation of this ice-mountain. The terrible revolution of Nature is sheer nonsense, and the ground ice of the Lena is cast up from the sea, and afterwards buried by the alluvial soil brought down by the floods, in the same manner as the huge blocks which Captain Parry found on the beach of Melville Island; this operation, however, could not take place on the face of the promontory in the tranquil sound of Kotzebue. What they discovered (without suspecting it) was, in fact, a real iceberg, which had been formed in the manner in which we conceive all icebergs are: a rill of water, falling in a little cascade from a precipitous height, is converted into a sheet of ice in the course of some severe winter; if such a sheet be not entirely melted in the short summer which follows, its volume will necessarily be increased in the ensuing winter, and thus the projection of the promontory, from year to year, will swell till the immense mass, by its own weight, and probably undermined by the constant dashing of the waves, breaks off, and is floated into the ocean. The thin stratum of soil which, in the present instance, covered the upper upper surface of the iceberg might have been carried upon it by the spreading of the original rill, which, if there be any truth in the miserable print annexed, is seen to trickle down the face of the ice in numerous little streamlets, proceeding from under the soil on the top, and which, when united at the base, form a very pretty river, with trees on its banks.

All our northern navigators affirm that stones, moss, and earth have been observed on the floating icebergs of Davis' Strait and Baffin's Bay. In like manner may the mammoth's teeth have been carried down by the upper stream and inclosed within the ice. Chamisso, however, does not say that these grinders and tusk (which more resemble those of the present race of elephants than such as are usually supposed to belong to the mammoth) were found within the ice, but near the ground ice on the point of land where they had bivouacked, adding that "fossil ivory is found here as in Northern Asia." How the remains of these huge animals came into these high latitudes we leave the geologists to settle.

On quitting this inlet, to which was properly given the name of Kotzebue's Sound (which they did on the 15th August), we naturally expected that, with a fine open sea, without the least appearance of ice on the water or snow on the land, and with the thermometer from 8 to 12 degrees of Réaumur (50 to 59 degrees of Fahrenheit), the "Rurick" would have directed her course to the northward, as far at least as Icy Cape, to which a couple of days would have carried her, instead of which she stood directly across for the Asiatic coast, "because," says Kotzebue, "I wished to become acquainted with its inhabitants, and to compare them with the Americans." This comparison had long before been made, and was certainly no object of the present voyage. Here were no discoveries to be made. He stood, however, over to East Cape, and having passed the remainder of the month of August among the Tchukutskoi, made the best of his way to Ounalaska.

We cannot help thinking that the Lieutenant committed a great error in judgment by spending a fortnight of the most favourable part of the season for making discoveries in these latitudes in Kotzebue's Sound. Had appearances been even more favourable than they were for a communication between this inlet and the Polar Sea, an enterprising navigator would have pushed forward, without a moment's loss of time, along the shore to the extreme north, as the ascertaining of this point, and the trending of the coast to the eastward, were the grand objects of the expedition, the postponing of which to another year, for the prosecution of one of minor importance (which might still have been examined before the winter set in), was, to say the least of it, imprudent. Besides, why did he not winter in Kotzebue's Sound, since it was found to be so perfectly safe, and so much superior to Norton Sound, from which he was instructed to proceed on his discovery the following year? And how are the instructions for wintering in Norton Sound consistent with those which, he afterwards tells us, directed him "to pass the winter months in the neighbourhood of the imperfectly known Coral Islands, to make discoveries there"? The latter was certainly the more agreeable, and we think he did right in adopting it.

Before we take leave of Behring Strait, we have a few remarks to offer on the information obtained by Kotzebue as connected with the main object of the expedition, and which alone induced Count Romanzoff to cause it to be undertaken. It may be recollected by some of our readers that about the time when our ships were fitting out for the Arctic expedition we were at some pains to assign grounds for the probability of a communication between the Atlantic and Pacific Oceans, on which alone the practicability of a north-west passage could be maintained, and that one of the arguments in favour of the affirmative was that a constant current being known to descend the Welcome into Hudson's Bay, seemed to require a constant current on the opposite side of America through Behring Strait to afford the necessary supply of water. Every circumstance that we inquired into on the side of the Pacific seemed to warrant this conclusion; the drift wood, the retiring of the ice to the northward, the temperature of the water, were all in favour of such a current; and this led to another conclusion, that the two continents of Asia and America could not be joined, as had been fancied, on grounds almost too absurd for serious refutation.

The observations of Kotzebue and Chamisso are highly satisfactory as to the perpetual current which sets to the northward through Behring Strait. They concur in affirming that it is this current which brings such quantities of drift wood (some of it consisting of the trunks of huge trees) to the shores of Saratcheff's Island and Kotzebue's Sound. M. Chamisso says that on "the breaking up of the ice in the Sea of Kamtchatka, the icebergs and fields of ice do not drift, as in the Atlantic, to the south, nor do they drive to the Aleutian Islands, but into the strait to the north;" and Kotzebue asserts that "the direction of the current was *always* north-east in Behring Strait." Again, he says, "the current, according to our calculation, had carried us 50 miles to the north-north-east in twenty-four hours, that is, above 2 miles an hour." When near the Asiatic side of the strait, they find it running with a velocity of not less than 3 miles an hour, and they confidently state that, even with a fresh north wind, it continued to run equally strong from the south. Now, if this happens in the summer season, when the melting of the ice is going on in the Polar Sea, which some would persuade us was the cause of the currents in Hudson's Bay, we have a right to ask them to explain the setting of the water from this melted ice in a contrary direction through Behring Strait.

M. Kotzebue thus concludes:—

"The constant north-east direction of the current in Behring Strait proves that the water meets with no opposition, and consequently a passage must exist, though perhaps not adapted to navigation. Observations have long been made that the current in Baffin's Bay runs to the south, and thus no doubt can remain that the mass of water which flows into Behring Strait takes its course round America, and returns through Baffin's Bay into the ocean."—(Vol. i, p. 243.)

We cannot omit recurring, on the present occasion, to a subject we have frequently noticed, but which, as we think. has never been satisfactorily accounted for; we mean the vast difference of temperature between the western and the eastern coasts of continents or large islands. Though Humboldt has taken a philosophic view of the subject, and in particular situations has, to a certain degree, explained the cause, yet his theory will not account for this extraordinary difference between two continents, separated only by a strait scarcely twice the width of that between Calais and Dover, which was felt so sensibly that the crossing of it was like passing from summer into winter. While all is verdure at Cape Prince of Wales, in America, the opposite point of East Cape, in Asia, is covered, as we are told, with "eternal ice." "The vegetation," says Chamisso, "in the interior of Kotzebue's Sound is considerably higher than in the interior of St. Lawrence Bay; the willows are higher, the grasses richer, all vegetation more juicy and stronger." "Ice and snow," says Kotzebue, "have maintained their rule here" (in Asia) "since last year, and in this state we find the old coast; while in America, even the summits of the highest mountains are free from snow; there the navigator sees the coast covered with a green carpet, while here, black mossy rocks frown upon him, with snow and icicles." In fact, a few hours' sailing directly to the westward sunk the thermometer from 59 to 43 degrees of Fahrenheit.

We can readily conceive why at Melville Island, surrounded with eternal ice, the thermometer should descend to 87 degrees below the freezing point, and still lower on the elevated plains in the interior of North America, where half the surface consists of frozen lakes and swamps,* but we cannot comprehend why the same warmth of the Great Pacific, which tempers the rigorous cold of the Frozen Ocean on the American side of Behring Strait, should refuse to mitigate the severity of the weather on the side of Asia, more especially as it appears, from repeated observations made on the present voyage, that the current from the south was equally strong on both sides of the strait.

* Captain Franklin observed it as low as 89 degrees below the freezing point in latitude 64°.

The difference is still greater between the climates of the two shores separated by the Atlantic, but then the sea is much wider. While on the eastern coast of North America all is desolation and sterility, even so low as the 55th degree of. latitude, and ice and snow mountain a perpetual existence at the 60th parallel, we find on the coast of Norway (10 degrees higher) that all is life and animation and beauty. "Altengaard," says the celebrated Von Buch, "is a surprising place. It is situated in the midst of a forest of Scotch firs, upon a green meadow, with noble views through the trees of the fiord, with its numerous points projecting one beyond the other into the vast sheet of water. and closed by the plains of Leyland and Langford. The surrounding woods are so beautiful and so diversified! We perceive through the boughs on the opposite side of the water the foaming torrent descending from the rocks, and communicating to the saw-mills perpetual motion. It appears, when we enter the wood from the beach, as if we were transported to the park of Berlin." Yet Altengaard is close upon the 70th parallel of latitude.

M. Chamisso seems to think that he has hit upon a more philosophical theory for this great difference of temperature in the same parallels of latitude than those of Humboldt, Von Buch, and Wallenberg, grounded on the sea and land breezes, the monsoons and trade winds; but as his ideas appear to us not a little crude, and as he declines to submit his "new theory to calculations, or try it by the touchstone of facts," it will be sufficient to refer our readers to it (vol. iii, p. 279). We have more respect for his observations on the sensible objects of the Creation, and readily subscribe to the correctness of his views in the following paragraph:—

"As, on the one hand, in proportion as you go farther in the land towards the north, the woods become less lofty, the vegetation gradually decreases, animals become scarcer, and, lastly (as at Nova Zembla), the reindeer and the *Glires* vanish with the last plants, and only birds of prey prowl about the icy streams for their food, so, on the other hand, the sea becomes more and more peopled. The *Algæ*, gigantic species of *Tang*, form inundated woods round the rocky coasts, such as are not met with in the torrid zone. But the waters swarm with animal life, though all aquatic animals seem to remain in a lower scale than their relatives of the same class on land. The *Medusæ* and *Zoophytes*, *Moluscæ* and *Crustaceæ*, innumerable species of fish, in incredibly crowded shoals; . the gigantic swimming mammalia, whales, physeters, dolphins, morse, and seals, fill the sea and its strand, and countless flights of water-fowls rock themselves on the bosom of the ocean, and in the twilight resemble floating islands."—(Vol. iii, p. 306.)

We have little to observe on the manners and character of the people who inhabit the shores of Behring Strait. They have long been supposed, and are now unquestionably ascertained, to belong to that extraordinary race of men generally known by the name of Esquimaux, and who, commencing at the Kolyma, and probably much farther to the westward of Asia, have settled themselves on the coast and islands of that continent, down to the Gulf of Anadyr, the islands of Behring Strait, the Aleutian Islands, the western coast of America from the promontory of Alaska, the northern coast along the Polar Sea, the shores and islands of Hudson's Bay, Baffin's Bay, and Davis' Strait, of Old Greenland and Labrador. Everywhere throughout this vast extent of sea-coast, where the gigantic mammalia above mentioned abound, and from which their food, raiment, dwellings, and utensils are derived, they are to be found. Of the deplorable circumstances which may have driven these people (evidently of Tartar origin) to dwell only among regions of "thick-ribbed ice" and snow, and to depend for their daily subsistence almost solely on the sea, history is silent, and it would be vain to form any hypothesis on the subject.

Miserable, however, as their condition appears to be, they are contented with it, and always cheerful; living in small independent hordes, and apparently on terms of a perfect equality. Civil and obliging to strangers, they are courteous to one another, and amidst their train oil and putrid fish carefully observe the decencies of domestic life. Woman here is not degraded from her rank in society by that curse which polygamy has entailed on the whole sex where it exists, whether in savage or half-civilized life. This common feature of Asiatic manners they have happily lost ; what is not a little remarkable, however, they have preserved a language of singular complication in its mechanism, which, with some little variety in the dialect, is spoken from the North-east Cape of Asia to the southern point of Old Greenland.

Captain Franklin found that his Esquimaux interpreter from the banks of the Chesterfield Inlet understood the vocabularies composed by the missionaries of Labrador; and Dr. Eschsoltz, surgeon of the "Rurick," was fully convinced of the coincidence of the Aleutian language with that of the Esquimaux. How has this community been maintained through ages between tribes so very widely separated, without any written character, and with little or no intercourse, when among nations apparently in a much higher state of civilization the languages are frequently so different as not to be generally understood ? Perhaps the fewness of their wants, and the very limited number of objects of sense by which they are surrounded (requiring but few words to express them), may partly explain a phenomenon so unusual in the history of the species.

It could not be expected that M. Kotzebue should have much new or interesting information to communicate respecting the Aleutian Islands, the coast of California, or the Sandwich Islands, at all of which he touched in his progress towards the tropical islands of the Pacific, where his intention was to pass the winter, and to prepare for a second attempt at northern discovery.

G

On the 1st January, 1817, a low woody island was discovered in latitude 10° 8' north, longitude 189° 4', reckoning from the meridian of Greenwich westerly. The natives came off and hovered round the ship in canoes; tall and well-shaped, with high foreheads and aquiline noses, they seemed to differ somewhat from the generality of the South Sea islanders; their hair, neatly tied up, was adorned with wreaths of flowers and coloured shells; and cylinders of green leaves or of tortoise-shells, 3 inches in diameter, hung from their ears. Two or three days afterwards they fell in with a chain of islands extending from latitude 6° to latitude 12°, longitude 187° to longitude 193° west, or rather a succession of groups, each consisting of a circular reef of coral rocks, out of which, at irregular distances, rose a number of small flat islands, richly covered with the bread-fruit, the pandanus, and cocoa-nut trees. Captain Krusenstern claims for Lieutenant Kotzebue the merit of having first discovered these groups; but we can scarcely permit ourselves to doubt that they are the same which were seen by Captain Marshall in the "Scarborough" in 1788, and by the "Nautilus" in 1799, and named on the charts the Nautilus, the Chatham, and Calvert's Islands. We readily admit, however, that "if Lieutenant Kotzebue be not the first discoverer of these islands, he is, at all events, the first who has made us acquainted with their true position;" and we are disposed to allow him the further merit of having thrown much additional light on the nature and formation of those singular coral groups which rise out of the Pacific in circular chains like *fairy rings* in a meadow, almost through its whole extent from east to west, and from the 30th parallel of northern to the same parallel of southern latitude.

It has long been known that the upper surface of these islands, usually known by the general name of Coral Rocks, is composed of calcareous fragments of a great variety of forms, the production of marine animals, and since the voyages of Cook, Flinders, D'Entrecasteaux, and others, it has been as generally supposed that these minute creatures began their wonderful fabrics at the very depth of the ocean, building upwards from the bottom, and that each generation, dying in its cells, was succeeded by others, building upon the labours of their predecessors, and thus rising in succession till they reached the surface. This was surmised to be the process from the circumstance of the sea being found so deep close to the external side of the reef as frequently to be unfathomable. It now appears that this is not precisely the case.

The facility with which the little vessel of Kotzebue entered through the open spaces in the surrounding reef or dam into the included lagoon enabled M. Chamisso to inspect more narrowly the nature of these extraordinary fabrics, and to give a more distinct and intelligible account of their origin and progress. From the circumstance of their being grouped only in certain spots of the Pacific, and always in an united though irregular chain, generally more or less approaching to a circle, he was led to conclude that the coral animals lay the foundation of their edifices on shoals in the ocean, or perhaps, more correctly speaking, on the summits of those submarine mountains which advance sufficiently near the surface to afford them as much light and heat as may be necessary for their operations.

The extreme depth at which they can perform their functions has not yet been ascertained, but it was found, on the late voyage of discovery, that in Baffin's Bay marine animals existed at the depth of 1,000 fathoms, and in a temperature below the freezing point. The outer edge of the reef exposed to the surf is the first that shows itself above water, and consists of the largest blocks of coral rock, composed of madrepores mixed with various shells and the spines of the sea hedgehog, which break into large tablets, and are so compact as to sound loudly under the hammer. On the sloping side of the inner ridge or reef the animals discovered in the act of carrying on their operations were the *Tubipora musica*, the *Millepora cœrulea*, *Distichopora*, *Actinias*, and various kinds of *Polypus*. The living branches of the *Lythophytes* were generally attached to the dead stems; many of the latter, however, crumbled into sand, which, accumulating on the inner declivity, constitutes a considerable part of the surface of the new islands.

The ridge or reef, when once above water on the windward side, extends itself by slow degrees till it has surrounded the whole plateau of the submarine mountain, leaving in the middle an inclosed lake into which are passages, more or less deep, communicating with the ocean; the islets formed on the reef or wall are smaller or larger, according to accidental circumstances. Chamisso observed that the smaller species of "corals" had sought a quiet abode within the lagoon, where they were silently and slowly throwing up banks which in process of time unite with the islets that surround them, and at length fill up the lagoon, so that what was at first a ring of islands becomes one connected mass of land. The progress towards a state fit for the habitation of man is thus described by the naturalist :—

"As soon as it has reached such a height that it remains almost dry at low water at the time of ebb, the corals leave off building higher; sea-shells, fragments of coral, sea-hedgehog shells, and their broken-off prickles are united by the burning sun, through the medium of the cementing calcareous sand, which has arisen from the pulverization of the above-mentioned shells into one whole or solid stone, which, strengthened by the continual throwing up of new materials, gradually increases in thickness, till it at last becomes so high that it is covered only during some seasons of the year by the high tides. The heat of the sun so penetrates the mass of stone when it is dry that it splits in many places and breaks off in flakes. These flakes, so separated, are raised one upon another by the waves at the time of high water. The always active surf throws blocks of coral (frequently of a fathom in length and 3 or 4 feet thick) and shells of marine animals between and upon the foundation stones. After this the calcareous sand lies undisturbed, and offers to the seeds of trees and plants cast upon it by the waves a soil upon which they rapidly grow to overshadow its dazzling white surface. Entire trunks of trees, which are carried by the rivers from other countries and islands, find here at length a resting-place after their long wanderings; with these come some small animals, such as lizards and insects, as the first inhabitants. Even before the trees form a wood, the real sea birds nestle here: strayed land birds take refuge in the bushes, and at a much later period, when the work has been long since completed, man also appears, builds his hut on the fruitful soil formed by the corruption of the leaves of the trees, and calls himself lord and proprietor of this new creation."—(Vol. iii, pp. 331-333.)

The reflections of Kotzebue are just and natural:—

"The spot on which I stood filled me with astonishment, and I adored in silent admiration the omnipotence of God, who had given even to these minute animals the power to construct such a work. My thoughts were confounded when I consider the immense series of years that must elapse before such an island can rise from the fathomless abyss of the ocean and become visible on the surface. At a future period they will assume another shape; all the islands will join, and form a circular slip of earth with a pond or lake in the circle; and this form will again change as these animals continue building, till they reach the surface, and then the water will one day vanish, and only one great island be visible. It is a strange feeling to walk about on a living island, where all below is actively at work. And to what corner of the earth can we penetrate where human beings are not already to be found? In the remotest regions of the north, amidst mountains of ice, under the burning sun of the Equator, nay, even in the middle of the ocean, on islands which have been formed by animals, they are met with."—(Vol. ii, p. 36.)

The inhabitants of this group seemed to differ little from those of Polynesia in general. The men were tall and well made; they wore their black hair neatly knotted upon the head, and decorated with wreaths of flowers, and had cylinders of tortoise-shell, also ornamented with flowers, hanging from the ears. The women were extremely bashful, retiring, and modest. Kotzebue and his associates went through every part of the group of islands without the least apprehension from the natives, whom they invariably found mild, inoffensive, and obliging. "I was unarmed," he says, "for I felt myself quite secure among these kind-hearted children of Nature, who, to amuse me, would play and dance before me." It was evident they had never before seen white men, for, on their first approach, they were dreadfully terrified, and it was some time before they could be prevailed on to visit the ship; the hogs and dogs on board greatly alarmed them, and were considered as huge rats, the only quadrupeds with which they were acquainted.

Among their most useful plants were the cocoa-nut tree, the pandanus, and the bread-fruit, which furnished them with food, raiment, and lodging.

"The fruit of the pandanus constitutes in Radack the food of the people. The compound fibrous stone-fruits which compose the conical fruit contain a spicy juice at their basis, the point where they are fixed. To obtain this juice, the fruit is first beaten with a stone, the fibres chewed, and pressed in the mouth. The fruit is also baked in pits, after the manner of the South Sea, not so much to eat it in this state as to prepare ' mogan ' from it, a spicy dry confectionery, which is carefully preserved as a valuable stock for long voyages. To prepare the 'mogan ' all the members of one or more families are employed. From the stone-fruits, as they come out of the baking-pit, the condensed juice is expressed by passing them over the edge of a shell, then spread out on a grate covered with leaves, exposed over a slight charcoal fire to the sun, and dried. The thin slices, as soon as they are sufficiently dried, are rolled up tight, and these rolls then neatly wrapped in the leaves of the tree and tied up. The kernel of this fruit is well tasted, but difficult to be obtained, and is often neglected. From the leaves of the pandanus the women prepare all sorts of mats, as well the square ones with elegant borders, which serve as aprons, as those which are used as ship's sails, and the thicker ones for sleeping upon."—(Vol. iii, p. 150.)

The naturalist seems to think that these children of Nature were somewhat restrained from the besetting vice of savages, that of appropriating to themselves the property of others, by a person of the name of Kadu, from the reef of Ulea (one of the numerous islets forming the great group of the Carolinas, and distant from this place at least 1,500 miles), and who, though he had never seen an European ship or European man, had heard much of both. This extraordinary character, notwithstanding all the entreaties of his friends, determined to accompany Lieutenant Kotzebue; and when they became enabled to understand each other, they learned from him that having one day left Ulea in a sailing-boat with three of his countrymen, a violent storm arose and drove them out of their course; that they drifted about the open sea for eight months, according to their reckoning by the moon, making a knot on a cord at every new moon. Being expert fishermen, they subsisted entirely on the produce of the sea, and when the rain fell laid in as much fresh water as they had vessels to contain it. " Kadu," says Kotzebue, " who was the best diver, frequently went down to the bottom of the sea, where *it is well known* that the water is not so salt, with a cocoa-nut (*shell*) with only a small opening."* When these unfortunate men reached the Isles of Radack, however, every hope and almost every feeling had died within them; their sail had long been destroyed, their canoe long been the sport of winds and waves; and they were picked up by the inhabitants of Aur in a state of insensibility. Three or four years had elapsed since their arrival, and Kadu had taken a wife by whom he had one child, notwithstanding which he came up to Kotzebue, and, with a firm and determined voice and look, said, "I will remain with you wherever you go." His friends endeavoured to dissuade him, and even to drag him from the ship; but his resolution was not to be shaken, and when the time of departure arrived, he took an affecting leave of his friends and family, distributed his little property among them, and embarked on board the "Rurick."

Before they left the group, however, Kotzebue thought it right to tell him that he had no intention of revisiting the Islands of Radack, and that he was about to proceed on a long and fatiguing voyage. "He threw his arms around me," says Kotzebue, "vowed to stay with me till death, and nothing remained for me but to keep him, and with a firm determination to provide for him as a father." M. Chamisso has given several anecdotes illustrative of the mild and amiable character of Kadu, who soon became a great favourite of the officers and men of the "Rurick." "We once only," says the naturalist, "saw this mild man angry;" and this was occasioned by some of the crew having removed a little collection of stones which he had formed to a place where he could not find them. He continued during the voyage to conduct himself with great propriety; but on the return of the ship to the same group, he as suddenly changed his mind of continuing with Kotzebue as he had previously formed that resolution, and determined to abide with his friends; the account which he received of the melancholy state of his little daughter after his departure was supposed to be the motive of this change; the reason assigned by himself, however, was that he wished to superintend the new plants and animals which had been collected for the use of the natives at the Sandwich Islands and other places visited by the "Rurick."

The "Rurick" sailed about the middle of March to renew her northern discovery, and on the 13th April had reached the latitude 44° 30′, "a frightful day," says Kotzebue, "which *blasted* all my fairest *hopes*." A tremendous storm had nearly overwhelmed his little vessel, and he was thrown with such violence against a projecting corner of his cabin that he was obliged to keep his bed for several days. On the 24th the ship reached Ounalaska, and on the 29th June, having received on board fifteen Aleutians, proceeded to the northward. On the 10th July they came in sight of St. Lawrence Island. Here Kotzebue inquired of the natives whether the ice had long left their shores. The answer was, "Only within the last three days." "My *hope*, therefore," he observes, "of penetrating Behring Straits was *blasted*" (the Lieutenant, or his translator, has no great choice of words), "as I could not expect that the sea would be cleared of ice for fourteen days." He stood, however, to the northward, and at midnight "perceived," he says, "to their terror firm ice, which extended as far as the eye could see to the north-east, and then to the north, covering the whole surface of the ocean."

Here he made up his mind, if that had not already been done, to lay aside all further attempt at discovery, and return to the more agreeable groups of coral islands. He thus states his case :—

"My melancholy situation, which had daily grown worse since we had left Ounalaska, received here the last blow. The cold air so affected my lungs that I lost my breath, and at last spasms in the chest, faintings, and spitting of blood ensued. I now for the first time perceived that my situation was worse than I would hitherto believe, and the physician seriously declared to me that I could not remain near the ice. It cost me a long and severe contest; more than once I resolved to brave death and accomplish my under-taking, but when I reflected that we had a difficult voyage to our own country still before us, and perhaps the preservation of the 'Rurick' and the lives of my companions depended on mine, I then felt that I must suppress my ambition. The only thing which supported me in this contest was the conscientious assurance of having 'strictly fulfilled my duty. I signified to the crew, in writing, that my ill-health obliged me to return to Ounalaska. The moment I signed the paper was the most painful in my life, for with this stroke of the pen I gave up the ardent and long-cherished wish of my heart."—(Vol. ii, p. 176.)

We have little more to offer on this unsuccessful voyage; but it appears to us that its abrupt abandonment was hardly justified under the circumstances stated. It would not be tolerated in England that the ill-health of the commanding officer should be urged as a plea for giving up an enterprise of moment, while there remained another officer on board fit to succeed him. But the great error, in our opinion, was committed in the first attempt. Had Kotzebue fortunately pushed on to the northward the preceding year, when the sea was perfectly open, and before his people had tasted the soft luxuries of the coral islands, he would unquestionably have succeeded in solving the problem as to the extreme north-west point of America, as Baron Wrangel has done that of the north-east point of Asia, and this would have been something; but we rather suspect that when the physician warned him against approaching the ice, the caution was not wholly disinterested on his

* Chamisso states this circumstance more cautiously; he brought up *cooler* water (he says) which, "*according to their opinion*," was likewise less salt.

part, and that the officers and men, like the successors of the immortal Cook, had come to the conclusion that "the longest way about was the nearest way home."

We cannot close this article without animadverting on the careless manner in which the "Voyage" has been "done into English." The naturalist, Chamisso, in seeming anticipation of what would happen, has entered his caveat against "translations of which he cannot judge," and "recognizes only the German text." In truth, he will find here more than enough to justify his precautions. The present translator joins to a style at once bald and incorrect a deplorable ignorance of his subject; hence the volume abounds in errors of the grossest kind. Many of them may unquestionably be attributed to the undue haste with which the work was produced; but surely it can never be worth the while of any respectable publisher to run a race with the Bridge Street press, the monthly erudities of which, though they may precede, cannot possibly supersede, translations made by competent persons, and brought out in a manner correspondent to the merit of the original works.

No. 4.

EXTRACT FROM THE "NORTH AMERICAN REVIEW" OF OCTOBER 1822.

Message from the President of the United States, transmitting the Information required by a Resolution of the House of Representatives of the 16th February last, in relation to Claims set up by Foreign Governments to Territory of the United States upon the Pacific Ocean, North of the 42nd Degree of Latitude, &c. April 17, 1822.

THE measures lately adopted by the Russian Government, in relation to the north-western coast of the American Continent, are of so extraordinary a character that we cannot refrain from examining the subject, and offering such comments as it naturally demands. We are sensible that a discussion relative to a country so remote, having within its limits but few objects to excite the curiosity, and only connected with the civilized world by an extremely limited commerce, might not ordinarily awaken much general interest. But it is also well known that particular causes have heretofore drawn to it the attention both of statesmen and philosophers, and we are not sure that the attempts to discover a north-west passage, or the dispute respecting Nootka Sound, involved more serious consequences than the efforts now making by Russia, in that quarter of the globe, to monopolize commerce and usurp territory.

A trade to the north-western coast of America, and the free navigation of the waters that wash its shores, have been enjoyed as a common right by subjects of the United States and of several European Powers, without interruption, for nearly forty years. We are by no means prepared to believe, or admit, that all this has been on sufferance merely; and that the *rights* of commerce and navigation in that region have been vested in Russia alone. If such be the fact, however—if Russia has always possessed the right to interdict this trade, we cannot but wonder at her forbearance in permitting it to be carried on for so long a time, manifestly to the injury of her own subjects. Had a monopoly of the fur trade, which Russia now aims at, been secured to the "Russian-American Company" thirty years ago, that Company, with any prudent management, might have attained at the present time the second rank, for wealth and power, in the commercial world, and been worthy not only of Imperial protection, but of Imperial attributes.

A short account of this trade, and sketch of its present state, may assist our readers in forming some estimate of the importance of this subject to the United States, merely in a commercial view, and independent of any question of territorial rights which it may be thought to involve. The third voyage of Cook having made us acquainted with countries of which little was before known, several enterprising individuals, allured by the prospect of a profitable traffic with the natives, engaged in voyages to the north-west coast as early as 1784. The citizens of the United States, then just recovering from the entire prostration of their commerce by the revolutionary war, and possessing more enterprise than capital, were not slow in perceiving the benefits likely to result from the participation in a branch of trade where industry and perseverance could be substituted for capital. In 1787 two vessels were fitted out in the port of Boston, the "Columbia," of 300 tons, and the "Washington," of 100 tons, burthen; the former commanded by Mr. John Kendrick, the latter by Mr. Robert Grey, since known as the first navigator who entered the River Columbia. Other vessels followed shortly after, and those intrusted with the management of these voyages soon acquired the necessary local knowledge to insure a successful competition with the traders of other nations (mostly English) who had preceded them. The habits and ordinary pursuits of the New Englanders qualified them in a peculiar manner for carrying on this trade, and the embarrassed state of Europe, combined with other circumstances, gave them, in the course of a few years, almost a monopoly of the most lucrative part of it. In 1801, which was perhaps the most flourishing period of the trade, there were sixteen ships on the north-west coast, fifteen of which were Americans, and one English. Upwards of 18,000 sea-otter skins, besides other furs, were collected for the China market in that year by the American vessels alone. Since that time the trade has declined, the sea-otter having become scarce, in consequence of the impolitic system pursued by the Russians, as well as by the natives, who destroy indiscriminately the old and the young of this animal, which will probably in a few years be as rarely met with on the coast of America as it is now on that of Kamtchatka and among the Aleutian Islands, where they abounded when first discovered by the Russians. There are at the present time absent from the United States fourteen vessels engaged in this trade, combined with that to the Sandwich Islands, which for several years past has been carried on to a considerable extent in sandal wood. These vessels are from 200 to 400 tons burthen, and carry from twenty-five to thirty men each, and they are usually about three years in completing a voyage. After exchanging with the natives of the coast for furs such part of their cargoes as is adapted to the wants or suited to the fancy of these people, the ships return to the Sandwich Islands, where a cargo of sandal wood is prepared, with which, and their furs, they proceed to Canton, and return to the United States with cargoes of teas, &c. The value at Canton of the furs, sandal wood, and other articles carried thither the last season by American vessels engaged in the trade was little short of 500,000 dollars. When it is considered that a comparatively small capital is originally embarked, that a great part of the value arises from the employment of so much tonnage, and so many men, for the long time necessary to perform a voyage, and that Government finally derives a revenue from that portion of the proceeds which is brought home in teas, equal to at least to the amount invested at Canton, we believe this trade will be thought too valuable to be quietly relinquished.

The publication of which the title is prefixed to this article contains certain documents, communicated by the President of the United States to Congress at their last Session. The most important of them is the Ukase issued by the Emperor of Russia in September 1821, and made known to our Government in February of the present year. We shall devote most of this article to some remarks on this Russian Edict, and the correspondence in relation to it between Mr. Adams, Secretary of State, and the Chevalier de Poletica, the Russian Minister to the United States.

The prohibitions and regulations contained in this Edict are very minute and particular, occupying nearly ten pages of a closely printed pamphlet, and divided into sixty-three sections; in the first and second of which, however, will be found the pith and marrow of the subject. These, together with the introduction, we transcribe. The others are of minor importance. They, however, authorize the forcible seizure, by Russian ships of war, by vessels belonging to the Company, or by individuals in their service, of all foreign vessels which may be *suspected* of violating these regulations, and direct that they be sent to the port of St. Peter and St. Paul, in Kamtchatka, for trial; and, if condemned, the crews are to be sent across Siberia, to some port on the Baltic, and permitted to return to their own country, if they can find the means.

" Edict of His Imperial Majesty, Autocrat of All the Russias.

" The Directing Senate maketh known unto all men: Whereas, in an Edict of His Imperial Majesty, issued to the Directing Senate, on the 4th day of September, and signed by His Imperial Majesty's own hand, it is thus expressed: ' Observing, from reports submitted to us, that the trade of our subjects on the Aleutian Islands and on the north-west coast of America appertaining unto Russia is subjected, because of secret and illicit traffic, to oppression and impediments; and finding that the principal cause of these' difficulties is the want of rules establishing the boundaries for navigation along these coasts, and the order of naval communication, as well in these places as on the whole of the eastern coast of Siberia and the Kurile Islands, we have deemed it necessary to determine these communications by specific regulations, which are hereto attached.

" ' In forwarding these regulations to the Directing Senate, we command that the same be published for universal information, and that the proper measures be taken to carry them into execution.

(Countersigned) " ' COUNT D. GURIEF,
" ' Minister of Finances.'

" It is therefore decreed by the Directing Senate that His Imperial Majesty's Edict be published for the information of all men, and that the same be obeyed by all whom it may concern."

The original is signed by the Directing Senate.
On the original is written, in the handwriting of His Imperial Majesty, thus:
" Be it accordingly,
" ALEXANDER."

" Section 1. The pursuits of commerce, whaling, and fishery, and of all other industry, on all islands, ports, and gulfs, including the whole of the north-west coast of America, beginning from Behring Straits, to the 51st degree of northern latitude, also from the Aleutian Islands to the eastern coast of Siberia, as well as along the Kurile Islands from Behring Straits to the south cape of the Island of Urup, viz., to the 45° 50' northern latitude, is exclusively granted to Russian subjects.

" Sec. 2. It is therefore prohibited to all foreign vessels not only to land on the coasts and islands belonging to Russia, as stated above, *but also to approach them within less than* 100 *Italian miles.* The transgressor's vessel is subject to confiscation, along with the whole cargo."

We doubt if pretensions so extravagant and unfounded—so utterly repugnant to the established laws and usages of nations, have been set up by any Government, claiming rank among civilized nations, since the dark ages of ignorance and superstition, when a Bull of the Holy See was supposed to convey the rights of sovereignty over whole continents, even in anticipation of their discovery. Russia claims the exclusive possession of the whole American Continent north of the 51st degree of latitude. We say the whole continent, for we search in vain for limits except the latitude of 51° on the south, and ' Behring Straits ' on the north. It is just possible that " His Imperial Majesty " may be content, *for the present,* to take the Rocky Mountains for his eastern boundary, though we are not sure, but we do him injustice in ascribing to him such narrow views. Even the attempts of Spain to usurp the exclusive navigation of the South Sea in the vicinity of her American possessions, arbitrary as they were, and violating as they did the indisputable rights of other nations, must, when examined with reference to the different periods when they were made, yield in absurdity to the claims now before us. We cannot forbear expressing our surprise that, in this enlightened age, when the general principles of national rights have been clearly defined, and are well understood, a Government, possessing the highest influence in the political world, and constantly referred to as the arbiter of national disputes, should prefer claims which can only be supported by the extraordinary notion of considering the Pacific Ocean a " close sea," where it is at least 4,000 miles across.

Mr. Adams, in answer to a note from M. de Poletica, accompanying a printed copy of the Russian Edict, expresses the surprise of the American Government at the extraordinary claims it sets forth, and after alluding to the friendly relations which have always existed between the two nations, says, " It was expected before any act which should define the boundaries between the territories of the United States and Russia on this continent, that the same would have been arranged, by Treaty, between the parties." We think this expectation a very reasonable one, and the different course which Russia has chosen to pursue evinces either ignorance of her own rights, or a disregard to those of others. Mr. Adams inquires if M. de Poletica is " authorized to give explanations of the grounds of right, upon principles generally recognized by the laws and usages of nations, which can warrant the claims and regulations contained in the Edict." M. de Poletica, in reply, declares himself " happy to fulfil this task." But as this letter purports to be a complete vindication of the claims of Russia, we prefer giving it entire, and shall follow it with some comments on the " historical facts " it contains, and the inferences which are drawn from them, and add some facts within our own knowledge which may have a bearing on the subject.

"The Chevalier de Poletica to the Secretary of State.

" (Translation.)

" Sir.   " Washington, February 28, 1822.

" I received two days since the letter which you did me the honour to address to me on the same day, by order of the President of the United States, in answer to my note of the 11th current, by which I discharged the orders of my Government in communicating to you the new Regulation adopted by the Russian-American Company, and sanctioned by His Majesty the Emperor, my august Sovereign, on the 4th (16th) September, 1821, relative to foreign commerce in the waters which border upon the establishments of the said Company, on the north-west coast of America.

" Readily yielding, Sir, to the desire expressed by you in your letter of knowing the rights and principles upon which are founded the determinate limits of the Russian possessions on the north-west coast of America, from Behring Strait to the 51st degree of north latitude, I am happy to fulfil this task by only calling your attention to the following historical facts, the authenticity of which cannot be contested.

" The first discoveries of the Russians on the north-west continent of America go back to the time of the Emperor Peter I. They belong to the attempt, made towards the end of the reign of this great Monarch, to find a passage from the Icy Sea into the Pacific Ocean.

" In 1728 the celebrated Captain Behring made his first voyage. The recital of his discoveries attracted the attention of the Government, and the Empress Anne intrusted to Captain Behring (1741) a new expedition in these same latitudes. She sent with him the Academicians Gmelin, Delile de la Crayere, Müller, Steller, Fisher, Krasilnicoff, Kræcheninicoff, and others, and the first chart of these countries which is known was the result of their labours, published in 1758. Besides the strait which bears the name of the chief of this expedition, he discovered a great part of the islands which are found between the two continents; Cape or Mount St. Elias, which still bears this name upon all the charts, was so called by Captain Behring, who discovered it on the day of the feast of this saint ; and his second, Captain Tchiricoff, pushed his discoveries as far as the 49th degree of north latitude.

" The first private expeditions undertaken upon the north-west coast of America go back as far as the year 1743.

" In 1763 the Russian establishments had already extended as far as the Island of Kodiak (or Kichtak). In 1778 Cook found them at Ounalaska, and some Russian inscriptions at Kodiak. Vancouver saw the Russian establishments in the Bay of Kinai. In fine, Captains Mirs, Portlock, La Peyrouse unanimously attest the existence of Russian establishments in these latitudes.

" If the Imperial Government had, at the time, published the discoveries made by the Russian navigators after Behring and Tchiricoff (viz., Chlodiloff, Serebreanicoff, Krassilnicoff, Paycoff, Poushcareff, Lazareff, Medwedeff, Solowieff, Lewasheff, Krenitsin, and others), no one could refuse to Russia the right of first discovery, nor could even any one deny her that of first occupation.

" Moreover, when D. José Martinez was sent, in 1789, by the Court of Madrid, to form an establishment in Vancouver's Island, and to remove foreigners from thence under the pretext that all that coast belonged to Spain, he gave not the least disturbance to the Russian Colonies and navigators; yet the Spanish Government was not ignorant of their existence, for this very Martinez had visited them the year before. The Report which Captain Malespina made of the results of his voyage proves that the Spaniards very well knew of the Russian Colonies, and in this very Report it is seen that the Court of Madrid acknowledged that its possessions upon the coast of the Pacific Ocean ought not to extend to the north of Cape Blanc, taken from the point of Trinity, situated under 42° 50' of north latitude.

" When, in 1799, the Emperor Paul I granted to the present American Company its first Charter, he gave it the exclusive possession of the north-west coast of America which belonged to Russia, from the 55th degree of north latitude to Behring Strait. He permitted them to extend their discoveries to the south, and there to form establishments, provided they did not encroach upon the territory occupied by other Powers.

" This Act, when made public, excited no claim on the part of other Cabinets, not even on that of Madrid, which confirms that it did not extend its pretensions to the 60th degree.

" When the Government of the United States treated with Spain for the cession of a part of the north-west coast, it was able to acquire by the Treaty of Washington the right to all that belonged to the Spaniards north of the 42nd degree of latitude; but this Treaty says nothing positive concerning the northern boundary of this cession, because, in fact, Spain well knew that she could not say that the coast as far as the 60th degree belonged to her.

" From this faithful exposition of known facts it is easy, Sir, as appears to me, to draw the conclusion that the rights of Russia to the extent of the north-west coast, specified in the Regulation of the Russian American Company, rest upon the three bases required by the general law of nations and immemorial usage among nations, that is, upon the title of first discovery; upon the title of first occupation; and, in the last place, upon that which results from a peaceable and uncontested possession of more than half a century; an epoch, consequently, several years anterior to that when the United States took their place among independent nations.

" It is, moreover, evident that if the right of the possession of a certain extent of the north-west coast of America, claimed by the United States, only devolves upon them in virtue of the Treaty of Washington of the 22nd February, 1819, and I believe it would be difficult to make good any other title, this Treaty could not confer upon the American Government any right of claim against the limits assigned to the Russian possessions upon the same coast, because Spain herself had never pretended to similar right.

" The Imperial Government, in assigning for limits to the Russian possessions on the north-west coast of America, on the one side Behring Strait, and on the other the 51st degree of north latitude, has only made a moderate use of an incontestable right, since the Russian navigators, who were the first to explore that part of the American Continent in 1741, pushed their discovery as far as the 49th degree of north latitude. The 51st degree, therefore, is no more than a mean point between the Russian establishment of New Archangel, situated under the 57th degree, and the American Colony at the mouth of the Columbia, which is found under the 46th degree of the same latitude.

" All these considerations united have concurred in inspiring the Imperial Government with an entire conviction that, in the last arrangements adopted in Russia relative to her possessions on the north-west coast, the legitimate right of no foreign Power has been infringed. In this conviction the Emperor, my august Sovereign, has judged that his good right, and the obligation imposed by Providence upon him to protect with all his power the interests of his subjects, sufficiently justified the measures last taken by His Imperial Majesty in favour of the Russian-American Company, without its being necessary to clothe them with the sanction of Treaties.

" I shall be more succinct, Sir, in the exposition of the motives which determined the Imperial Government to prohibit foreign vessels from approaching the north-west coast of America belonging to Russia, within the distance of at least 100 Italian miles. This measure, however severe it may at first view appear, is after all but a measure of prevention. It is exclusively directed against the culpable enterprises of foreign adventurers, who, not content with exercising upon the coasts above mentioned an illicit trade very prejudicial to the rights reserved entirely to the Russian-American Company, take upon them besides to furnish arms and ammunition to the natives in the Russian possessions in America, exciting them likewise in every manner to resistance and revolt against the authorities there established.

" The American Government doubtless recollects that the irregular conduct of these adventurers, the majority of whom was composed of American citizens, has been the object of the most pressing remonstrances on the part of Russia to the Federal Government from the time that Diplomatic Missions were organized between the two countries. These remonstrances, repeated at different times, remain constantly without effect, and the inconveniences to which they ought to bring a remedy continue to increase.

" The Imperial Government, respecting the intentions of the American Government, has always abstained from attributing the ill-success of its remonstrances to any other motives than those which flow, if I may be allowed the expression, from the very nature of the institutions which govern the national affairs of the American Federation. But the high opinion which the Emperor has always entertained of the rectitude of the American Government cannot exempt him from the care which his sense of justice towards his own subjects imposes upon him. Pacific means not having brought any alleviation to the just grievances of the Russian American Company against foreign navigators in the waters which environ their establishments on the north-west coast of America, the Imperial Government saw itself under the necessity of having recourse to the means of coercion, and of measuring the rigour according to the inveterate character of the evil to which it wished to put a stop. Yet it is easy to discover, on examining closely the last Regulation of the Russian-American Company, that no spirit of hostility had anything to do with its ormation. The most minute precautions have been taken in it to prevent abuses of authority on the part of Commanders of Russian cruizers appointed for the execution of said

1

Regulation. At the same time, it has not been neglected to give all the timely publicity necessary to put those on their guard against whom the measure is aimed.

"Its action, therefore, can only reach the foreign vessels which, in spite of the notification, will expose themselves to seizure by infringing upon the line marked out in the Regulation. The Government flatters itself that these cases will be very rare; if all remain as at present appears, not one.

"I ought, in the last place, to request you to consider, Sir, that the Russian possessions in the Pacific Ocean extend, on the north-west coast of America, from Behring Strait to the 51st degree of north latitude, and on the opposite side of Asia and the islands adjacent from the same strait to the 45th degree. The extent of sea of which these possessions form the limits comprehends all the conditions which are ordinarily attached to *shut seas* ('mers fermées'), and the Russian Government might consequently judge itself authorized to exercise upon this sea the right of sovereignty, and especially that of entirely interdicting the entrance of foreigners. But it preferred only asserting its essential rights, without taking any advantage of localities.

"The Emperor, my august Sovereign, sets a very high value upon the maintenance of the relations of amity and good understanding which have till now subsisted between the two countries. The dispositions of His Imperial Majesty in this regard have never failed appearing at all times when an occasion has presented itself in the political relations of the United States with the European Powers, and surely in the midst of a general peace Russia does not think of aiming a blow at the maritime interests of the United States; she who has constantly respected them in those difficult circumstances in which Europe has been seen to be placed in the latter times, and the influence of which the United States have been unable to avert.

"I have, &c.
(Signed) "PIERRE DE POLETICA."

Before proceeding to remark on this letter, we must call the particular attention of our readers to the conformation of the west coast of America, within the disputed limits, by which the confusion and apparent contradictions in which the subject has been involved may be avoided. We further desire that our conceptions of the question really at issue may be distinctly understood. It is not, we apprehend, whether Russia has any Settlements that give her territorial claims on the Continent of America. This we do not deny— but it is *whether the location of those Settlements and the discoveries of her navigators are such as they are represented to be; whether they entitle her to the exclusive possession of the whole territory north of* 51°, *and to sovereignty over the Pacific Ocean beyond that parallel.* The extremity of the Peninsula of Alaska is in about the latitude 55° and longitude 162° west from Greenwich. On the western side of the peninsula the land runs nearly north, to the Straits of Behring; on the eastern side it tends northward and eastward to the entrance of Cook's River, in latitude 59°, longitude 152°, and Prince William's Sound, in latitude 60° 30', longitude 146°; thence east, southerly to the Behring Bay of Cook and Vancouver; and more southerly to Cross Sound and Norfolk Sound, the latter in latitude 57°, longitude 135°. Cape Scott in the latitude of 51°, to which the Russian claim now extends, is in the longitude of 128°; making a difference between that and the points of Alaska of 34°, or more than 1,200 miles. The coast between these two points forms an immense bay, which extends north beyond the 61st degree of latitude, and is nearly twice as broad across its entrance as the Bay of Bengal. The Aleutian Islands, lying southward of Alaska, are scattered between the Continents of Asia and America, and extend to the latitude 51°. The large Island of Kodiak, on which are the principal Russian Settlements, lies near the eastern side of the Peninsula of Alaska, between the parallels of 57° and 58°. Having no disposition to question the claims of Russia, where they have a plausible foundation, we shall, in this discussion, fix the boundary at Behring Bay, in latitude 59° 30', and longitude 140°; and leaving her in undisputed possession of that bay, and the whole country north-westward of it, shall confine our remarks to that part of the coast lying to the southward and eastward of it; which we undertake to prove was first seen and explored by the navigators of other nations, and that a commerce was carried on by them with the native inhabitants, long before the Russians had any intercourse with them whatever.

According to M. de Poletica the "rights of Russia" to this coast rest upon "three bases," viz., "the title of first discovery," "the title of first occupation," and "upon that which results from a peaceable and uncontested possession of more than half a century." We shall examine these "titles" in the order in which they are placed.

It is not pretended that Behring extended his excursions beyond the bay which bears his name, and his discoveries are therefore irrelevant to the discussion; but the assertion that "his second captain, Tchiricoff (in 1741), pushed his discoveries to the 49th degree of north latitude," is deserving particular consideration, because it will be found that the asserted Russian "title of first discovery," rests wholly on the voyage of this navigator. We have not met with any account of this voyage from which the slightest inference can be drawn that Tchiricoff saw the American coast in the parallel of 49°; but, on the contrary, all the accounts which we have seen concur in fixing the southern limits of his *continental* researches north of 55°. The earliest account we can find is in a Memoir of Philippe Buache, read to the French Academy in 1752, and published at Paris in 1753. This Memoir is accompanied by a Chart, prepared by M. de Lisle, formerly First Professor of Astronomy in the Imperial Academy of St. Petersburgh, and brother to Delile de la Croyere, one of the Academicians who accompanied Tchiricoff. On this Chart is marked the route of that navigator from Kamtchatka to America, and of his return. It appears from this that they discovered the coast of America on the 15th July, 1741, about the latitude 55° 30', and sent a boat, with the pilot Dementiew and ten men, with orders to land. This boat not returning, after several days a second one was sent, with four men, who shared the fate of the first, and nothing was heard of them till 1822, when they were fortunately discovered by M. de Poletica in the latitude of 48° and 49°! After waiting in vain for the return of his boats, Tchiricoff left the coast of America, and on his return discovered land in latitude 51°. This could be no other than the southernmost of the Aleutian Islands; and the circumstance of the natives coming off to him in *skin* canoes confirms this supposition, as no canoes of that description have ever been found on the American coast in that parallel. The authenticity of this account of Tchiricoff's voyage can hardly be questioned. It was published a few years only after his return, and it is stated that M. de Lisle had received the manuscripts of his brother, who died at Kamtchatka shortly after the termination of the voyage. Possibly this Chart and Memoir may not have met the eye of M. de Poletica, or he would not have asserted that "the first Chart of these countries was published in 1758." Müller, who was in the expedition on board Behring's ship, gives nearly the same account as the above of Tchiricoff's voyage, placing his land-fall in latitude of 56°. Cox, Burney, and all writers on this subject whom we have met with have adopted these accounts, and we cannot even conjecture on what authority M. de Poletica pushes Tchiricoff's discoveries to 49°.

The formidable host of navigators cited by M. de Poletica does not appal us. If our readers will look into "Cox's Account of the Russian Discoveries," and examine the relation there given of most of these voyages, they will find it difficult to believe that any discoveries resulting from them remain unpublished, or that they have any bearing on the question before us. There is not the slightest probability that any of those navigators penetrated so far eastward as Behring Bay. In support of this opinion we have the authority of the learned M. Fleurieu, the most intelligent writer on this subject of the last century. In his "Historical Introduction" to the voyage of Marchand, published in 1801, speaking of the Russian navigators alluded to by M. de Poletica, he says, "the principal object of all these voyages was the examination of that long archipelago known under the collective name of the Aleutian or Fox Islands, which the Russian Charts divide into several archipelagoes under different names; of all that part of the coast which extends east and west under the parallel of 60°, and comprehends a great number of islands situated to the south of the mainland, some of which were visited and others only perceived by Behring; lastly, of the Peninsula of Alaska, and of the lands situated to the *north* of this peninsula as far as the 70th degree. It is on these Aleutian Islands and on upwards of 300 leagues of the coast, *which extends beyond the Polar Circle,* that the indefatigable Russians have formed those numerous Settlements," &c. From all these facts we feel fully warranted in the conclusion that no Russian navigator, except Tchiricoff, had seen the coast *eastward of Behring Bay,* previous to the Spanish voyages of Perez in 1774; Heceta, Ayala, and Quadra in 1775; that of Cook in 1778; or even so late as 1788, when it was first visited by vessels from the United States. Thus much for the Russian "title of first discovery;" that of "first occupation" comes next.

We have no doubt but Russian fur-hunters formed establishments at an early period on the Aleutian Islands and neighbouring coast of the continent; but we are equally certain that it can be clearly demonstrated that no Settlement was made eastward of Behring Bay till the one at Norfolk Sound in 1799. The statements of Cook, Vancouver, Mears (Mirs), Portlock, and La Pérouse prove what we readily admit that, previous to 1786, the Russians had Settlements on the Island of Kodiak and in Cook's River; but we shall take leave to use the same authorities to establish the fact that none of these Settlements extended so far east as Behring Bay. Vancouver, when speaking of Port Etches, in Prince William's Sound (June 1794), says (vol. iii, p. 173), "from the result of Mr. Johnstone's inquiries it did not appear that the Russians had formed any establishments *eastward of this station,* but that their boats made excursions along the exterior coast as far as Cape Suckling, and their galiots much farther." Again, p. 199, " we, however, clearly understood that the Russian Government had little to do with these Settlements; that they were solely under the direction and support of independent mercantile Companies; and that Port Etches, which had been established in course of the preceding summer, *was the most eastern Settlement on the American coast."*

In a subsequent letter to Mr. Adams, M. de Poletica says: " But what will dispel even the shadow of doubt in this regard " (title by occupation) " is the *authentic fact* that, in 1789, the Spanish packet 'St. Charles,' commanded by Captain Haro, found in the latitude 48 and 49, Russian establishments to the number of *eight,* consisting in the whole of twenty families, and 460 individuals. *These were the descendants of the companions of Tchiricoff, who was supposed till then to have perished."* This, if true, is, we allow, conclusive evidence of the Russian "title by occupation." It is certainly the most important fact brought forward by M. de Poletica. In truth it is the only one that, in our opinion, has a direct bearing on the question, and on its correctness we are willing to rest the issue. Nootka Sound lies in latitude 49° 30', Clayoquot, or Port Cox, in 49°, and Classet, at the entrance of the Straits of Juan de Fuca, in 48°. Nootka was first visited by the Spanish navigator Perez in 1774, by Cook in 1778; from 1784 to 1789 it was frequented by English, Portuguese, and American vessels; in 1788 Captain Mears built there a vessel, and made the Settlement which, subsequently, came near causing a rupture between Great Britain and Spain; in 1789 a Spanish Settlement was made by Martinez, and continued till 1794. During this period Nootka, Clayoquot, and Classet were the common rendezvous for the ships and fur-traders of all nations; vessels were built by citizens of the United States both at Nootka and Clayoquot; in 1790 the Settlements at Nootka became the subject of investigation in the British Parliament, and volumes were written on it. Now we ask M. de Poletica, or any man of common intelligence, if it is within the bounds of probability—if it is even possible—that eight Russian establishments, containing 462 individuals, should have existed in 1789 in the centre of these operations, on the very spot for which two powerful nations were contending, and no allusion be made to the circumstances during the whole discussion, no mention be made of them by any of the numerous writers on the subject, and no intimation of the fact in the journals of Cook, Mears, Dixon, and Vancouver, who speak of Russian establishments on other parts of the coast, and are altogether silent respecting these, which, had they existed, would have been of more importance than all the other Russian Settlements in that quarter of the globe?

We have recently conversed with a son of Captain Kendrick, who was with his father in the "Columbia" in 1787, and remained a considerable time at Nootka in the Spanish service, and with another individual of great respectability, now residing near Boston, who, in 1792, built and equipped a small vessel at Nootka for commercial purposes. Both these individuals were personally intimate with Captain Haro at Nootka, but never heard an intimation of his having discovered Russian establishments in that vicinity; yet such a fact must have been highly interesting to the Spaniards, who intended their Settlement to be permanent, and to the Americans, who were actively engaged in the fur trade; and, therefore, very likely to become a subject of discussion.

In 1799 the writer of this article visited the north-west coast on commercial pursuits. In the course of that year he entered the several ports situated in the 48th and 49th degrees of latitude; was personally acquainted with the Chiefs and many of the natives; acquired considerable knowledge of their language and customs, but saw no vestige of M. de Poletica's Russian establishments, nor perceived the slightest indication of Russians having ever set foot in the country or visited its shores. These facts might be deemed sufficient, but we shall offer one still more directly to the point. In the summer of 1799 the writer, then off Behring Bay, in latitude 59° 30', fell in with M. Baranoff, at that time, and for many years before and afterwards, Commander-in-chief of all the Russian establishments in that part of the world. He visited the American ship, and passed a day on board. Through an Englishman in his service, who acted as interpreter, a full and free communication took place. M. Baranoff stated that he was from Oonalaska, which he left in company with a galiot and a large fleet of skin-canoes, from whom he separated, in a fog, a few days before, and that they were all bound for Norfolk Sound for the purpose of forming a Settlement or hunting-post. Learning that the writer had been at that place a short time previous, he showed great solicitude to obtain information, particularly respecting the native inhabitants, of whom he appeared to be much in dread, declaring his apprehensions that they would destroy his hunters and defeat his plans. He further stated that a hunting party having a short time before extended their excursion to the neighbourhood of Norfolk Sound, had found the sea-otters so abundant as to induce him to undertake what he considered a most perilous enterprise, and *he expressly declared that this was the first attempt ever made by the Russians to establish a post so far to the southward and eastward.* This, though not a "historical fact," is one for the correctness of which we hold ourselves pledged. It would thus seem that M. Baranoff knew nothing of the extensive Russian establishments in 48° and 49°, and we may, without injustice, regard as wholly gratuitous on the part of M. de Poletica the discovery of the long-lost companions of Tchiricoff. We are tempted, moreover, to dwell a moment on the unparalleled increase ascribed to this party. Four hundred and sixty descendants from fifteen men in forty-seven years would afford a duplication of numbers in a little more than nine years, a statement we should not dare to make in the hearing of Mr. Godwin. But what has become of these "eight establishments" at the present time? By the same ratio of increase they would now contain about 4,000 souls; why are they left without the pale of Imperial protection? If they do not exist, why, when, and to what place were they removed? The plain truth is, that in fixing the situation of the eight establishments discovered by Captain Haro, M. de Poletica has made the mistake (a trifling one it may seem on a Russian Map) of *ten degrees* of latitude. They were actually found in latitude *fifty*-eight and *fifty*-nine, instead of 48° and 49°, and distant more than 1,000 miles from the situation assigned them by the Russian Minister. This fact appears beyond a doubt from the account of the voyage of Captain Haro given by M. Fleurieu in the "Historical Introduction" before referred to. It is there stated, on the authority of two original letters, the one from San Blass, dated the 30th October, 1788 (a few days after the return of Haro), the other from the city of Mexico, dated the 28th August, 1789, that Don Haro found, between the latitudes *fifty*-eight and *fifty*-nine, eight Russian establishments, each composed of between sixteen and twenty families, forming a total of 462 individuals. It is added, "that the strangers had succeeded in habituating to their customs and manners 600 of the natives of the country, and received a tribute from them for the Empress of Russia." For this part of the account M. de Poletica has substituted his own speculations concerning the lost companions of Tchiricoff. In a note M. Fleurieu remarks that, "in the letter from St. Blass, it is mentioned that the Settlements are situated between the latitudes of 48° and 49°, but it is either the fault of the copy, or it is by design, that the latitudes have been improperly indicated." M. de Humboldt, in his "Political Essay on the Kingdom of New Spain," vol. ii, p. 320, mentions the voyage of Don Haro in the "St. Carlos," and essentially confirms the account already given. As he had access to the manuscript account of the voyage, we presume his authority will not be questioned. Page 339 he says, "No European nation has yet formed a solid establishment on the immense extent of coast from Cape Mendocino (latitude 42°) to the *fifty-ninth* degree of latitude : *beyond this limit the Russian factories commence*," &c. We have been thus particular respecting the discoveries made by Captain Haro, because M. de Poletica considers them as "dispelling even the shadow of a doubt" in relation to the Russian "title by occupation" even farther south than 51°. As we fully agree with him that they do dispel all doubt on the subject, and as this is probably the only point in which we shall agree, we trust our readers will pardon us for dwelling on this coincidence of opinion.

The minute investigation we have bestowed on the Russian "title by first occupation" has sufficiently taxed the patience of our readers, and we spare them an examination of that which "results from a peaceable possession of more than half a century," for it is obvious in the present case that unless the fact of occupation is clearly established the claim to "peaceable possession" must fall. We readily concede to Russia priority of discovery, first occupation, and are by no means disposed to disturb her "peaceable possession" of the Aleutian Islands and adjacent coast, including Cook's River, Prince William's Sound, and Behring Bay. We are not remarkably disinterested in making this concession, for, to all practical purposes, we would as soon contend for one of the floating icebergs that are annually detached from the polar masses. The trade carried on by citizens of the United States with those places was never very valuable, and for many years has been altogether abandoned. In a territorial point of view, it is of little importance whether those distant regions are inhabited by the aboriginal savage or the Siberian convict. As to the fact, however, we give a short quotation from Vancouver to show that in 1794 the Russians were very far from having "peaceable possession" even of Behring Bay.[*] In relating transactions at that place, when in company with a large hunting party of Russian Indians, he says, "Portoff embraced this occasion to inform M. Puget that, on the evening of the 28th, while he and his whole party were on one of the small islands in Port Mulgrave" (situated in Behring Bay). "they were surprised by a visit from about fifty of the natives ; and, notwithstanding the superior numbers of his party (about 900!), he had so little confidence in the courage of the Kodiak and Cook's Inlet Indians that he was extremely anxious to be quit of such dangerous visitors, and *had determined on returning to Kodiak as soon as the 'Chatham' should leave the bay.*" The destruction of the Settlement at Norfolk Sound in 1802 is as little calculated to confirm the fact of peaceable possession at that period. In short, it is perfectly well known to every navigator, Russian as well as others, who has visited that part of the world that no Russian settlement now exists, or *ever did exist*, between the latitudes of 58° and 42′, except the one so often mentioned at Norfolk Sound. On what, then, rests the Russian claim to any part of the country between those parallels? Simply on the facts that Tchiricoff, in 1741, saw land in 55° 36′, and that M. Baranoff, in 1799, made a Settlement at Norfolk Sound, which was destroyed in 1802, and re-established in 1804. Such, we conceive, is the plain result of an investigation of the very authorities which M. de Poletica himself has adduced.

We are not among those who believe that a distant view of a cape or mountain—or dropping the first anchor in a bay or harbour—nay, we carry our incredulity so far as to doubt if the magical ceremony of landing on a coast, hoisting a piece of bunting, cutting an inscription, or even that last great act of Empire, burying a bottle, can invest the nation, whose flag the navigator happens to bear, with the rights of sovereignty over a country inhabited by a brave and independent people, whose right to the soil which they possess, and the freedom they enjoy, is coeval with time itself. We therefore attach no importance to the circumstance of land being seen by Tchiricoff in 1741 ; but if M. de Poletica does, we are perfectly willing to try titles with him on the score of discovery. It is well known that Spain, by the IIIrd Article of the Treaty of 1819, ceded to the United States all her rights to the western coast of America north of 42°. It follows that all the discoveries made by her navigators beyond that limit now belong to the United States. It is a "historical fact," and one too well authenticated to admit of doubt, and it is stated by M. de Humboldt in the work before quoted (p. 315), that "Francisco Gali, in his voyage from Macao to Acapulco, discovered in *fifteen hundred eighty-two* the north-west coast of America, under the 57° 30′." —"On correcting the old observations by the new in places of which the identity is ascertained, we find that Gali coasted part of the archipelago of the Prince of Wales, or that of King George." Here we find that the land was discovered and its shores examined 159 years before the voyage of Tchiricoff, and from 2 degrees farther north than the cape seen by that navigator, a fact that puts the Russian claim to discovery out of the question. As little do we believe in the validity of the claims resulting from the occupation of Norfolk Sound in 1799. This sound was first discovered and examined by the Spanish expedition under Heceta, Ayala, and Quadra in 1775, and received the name of "Bay of Guadalupa." A few years afterwards it was visited for commercial purposes, and, abounding in valuable furs, soon became the general resort of all those engaged in that trade. It was frequented by the vessels of Great Britain, France, and the United States several years before the Russians had extended their excursions so far eastward, and it is therefore clear that at that time they had no claim on the ground of occupation. If, then, prior to 1799 Russia possessed no rights on this part of the coast but such as were common to and enjoyed by other nations, we confess ourselves unable to perceive why the establishing of a few hunters and mounting some cannon in the corner of Sitka Bay should

K

give her the right of restraining an intercourse and interdicting a commerce which had hitherto been free as air, and prohibiting the approach of vessels of other nations to shores which the navigators of such nations first discovered and explored! The claim of Russia to sovereignty over the Pacific Ocean north of latitude 51° on the pretence of its being a "*close sea*" is, if possible, more unwarrantable than her territorial usurpations.

Mr. Adams, in noticing it, merely states the fact that "the distance from shore to shore on this sea in latitude 51° is not less than 90 degrees of longitude, or 4,000 miles!" A volume on the subject could not have placed the absurdity of these pretensions more glaringly before us. M. de Poletica, in his third letter, declines further discussion on this subject, "as the Imperial Government," he says, "has not thought fit to take advantage of that right." If interdicting the navigation of this sea to the distance of 100 miles from the shore is not taking advantage of the right to consider it a "close sea," we ask M. de Poletica to point out to us the "laws and usages of nations" by which such a measure can be justified.

We have thus attempted to lay before our readers the character of the Russian claims to the north-west coast of America. It is difficult to conjecture what are the ultimate views of the Russian Government in relation to this coast. The ostensible object is, evidently, a monopoly of the fur trade. It is well known to the Russian Fur Company that nearly all the sea-otter skins, and most of the other valuable furs, are procured north of the 51st degree, and if "foreign adventurers" can be prevented from approaching that part of the coast, the Company would soon be left in undisturbed possession of the whole trade, for south of 51° it is not of sufficient value to attract a single vessel in a season. This would not only secure to them a monopoly in the purchase, but give them the control of the Chinese market for the most valuable furs, which would be still more important. But we suspect a deeper design than the monopoly of a few otter-skins, for which the interests of the Fur Company are made a convenient cover. We have the authority of Humboldt for stating that, in 1802, the Russian Government limited their territorial claims to the north of 55°. They are now extended to 51°, and M. de Poletica informs us that this is only "a moderate use of an incontestable right," intimating that the just claims of Russia extend still further south. If these usurpations are submitted to, is it improbable that a further use may be made of "incontestable rights"? If the eight establishments existed in 1789 where the Russian Minister places them, no one would deny their right of possession at that time as far as 48°. The nearest European Settlement was then the Spanish one of St. Francisco, in 38°. The point, equi-distant from these two, is the 43rd degree, which, according to the principle asserted by M. de Poletica, would have been the Russian boundary in 1789. With the ingenuity which that gentleman has displayed, it would not be difficult to extend the Russian claims quite to the borders of California, and establish them there as satisfactorily as he has done to the 51st degree. The Russians have already made a considerable Settlement on Spanish territory at Port Bodega, in latitude 40°; and it is *possible* that, guided by the same spirit of philanthropy which prompted the dismemberment of Poland, the august Emperor may choose to occupy the fertile but defenceless Province of California, and annex it to his already extensive dominions. Notwithstanding the friendly relations that exist between the United States and Russia, we should deem it a serious evil to have, on our western frontiers, a formidable population, subjects of an ambitious and despotic Government; and all the veneration we feel for the great leader of the "Holy Alliance" awakens no desire to witness a nearer display of his greatness and power.

Great Britain, we apprehend, will not be more desirous of such neighbours than the United States, and she may think fit to advance claims that will be found to conflict with those of Russia. The subject has recently been noticed in the British Parliament, and appears to have created considerable excitement. In justice to the memory of her celebrated navigators, Cook and Vancouver, we must declare that the world is more indebted to their indefatigable labours for a correct knowledge of this coast than to those of all other navigators who have ever visited it. Her subjects were the first Europeans who engaged in the fur trade, and a free access to the *interdicted shores* is at the present time quite as important to them as to those of any other Power. Since the commencement of the present century the British "North-West Company," following the steps of the enterprising McKenzie, have extended their trading posts westward of the Rocky Mountains, and established them, from the Columbia River to the latitude of 55°, on the borders of several lakes and rivers that empty into the Pacific Ocean. At first the supplies for these posts were carried from Canada by way of the lakes and the Unjagah, or "Great Peace River," that has its source near the Pacific, and runs eastward through the Rocky Mountains. This mode of transportation was found hazardous and expensive, and arrangements were made about 1814 by the Company with the proprietors of a Settlement made by American citizens at the mouth of the Columbia, by which the Company became possessed of that Settlement. Since that time the posts westward of the Rocky Mountains receive their supplies through that channel. Hitherto most of these supplies have been shipped from London to Boston, and sent to the mouth of the Columbia in American vessels. From an intimation in the fifty-second number of the "Quarterly Review" we are prepared to learn that the United North-West and Hudson Bay Companies have extended their Settlements still further, and already fixed themselves on the borders of the Pacific. They will soon discover that the most direct and easy route for conveying supplies to all their northern establishments west of the Rocky Mountains, and even to some of those on the eastern side of that range, will be by means of the river called by Mr. Harmon the "Nate-ote-tain," which empties into the Pacific a little south of 54°, and by "Nass River," which disembogues in a large bay on the eastern side of "Observatory Inlet," about the latitude of 55°. The Indians of the coast describe both these rivers as communicating with "cûwon teêdor hûntles" (great inland waters), and represent the navigation of them as safe and easy for loaded canoes, with the exception of some short portages at the rapids and falls. They make frequent journeys to trade with the Teêdor Hardï (inland people), who are said to reside in numerous villages on the banks of these rivers and the adjoining lakes. The free navigation of these streams will be highly important to the United Fur Company, and the British Administration of the present day must be actuated by a very different spirit from that which thirty years ago prompted the expenditure of millions in preparing to resent the outrage committed at Nootka, if they do not resist the usurpations of Russia; usurpations which would compel the British Company to abandon the Settlements already made, and forego the advantages resulting from free access to the shores of the continent north of 51°.

France has likewise an interest in resisting the pretensions of Russia. She has made several efforts to carry on a trade to this coast since it was visited by her distinguished navigator, the unfortunate La Pérouse. The voyage of Marchand in the "Solide" was made between 1790 and 1793, and a French vessel was cut off by the tribe of Coyer near the south part of Queen Charlotte's Islands about the same time. In 1819 the attempt was renewed. A vessel from France in course of that season collected a cargo of furs on the coast, and carried them to Canton. These, however, are all the attempts of that nation which have come to our knowledge. One section of the Ukase appears to us little short of an actual declaration of hostilities against every nation carrying on a trade to the north-west coast. It is as follows :—

"Section 26. The commander of a Russian vessel, *suspecting* a foreign one to be liable to confiscation, must inquire and *search* the same, and, finding her guilty, take possession of her. Should the foreign vessel resist, he is to employ, first *persuasion*, then *threats*, and at last *force;* endeavouring, however, at all events, to do this with as much reserve as possible. If the foreign vessel employ force against force, then he shall consider the same as an evident enemy, and force her to surrender according to the naval laws."!

It might have been expected that no attempt would be made to enforce regulations so deeply affecting the interest and supposed rights of other nations, pending the discussions they had given rise to; but the closing part of the correspondence precludes the hope of even this *appearance* of justice. Mr. Adams, in concluding his last letter, says, "The President is persuaded that the citizens of this Union will remain unmolested in the prosecution of their lawful commerce, and that no effect will be given to an interdiction manifestly incompatible with their rights." To this M. de Poletica answers, "I cannot dissemble, Sir, that this same trade beyond the 51st degree will meet with difficulties and inconveniences for which the American owners will only have to accuse their own imprudence," &c. If we understand this threat, it is meant to prepare us for the immediate execution of the Imperial Ukase. We thank M. de Poletica for this candid avowal of the hostile intentions of his Government, and, with equal frankness, assure him that those engaged in the trade to the north-west coast have always considered it a lawful commerce; and having been confirmed in that opinion by the official declaration of the Executive of the United States that, "from the period of the existence of the United States as an independent nation, their vessels have freely navigated those seas, and *the right to navigate them is a part of that independence,*" and that "the right of the citizens of the United States to hold commerce with the aboriginal natives of the north-west coast of America, without the territorial jurisdiction of other nations, even in arms and ammunitions of war, is as clear and indisputable as that of navigating the seas," they are not disposed to surrender these rights without a struggle. The American vessels employed on the north-west coast are well armed, and amply furnished with the munitions of war. Separated from the civilized world, and cut off for a long time from all communication with it, they have been accustomed to rely on their own resources for protection and defence; and to consider and *treat* as enemies all who attempt to interrupt them in the prosecution of their lawful pursuits. To induce them to relinquish this commerce "persuasion" will be unavailing, "threats" will be disregarded, and any attempts at coercion will be promptly resisted unless made by a force so superior as to render resistance hopeless, in which event they will look with confidence to their Government for redress and support.

We have already devoted to this article more of our pages than so dry a subject may be thought to merit; but we cannot close without noticing the remarks made by M. de Poletica upon what he is pleased to call "the culpable enterprises of foreign adventurers," whom he accuses of carrying on an "illicit trade" of "furnishing arms and ammunition to to the natives in the Russian possessions in America," and of "exciting them in every manner to resistance and revolt against the authorities there established."

In answer to the first charge, we would observe that the trade carried on by citizens of the United States with the Russian Settlements on the north-west coast has the sanction of their own Government, and till now has never been prohibited by that of Russia. It is done openly, and with the consent of the "established authorities" at the several places, who are themselves, in most instances, parties to all commercial transactions. But for the supplies which this trade has furnished, some of the Russian Settlements must have been abandoned; and from Langsdorff's account of the situation of "New Archangel," it appears that, in 1805, the people would have perished from famine had they not been relieved by

American traders. At this moment American vessels are engaged by contract with the servants of the Russian Fur Company in supplying their Settlements with the necessaries and comforts of life. It is a perversion of language to call such a trade "illicit."

On no better foundation rests the charge of "furnishing arms and ammunition to the natives in the *Russian possessions.*" The natives who have been subjected to the Russian power are too wretchedly poor to purchase arms, or indeed anything else. That supplies of this nature are furnished in large quantities to the independent aboriginal inhabitants is certainly true. No arguments are necessary to prove our unquestionable right to continue such supplies, and Russia might with equal justice complain of our furnishing the Chinese with furs as "prejudicial to rights," which the "Russian-American Company" seem disposed to "reserve entirely" to themselves.

The *general* charge of "exciting the natives to *revolt* against the established authorities" may be sufficiently answered by as broad a denial. The only specification we have met with is the following relation, given by the Russian navigator Lisiansky, of the destruction of the Settlement at Norfolk Sound in 1802 by the Sitka Indians:—

"With so fair a face of friendship no enmity could be suspected, and the fort was occasionally left in a sort of unprotected state, the Aleutians and Russians being engaged in hunting the sea-otter, or in the still more necessary business of procuring a supply of provisions for the winter. It was an opportunity of this nature which the Sitcans embraced for the execution of their nefarious plan; and so secret were they in its management that, while some stole through the woods, others passed in canoes by different creeks to the place of rendezvous: they were about 600 in number, and all were provided with fire-arms. Though the attack was wholly unexpected, the few Russians in the fort courageously defended it. But vain was defence against such numbers: it was quickly taken by storm. The assault commenced at noon, and in a few hours the place was levelled to the ground. Among the assailants were three seamen belonging to the United Sates, who, having deserted from their ship, had entered into the service of the Russians, and then took part against them. These double traitors were among the most active in the plot. They contrived combustible wads, which they lighted, and threw upon the buildings where they knew the gunpowder was kept, which took fire and were blown up. Every person who was found in the fort was put to death."

M. Lisiansky does not favour us with his authority for implicating the Americans in this transaction, of which we have received a very different account from a source which leaves not a doubt in our minds of its authenticity, and which we subjoin to show that "foreign adventurers" have, contrary to the dictates of sound policy and their own interest, taken part with the Russians against the aboriginal natives.

The intolerable tyranny exercised by the Russians over the Sitka Indians in seizing their Chiefs and loading them with irons on the most frivolous pretences, in taking possession of their hunting-grounds, and attempting, by every means in their power, to subject them to the most abject slavery, roused the indignation of that tribe, and they resolved to destroy their oppressors, or perish in the attempt. Having by an appearance of submission lulled the suspicions of the Russians, they determined in the summer of 1802 to make the attack. At that time there resided at the Russian Settlement six American seamen who had deserted from the ship "Jenny," of Boston, and *been secreted by the Russians till after her departure.* These seamen were invited by the Indians to visit the village of Sitka, and, on arriving there, were informed of the meditated attack, and their assistance solicited. This was *positively refused.* They were then assured that no injury should be done to them, whatever might be the event, but that they must remain at the village under guard till the event was known. The Indians succeeded in surprising and destroying the fort, and under the excitement of the moment put to death every Russian whom they found. The Aleutian women and some children who were living with the Russians were made prisoners. A few days afterwards two American vessels and one English entered Norfolk Sound. The Indians immediately brought the six Americans on board in safety, but refused to comply with a demand, made by the commanders of these vessels, for the Aleutian women and other captives taken in the fort; and coercive measures were finally resorted to, and hostilities commenced, by these "foreign adventurers," to obtain the release of Russian subjects! This was accomplished, and upwards of thirty individuals were received on board, and carried in one of the vessels to the Russian Settlement at Kodiak. The writer was at that time in the vicinity of Norfolk Sound, and received this account from the Sitka Indians and from the officers of the American vessels, some of whom are now living in Boston. But had the conduct of the Americans been otherwise, we cannot admit that *any* transactions in Norfolk Sound would support the charge of "exciting revolt" in the "*Russian possessions;*" for the whole of her possessions there are limited to the range of the cannon-shot of her fort. The whole extent of coast from latitude 58° to the Straits of Juan de Fuca, in 48°, is inhabited by numerous powerful and warlike tribes, perfectly free and independent of Russian authority. Possessing in a high degree the nobler traits of savage character, and devotedly attached to liberty, they prize personal freedom more highly than life itself.

The courage and constancy of the Sitka Indians, when attacked by the Russians in 1804, is a striking instance of their intrepidity and deep-rooted love of independence, and warrants the conclusion that to secure "the peaceable possession" of that country to Russia, something more will be requisite than the "*Be it accordingly*" of her Emperor, or the arguments of her Envoy. The following is from the account of that transaction by

Lisiansky, who commanded the "Neva," a Russian ship of war, engaged in the expedition:—

"In the afternoon of the 26th a canoe, with three young men in it, came alongside the American ship.* Being informed that one of these youths was the son of our greatest enemy, I could not resist the desire I felt to have him in my power; and the moment the canoe left the 'O'Cain' I dispatched a jolly-boat in pursuit of it; but the natives rowed so lustily that they outstripped the boat, and when our party fired upon them they intrepidly returned the fire, showing us thereby with what sort of persons we should have to deal." Again, "he (the Ambassador) was then sent back with the same answer as before, that we required, as a necessary preliminary to pacification, that the Chiefs themselves should come to us. At noon we saw thirty men approaching, all having fire-arms. They stopped when at the distance of musket-shot from the fort, and commenced their parley, which, however, was quickly terminated, *as they would not agree to a proposal made by M. Baranoff that we should be permitted to keep perpetual possession of the place at present occupied by us, and that two respectable persons should be given as hostages.* On the conclusion of this interview the savages, who were sitting, rose up, and after singing out three several times, 'Oo, Oo, Oo!' meaning 'End, end, end!' retired in military order. However, they were given to understand by our interpreters that we should instantly move our ships close to their fort (for their Settlement was fortified by a wooden fence), and they would have no one but themselves to reproach for any consequences that might ensue.

"On the 1st October we carried this menace into execution by forming a line with four of our ships before the Settlement. I then ordered a white flag to be hoisted on board the 'Neva,' and presently we saw a similar one on the fort of the enemy. From this circumstance I was not without hope that something might yet occur to prevent bloodshed; but finding no advances on their part I ordered the several ships to fire into the fort. A launch and a jolly-boat, armed with a 4-pr., under the command of Lieutenant Arboosoff, were then sent to destroy the canoes on the beach, some of which were of sufficient burthen to carry sixty men each, and to set fire to a large barn not far from the shore, which I supposed to contain stores. Lieutenant Arboosoff, finding he could do but little execution from the boats, landed, and taking with him the 4-pr., advanced towards the fort. M. Baranoff, who was then on board the 'Neva,' seeing this, ordered some field-pieces to be landed, and, with about 150 men, went himself on shore to aid the Lieutenant. The savages kept perfectly quiet till dark, except that now and then a musket was fired off. This stillness was mistaken by M. Baranoff, and, encouraged by it, he ordered the fort to be stormed, a proceeding, however, that had nearly proved fatal to the expedition, for as soon as the enemy perceived our people close to their walls, they collected in a body, and fired upon them with an order and execution that surprised us. The Aleutians who, with the aid of some of the Company's servants, were drawing the guns along, terrified at so unexpected a reception, took to their heels, while the commanders. left with a mere handful of men belonging to my ship, judged it prudent to retire, and endeavour to save the guns. The natives, seeing this, rushed out in pursuit of them, but our sailors behaved so gallantly that, though almost all wounded, they brought off the field-pieces in safety. In this affair, out of my own ship alone, a Lieutenant, a Master's Mate, a Surgeon's Mate, a Quartermaster, and ten sailors of the sixteen who accompanied them, were wounded, and two killed; and if I had not covered this unfortunate retreat with my cannon, not a man would probably have been saved. The Russians finally prevailed, by the superiority of their artillery, and this was the closing scene.

"When morning came I observed a great number of crows hovering about the Settlement. I sent on shore to ascertain the cause of this, and the messenger returned with news that the natives had quitted the fort during the night, leaving in it alive only two old women and a little boy. It appears that, judging of us by themselves, they imagined that we were capable of the same perfidiousness and cruelty, and that if they had come out openly in their boats, as had been proposed, we should have fallen on them in revenge for their past behaviour. They had, therefore, preferred running into the woods, leaving many things behind, which, from their haste, they had been unable to take away.

"It was on the 8th that the fate of Sitka Fort was decided. After everything that could be of use was removed out of it, it was burned to the ground. Upon my entering it before it was set on fire, what anguish did I feel when I saw, like a second massacre of innocents, numbers of young children lying together murdered, lest their cries, if they had been borne away with their cruel parents, should have led to a discovery of the retreat to which they were flying. O, man, man! of what cruelties is not thy nature, civilized or uncivilized, capable?"

Whether M. Lisiansky means this exclamation for the invaders or their victims does not appear.

Lisiansky adds, "We have reason to believe, from information we obtained, that the chief cause of their flight was the want of powder and ball; and that if these had not failed them, they would have defended themselves to the last extremity." Such we know to have been the fact, and but for this they would, with a heroism worthy a better fate, have perished in defending their invaded rights.

The writer was at that time near the scene of these transactions, and received from the

* The American ship "O'Cain," of Boston, was then lying in Norfolk Sound.

L

Indians daily accounts of passing events. They were in substance much the same as those given by Lisiansky, with this addition, that having so often experienced the perfidy and cruelty of the Russians, they placed no confidence in any promises made by them, and well knew that *slavery* must follow submission. Finding themselves without means of defence, they determined to abandon their country, retreat into the interior, and thus preserve their independence by the sacrifice of their possessions. Those who were too old or too young to support the fatigues and sufferings of the contemplated journey were dispatched on the spot, " and," added the Chief who gave this account, *"their innocent blood be on the heads of those who caused the deed."* We shall offer no apology for introducing the following anecdote as a further illustration of the character of these people.

In the summer of 1804 several tribes collected at " Nass," where a sort of fair is annually held. At this time an affray took place between individuals of the Cockalane tribe, who reside on the main, near the entrance of Observatory Inlet, and of the Skettageets tribe, who inhabit the opposite shores of Queen Charlotte's Islands, in which Cockalane, the great Chief of his nation, was unfortunately killed. In the course of the following winter, when the inclemency of the season prevented all intercourse between the Indians of the main and those of the islands, the writer visited Skettageets. Inquiry being made by the Chiefs respecting the intentions of the Cockalane tribe, they were told that early in the spring the friends of the deceased Chief were determined to attack them with an irresistible force, and destroy the whole Skettageets nation. Elsworsh, a distinguished young Chief, heard this account with great calmness, and expressed doubts of the ability of their enemies to execute these threats. Being assured that they were highly exasperated, and resolved on vengeance, he replied, with a countenance and manner that expressed his feelings more forcibly than language, " It is well, let them come—let them attack—let them destroy us—it is well—we are but passing clouds," and added, pointing to the sun, " Where is the man, like yonder sun, who never dies ?"[*]

Let us not be suspected of representing these people in too favourable a light. They share, of course, the passions and vices that usually prevail in the savage state. Implacable hatred and thirst for revenge, engendered by real or supposed injuries, too often excite them to deeds at which humanity shudders. We have known in their intercourse with foreigners instances of unprovoked outrage and violence. But we have more frequently met with *ex parte* accounts of their treachery and ferocity where circumstances have been known to us that gave a very different colouring to their conduct. They are a people more " sinned against " than " sinning." We should rejoice if the dark shades of their character could be dispelled by the mild influence of Christianity, without endangering that independence which is the ground-work of every virtue they possess; but our knowledge of their habits and feelings give us little hope of its accomplishment, and our fears that any change encouraging white people to settle among them would lead to their destruction leave us no wish that it should be attempted.

The march of civilization seems the signal for their disappearance, and there is something mournful in the reflection that at no distant period this race of men, which physiologists reckon as one of the distinct varieties of mankind, will exist only in the pages of history.

We have already extended this article beyond reasonable bounds, or we should have offered some remarks on the letter of Mr. Prevost to the Secretary of State respecting the Columbia River. We do not subscribe to all the opinions of that gentleman, and doubt the accuracy of the information he received in relation to some facts he has stated. But as we cannot go into the subject at large, we shall only notice an unimportant error in relation to the language, which, he says, " bears a strong analogy with that of Nootka." This mistake (if it be one) may be easily accounted for, when it is known that the natives of Columbia River have frequent intercourse with the Indians of Classett, who speak the Nootka language, and that the first " foreign adventurers " who visited the river had previously acquired a knowledge of that language. It was natural that their intercourse should be carried on in a language of which both had some knowledge, and this has been the case to a certain extent ever since. A comparison of the following numerals in the Nootka language and in that spoken at the mouth of the Columbia will show an essential difference :—

English.	*Nootka.*	*Cheenook.*[†]
One.	Sawac.	Eel.
Two.	Athlor.	Möxt.
Three.	Cutsar.	Clüne.
Four.	Moo.	Luet.
Five.	Suchar.	Quánim.
Six.	Nöopoo.	Tückum.
Seven.	Athlarpoo.	Sinnmixt.
Eight.	Athlacquelth.	Stöötkëën.
Nine.	Tsawacquelth.	Quicëtu.
Ten.	Hëioo.	Taltlelum.

---

[*] " Keütlännu Këëset, Lluë cooteanöng, come howëëne cardie."
[†] Mouth of the Columbia.

No. 5.

EXTRACTS FROM THE "HISTORICAL REVIEW OF THE FORMATION OF THE RUSSIAN-AMERICAN COMPANY, AND THEIR PROCEEDINGS UP TO THE PRESENT TIME" (IN RUSSIAN), BY P. TIKHMENIEFF, ST. PETERSBURGH, 1861, PART I, CHAPTER VIII, PAGES 257–261.

(Translation.)

THE boundaries of the Russian possessions on the north-west coast of America, defined in the Charter renewed to the Company by the Emperor in 1821, were somewhat altered in consequence of disputes which arose with the United States of America and with England. In the Conventions concluded by Russia with the United States' Government on the 5th (17th) April, 1824, and with England on the 16th (28th) February, 1825, it was stipulated that the boundary of the Russian dominions on the south should extend from the southern limit of Prince of Wales' Island (54° 40' north latitude), and between 131° and 133° west longitude from Greenwich to the north along the Portland Channel to that point of land which touches the 56th parallel of latitude. By the former of these Conventions the citizens of the United States were given the right, for a period of ten years, to fish in the waters of the Colony, and to trade with the inhabitants of the coast.

This latter provision provoked from the Company a complaint that the privileges granted to them by the Emperor had been infringed in a manner which threatened the prosperity of the Colony, and even the very existence of the Company.

In a letter addressed to the Foreign Office, Admiral Mordvinoff, a shareholder of the Company, spoke very strongly in defence of the rights of the Company, and called attention to the fact that certain parts of the Convention were not at all clear, and might give rise to many disputes. The Foreign Office replied that our Government had two very good reasons for granting to the citizens of the United States the right to trade and fish in the waters of the Colony for a period not exceeding ten years, namely, first, because the Government of the United States asked, not without reason, for something in return for the great advantages conceded to Russia by the other parts of the Convention, in particular by Article V; and, in the second place, because, as the Company had not hitherto been able to prevent the Americans from continuing the trading and fishing in the waters of the Colony, which they had carried on for many years, it would be much better that the Company should give their formal consent to such trading and fishing than that they should see their prohibition disregarded, and trade and fishing continue as before, as if by a natural and indefeasible right. Besides, a great advantage would be gained by the formal grant of this privilege for a certain period, because, in return, the United States' Government would be ready to admit formally that, at the end of the stipulated period, the Company would have a perfect right to prohibit trading and fishing by Americans in the waters of the Colony, and punish those who disregarded the prohibition.

As the Convention had not yet been ratified, the Emperor, on the representation of the Company that they would be injured by that part of the Convention to which we have referred, ordered inquiry to be made into the matter by a Special Commission. In the Protocol of the Commission, which was approved by the Emperor, it was declared, inter alia, that the provision of the Convention granting to the citizens of the United States the right to fish in the waters of the Colony, and to trade with the inhabitants of the coast, must not be understood as giving them a right to approach the coast of Eastern Siberia, and the Aleutian and Kurile Islands, which had long been recognized by the other Powers as being under the exclusive dominion of Russia, and that that provision only applied to the disputed territory on the north-west coast of America, between 54° 40' and 57°.

In consequence of this declaration, the Head of the Foreign Office and the Commission were of opinion that, in order to safeguard the rights of the Company, and to obviate the possibility of the Convention being wrongly interpreted, the Russian Minister to the United States should be instructed to make a formal explanatory declaration on the occasion of the exchange of the ratifications of the Convention. The Minister reported that he did not see his way to carrying out these instructions, and that the only way in which he could explain the provision in question to the Washington Cabinet was by a verbal note; he added that a formal declaration might give rise to serious disputes, prevent the ratification of the Convention, and produce an effect which was not intended, by arousing suspicions which would otherwise never be entertained. The Convention was accordingly ratified.

*　　　*　　　*　　　*　　　*　　　*

[At the end of the ten years' period the American Government asked for a renewal of the privileges; the Russian Government refused, stating that such a renewal would not be in the interest of the Russian-American Company. The American Government then inquired what steps the Russian Government proposed to take, and were informed that the authorities of the Russian Colonies had been instructed to prevent American vessels from visiting the inland seas, gulfs, harbours, and bays to the north of 54° 40′ north latitude.]* '

EXTRACTS FROM THE "HISTORICAL REVIEW OF THE FORMATION OF THE RUSSIAN-AMERICAN COMPANY, AND THEIR PROCEEDINGS UP TO THE PRESENT TIME" (IN RUSSIAN), BY P. TIKHMENIEFF, ST. PETERSBURGH, 1863, PART II, PAGES 130–139.

(Translation.)

In 1812 Etolin, Governor of the Colony, informed the Company that in the course of his tour of inspection he had come across several American ships. Although circumstances had prevented his communicating with them at the time, he had reason to believe that they were whalers. In corroboration of this he stated that for some time he had been constantly receiving reports from various parts of the Colony of the appearance of American whalers in the neighbourhood of the harbours and shores of the Colony.

Amongst these reports the most noteworthy was that of Captain Kadnikoff, the commander of the Company's ship "Nasliednik Alexander," who stated that, on a voyage from Sitka to Okhotsk, he had hailed a whaler flying the American flag. The master informed him that he had come from the Sandwich Islands in company with thirty other ships to whale on both sides of the western extremity of the Peninsula of Alaska and the eastern islands of the Aleutian group belonging to that peninsula, and that as many as 200 whalers were coming from the United States the same year. Captain Kadnikoff also ascertained from the master that in 1841 he had whaled in the same waters in company with fifty other ships, and that his ship secured thirteen whales, from which 1,000 barrels of oil were obtained.

The Company addressed an energetic representation to the Foreign Office, calling upon the Government to prevent the Americans from fishing in the waters of the Colony in contravention of the Convention. The Foreign Office replied :† " The claim to a *mare clausum*, if we wished to advance such a claim in respect to the northern part of the Pacific Ocean, could not be theoretically justified. Under Article I of the Convention of 1824 between Russia and the United States, which is still in force, American citizens have a right to fish in all parts of the Pacific Ocean. But under Article IV of the same Convention, the ten years' period mentioned in that Article having expired, we have power to forbid American vessels to visit inland seas, gulfs, harbours, and bays for the purposes of fishing and trading with the natives. That is the limit of our rights, and we have no power to prevent American ships from taking whales in the open sea."

Of course this decision, which made it impossible for the Company to restrain in any way the licence of the whalers, gave the latter an excuse for continuing to act exactly as they chose within the limits of the Colony. From 1843 to 1850 there were constant complaints by the Company of the increasing boldness of the whalers. They were not content with landing on the Aleutian and Kurile Islands, cutting wood wherever they chose, boiling blubber on the shore, and thereby inflicting real damage on the fur industry (especially in the case of the otter, for the least smoke is sufficient to drive it from the coast); they went still further in their arbitrary proceedings. On more than one occasion they destroyed huts belonging to the natives or to the Company, and on receiving notice of the Regulations and Circulars in force prohibiting whaling off the shores of the Colony, they replied with threats or contemptuous language. The whalers asserted that the sea in all latitudes and longitudes was the common property of all; besides, they said, they had a right to exercise their industry under their national flag. Traffic in furs was openly carried on between the natives and the American captains, and when the Colonial authorities made some whalers leave Novoarkhangelsk on that account. they quietly continued the traffic in the Bay of Sitka, and disregarded all protests. The following case also deserves to be noticed : In 1847 one of the whalers came to Behring Island, and on the captain being told that he must not traffic in seal-skins‡ on a neighbouring small island, he ordered the overseer of the island to be turned off his ship, and immediately went on shore with his men, with the evident intention of disregarding the prohibition. ,

It was only when active steps were taken to resist them that the whalers left, but before going they cut down a plantation which had been grown with great trouble, the island being without other trees or shrubs. Few of the districts of the Colony escaped the visits of the whalers, which were everywhere accompanied by acts of violence on their part.

Whenever complaints of such acts reached the Company, they took all the steps in their power to protect the country under their administration ; but all their efforts led to no satisfactory result. In 1843, almost immediately after the first protest of the Company,

* The passages in brackets are abstracts of the Russian text.
† Letter from the Department of Manufactures and Internal Trade, December 14, 1842, No. 5191. Dielo Arkh. Kom. 1842 goda, No. 14, str. 7.
‡ The Russian word is " sivutsh," for which the equivalent given in the dictionary is " otary," " sea-lion."

the Colonial authorities were alarmed at the large number of whalers engaged round the shores of Kadiak, as the Company's fur trade was certain to suffer from their presence. M. Etolin accordingly resolved once more to ask the Company to furnish him with more definite instructions in regard to the whalers, *i.e.*, to define the rights of the Governor of the Colony with reference to those captains who, in spite of the prohibition, should enter the bays, harbours, and gulfs of the Russian possessions, or land on the islands. While awaiting a decision in the matter, he resolved to arm one of the ships of the colonial flotilla to act as a cruizer in the waters most infested by the foreign vessels. The cruizer was ordered to avoid most carefully anything which might give rise to a conflict, and to confine herself strictly to observing the whalers. She was on no account to resort to force unless it became necessary to resist an attack. Apart from this measure, M. Etolin suggested the expediency of obtaining the permission of the Government for the colonial cruizer to fly the flag of the Imperial Navy, as that flag would, in certain eventualities, inspire more respect. Finally, he considered that the claim of foreigners to take whales in Russian waters ought certainly to be limited by a line drawn at a distance of at least 3 leagues, or 9 Italian miles, from the shores of the Colony. As an example of the justice of fixing such a limit, and of the advantages to be obtained therefrom, he adduced New Holland and other British possessions, where no whaler would dare to take whales within the 3-league limit.

Unfortunately, these efforts to defend the rights of the Company were not attended with more success than those previously made. Although the Foreign Office, at the request of the Company, informed the Government of the United States of the establishment of cruizers in the Russian Colonies for the purpose of insuring the observation of the Convention of 1824 by foreign ships, no decision was arrived at in regard to the fixing of a limit for whaling, or with reference to the proposal that the Company's cruizer should fly the flag of the Imperial Navy. On the other hand, the Government took occasion to impress upon the Company the importance of great caution being observed by the colonial cruizers in all that concerned foreign ships.

The exact words of the letter from the Foreign Office are as follows: "The fixing of a line at sea within which foreign vessels should be prohibited from whaling off our shores would not be in accordance with the spirit of the Convention of 1824, and would be contrary to the provisions of our Convention of 1825 with Great Britain. Moreover, the adoption of such a measure, without preliminary negotiation and arrangement with the other Powers, might lead to protests, since no clear and uniform agreement has yet been arrived at among nations in regard to the limit of jurisdiction at sea."

In 1847 a representation from Governor Tebenkoff in regard to new aggressions on the part of the whalers gave rise to further correspondence. Some time before, in June 1846, the Governor-General of Eastern Siberia had expressed his opinion that, in order to limit the whaling operations of foreigners, it would be fair to forbid them to come within 40 Italian miles of our shores, the ports of Petropavlovsk and Okhotsk to be excluded, and a payment of 100 silver roubles to be demanded at those ports from every vessel for the right of whaling. He recommended that a ship of war should be employed as a cruizer to watch foreign vessels. The Foreign Office expressly stated as follows in reply: "We have no right to exclude foreign ships from that part of the great ocean which separates the eastern shore of Siberia from the north-western shore of America, or to make the payment of a sum of money a condition to allowing them to take whales." The Foreign Office were of opinion that the fixing of the line referred to above would reopen the discussions formerly carried on between England and France on the subject. The limit of a cannon-shot, that is about 3 Italian miles, would alone give rise to no dispute. The Foreign Office observed, in conclusion, that no Power had yet succeeded in limiting the freedom of fishing in open seas, and that such pretensions had never been recognized by the other Powers. They were confident that the fitting out of colonial cruizers would put an end to all difficulties; there had not yet been time to test the efficacy of this measure.

[Soon after this the whalers began to turn their chief attention to the Sea of Okhotsk.]

In 1850 the corvette "Olivutsa," of the Russian navy, was sent by the Government to cruize in the Northern Pacific. The Company were invited to offer suggestions with regard to the instructions to be given to cruizers.

The following is an extract from their suggestions: "In order to prevent the complete extermination of the whales in the Sea of Okhotsk it is most desirable that an armed cruizer should always be stationed at the Shantar Islands to keep away foreign whalers, at all events until such time as it is found possible altogether to prohibit whaling by foreign ships in that sea." (16th November, 1853, No. 970; Dielo Arkh. Kom. 1842 goda, No. 14, str. 181.)

Some time before the Company had written to the Foreign Office (22nd March, 1853, No. 368, the same Dielo, p. 163): "If it is found impracticable entirely to prohibit for a time fishing by foreigners in the Sea of Okhotsk, as an inland sea, would it not, at any rate, be possible officially to prohibit whalers from coming close to our shores and whaling in the bays and among the islands, detaching one of the cruizers of the Kamtchatka flotilla for this service?"

The instructions to cruizers were approved on the 9th December, 1853. The cruizers were to see that no whalers entered the bays or gulfs, or came within 3 Italian miles of our shores, that is, the shores of Russian America (north of 54° 41'), the Peninsula of Kamtchatka, Siberia, the Kadjak Archipelago, the Aleutian Islands, the Pribyloff and Commander Islands, and the others in Behring Sea, the Kuriles, Sakhalin, the Shantar

Islands, and the others in the Sea of Okhotsk to the north of 46° 30' north. The cruizers were instructed constantly to keep in view that " our Government not only does not wish to prohibit or put obstacles in the way of whaling by foreigners in the northern part of the Pacific Ocean, but allows foreigners to take whales in the Sea of Okhotsk, which, as stated in these instructions, *is, from its geographical position, a Russian inland sea.*"*

EXTRACTS FROM THE "HISTORICAL REVIEW OF THE FORMATION OF THE RUSSIAN-AMERICAN COMPANY, AND THEIR PROCEEDINGS UP TO THE PRESENT TIME" (IN RUSSIAN), BY P. TIKHMENIEFF, ST. PETERSBURGH, 1863, PART I, PAGES 252, 250.

(Translation.)

According to reports from the Colony the number of Russians, half-breeds, and natives under the administration of the Company was, on the 1st January, 1819, as follows :—

					Russians.		Half-breeds.	
Locality.					Males.	Females.	Males.	Females.
Novarkhangelsk	..	..	..	..	198	11	93	111
Kadiak and neighbouring islands		..	..	..	73	..	39	..
Ukamok Island	..	..	..	..	2	..	..	..
Katmai Factory	..	..	..	..	4	..	..	..
Sutkhom Factory	..	..	..	..	3	..	1	..
Fort Voskresensky	..	..	..	..	2	..	..	..
„ Constantine	..	..	..	..	17	..	..	..
„ Nicholas	..	..	..	..	11	..	..	..
„ Alexander	..	..	..	..	11	..	..	..
Ross Settlement	..	..	..	..	27	..	..	..
Seal Islands	..	..	..	..	27	..	..	..
Nushagak	..	..	..	..	3	2	..	..
Total	..	..	..	..	378	13	133	111

NATIVES.

Locality.							Males.	Females.	Total.
At Kadiak	..	..	..	..	..	..	1,483	1,769	3,252
At Novarkhangelsk (Aleuts)	..	..	..	..	..	285	61	346
Aliaksintsi	..	..	..	..	..	..	402	467	869
Tshugatsh	..	..	..	..	..	..	172	188	360
Kenaitsi	..	..	..	..	..	..	723	748	1,471
Ugalentsi	..	..	..	..	..	..	51	66	117
Miednovtsi	..	..	..	..	..	..	294	273	567
On the Fox (Lisy) Islands	..	..	..	..	..	464	559	1,023
On the Seal Islands (Aleuts)	..	..	..	..	..	198	181	379
Totals	..	..	..	..	..	..	4,062	4,322	8,384

---

* These words are in italics in the original.

No. 6.

SPEECH BY THE HON. CHARLES SUMNER, OF MASSACHUSETTS, ON THE
CESSION OF RUSSIAN AMERICA TO THE UNITED STATES IN 1867.
H. R. EX. DOC. 177, 40TH CONGRESS, 2ND SESSION, PAGES 124–189.

Mr. President,

YOU have just listened to the reading of the Treaty by which Russia cedes to the
United States all her possessions on the North American Continent in consideration
of 7,200,000 dollars, to be paid by the United States. On the one side is the cession of a
vast country with its jurisdiction and its resources of all kinds, on the other side is the
purchase-money. Such is this transaction on its face.

Boundaries and Configuration.

In endeavouring to estimate its character I am glad to begin with what is clear and
beyond question. I refer to the boundaries fixed by the Treaty. Commencing at the
parallel of 54° 40′ north latitude, so famous in our history, the line ascends Portland
Channel to the mountains, which it follows on their summits to the point of intersection
with the 141° west longitude, which line it ascends to the Frozen Ocean, or, if you please,
to the North Pole. This is the eastern boundary, separating this region from the British
possessions, and it is borrowed from the Treaty between Russia and Great Britain in 1825,
establishing the relations between these two Powers on this continent. It will be seen
that this boundary is old; the rest is new. Starting from the Frozen Ocean, the western
boundary descends Behring Straits, midway between the two islands of Krüsenstern and
Ratmanov, to the parallel of 65° 30′, just below where the Continents of America and Asia
approach each other the nearest; and from this point it proceeds in a course nearly
south-west through Behring Straits, midway between the Island of St. Lawrence and Cape
Chonkotski, to the meridian of 172° west longitude, and thence, in a south-westerly
direction,-traversing Behring Sea, midway between the Island of Attou on the east, and
Copper Island on the west, to the meridian of 193° west longitude, leaving the prolonged
group of the Aleutian Islands in the possessions now transferred to the United States, and
making the western boundary of our country the dividing line which separates Asia from
America.

Look at the map and see the configuration of this extensive region, whose estimated
area is more than 570,000 square miles. I speak by the authority of our own Coast
Survey. Including the Sitkan Archipelago at the south, it takes a margin of the mainland, fronting on the ocean 30 miles broad and 300 miles long, to Mount St. Elias, the
highest peak of the continent, when it turns with an elbow to the west, and then along
Behring Straits northerly, when it rounds to the east along the Frozen Ocean. Here are
upwards of 4,000 statute miles of coast, indented by capacious bays and commodious
harbours without number, embracing the Peninsula of Alaska, one of the most remarkable
in the world, 50 miles in breadth and 300 miles in length; piled with mountains, many
volcanic, and some still smoking; penetrated by navigable rivers, one of which is among
the largest of the world; studded with islands which stand like sentinels on the coast, and
flanked by that narrow Aleutian range which, starting from Alaska, stretches far away to
to Japan, as if America were extending a friendly hand to Asia. This is the most general
aspect. There are details specially disclosing maritime advantages and approaches to the
sea, which properly belong to this preliminary sketch. According to accurate estimates
the coast-line, including bays and islands, is not less than 11,270 miles. In the Aleutian
range, besides innumerable islets and rocks, there are not less than fifty-five islands
exceeding 3 miles in length; there are seven exceeding 40 miles, with Ounimak, which is
the largest, exceeding 73 miles. In our part of Behring Sea there are five considerable
islands, the largest of which is St. Lawrence, being more than 96 miles long. Add to all
these the group south of the Peninsula of Alaska, including the Shumagins and the
magnificent Island of Kodiak, and then the Sitkan group, being archipelago added to
archipelago, and the whole together constituting the geographical complement to the West
Indies, so that the north-west of the contingent answers archipelago for archipelago to the
south-east.

Discovery of Russian America by Behring, under instructions from Peter the Great.

The title of Russia to all these possessions is derived from prior discovery, which is
the admitted title by which all European Powers have held in North and South America,
unless we except what England acquired by conquest from France, but here the title

cf France was derived from prior discovery. Russia, shut up in a distant interior, and struggling with barbarism, was scarcely known to the other Powers at the time they were lifting their flags in the Western Hemisphere. At a later day the same powerful genius which made her known as an Empire set in motion the enterprise by which these possessions were opened to her dominion. Peter the Great, himself a ship-builder and a reformer, who had worked in the ship-yards of England and Holland, was curious to know if Asia and America were separated by the sea, or if they constituted one undivided body with different names, like Europe and Asia. To obtain this information he wrote with his own hand the following instructions, and ordered his Chief Admiral to see them carried into execution:—

"One or two boats with decks to be built at Kamtschatka, or at any other convenient place, with which inquiry should be made in relation to the northerly coasts, to see whether they were not contiguous with America, since their end was not known ; and this done, they should see whether they could not somewhere find a harbour belonging to Europeans or an European ship. They should likewise set apart some men who should inquire after the name and situation of the coasts discovered. Of all this an exact journal should be kept, with which they should return to St. Petersburgh."—(Müller's "Voyages from Asia to America," by Jeffreys, p. 45.)

The Czar died in the winter of 1725, but the Empress Catharine, faithful to the desires of her husband, did not allow this work to be neglected. Vitus Behring, a Dane by birth, and a navigator of some experience, was made Commander. The place of embarkation was on the other side of the Asiatic Continent. Taking with him officers and ship-builders, the navigator left St. Petersburgh by land on the 5th February, 1725, and commenced the preliminary journey across Siberia, Northern Asia, and the Sea of Okhotsk to the coast of Kamtschatka, which they reached after infinite hardships and delays, sometimes with dogs for horses, and sometimes supporting life by eating leather bags, straps, and shoes. More than three years were passed in this toilsome and perilous journey to the place of embarkation. At last, on the 20th July, 1728, the party was able to set sail in a small vessel called the "Gabriel," and described as "like the packet-boats used in the Baltic." Steering in a north-easterly direction, Behring passed a large island, which he called St. Lawrence, from the saint on whose day it was seen. This island, which is included in the present cession, may be considered as the first point in Russian discovery, as it is also the first outpost of the North American Continent. Continuing northward, and hugging the Asiatic coast, Behring turned back only when he thought he had reached the north-eastern extremity of Asia, and was satisfied that the two continents were separated from each other. He did not penetrate further north than 67° 30'.

In his voyage Behring was struck by the absence of such great and high waves as in other places are common to the open sea, and he observed fir trees swimming in the water, although they were unknown on the Asiatic coast. Relations of inhabitants, in harmony with these indications, pointed to "a country at no great distance toward the east." His work was still incomplete, and the navigator before returning home put forth again for this discovery, but without success. By another dreary land journey he made his way back to St. Petersburgh in March 1730, after an absence of five years. Something was accomplished for Russian discovery, and his own fame was engraved on the Maps of the world. The straits through which he sailed now bear his name, as also does the expanse of sea which he traversed on his way to the straits.

The spirit of discovery continued at St. Petersburgh. A Cossack Chief undertaking to conquer the obstinate natives on the north-eastern coast, proposed also "to discover the pretended country on the Frozen Sea." He was killed by an arrow before his enterprise was completed. Little is known of the result, but it is stated that the navigator whom he had selected, by name Gwosdew, in 1730 succeeded in reaching a "strange coast" between 65° and 66° of north latitude, where he saw people, but could not speak with them for want of an interpreter. This must have been the coast of North America, and not far from the group of islands in Behring Straits, through which the present boundary passes, separating the United States from Russia, and America from Asia.

The desire of the Russian Government to get behind the curtain increased. Behring volunteered to undertake the discoveries that remained to be made. He was created a Commodore, and his old Lieutenants were created Captains. The Senate, the Admiralty, and the Academy of Sciences at St. Petersburgh all united in the enterprise. Several Academicians were appointed to report on the natural history of the coasts visited, among whom was Steller the naturalist, said to be "immortal" from this association. All of these, with a numerous body of officers, journeyed across Siberia, Northern Asia, and the Sea of Okhotsk, to Kamtchatka, as Behring had journeyed before. Though ordered in 1732, the expedition was not able to leave the western coast until the 4th June, 1741, when two well-appointed ships set sail in company "to discover the Continent of America." One of these, called the "St. Paul," was under Commodore Behring; the other, called the "St. Peter," was under Captain Tschirikow. For some time the two kept together, but in a violent storm and fog they were separated, when each continued the expedition alone.

Behring first saw the Continent of North America on the 18th July, 1741, in latitude 58° 28'. Looking at it from a distance, "the country had terrible high mountains that were covered with snow." Two days later he anchored in a sheltered bay near a point which he called from the saint-day on which he saw it, Cape St. Elias. He was in the shadow of Mount St. Elias. On landing he found deserted huts, fire-places, hewn wood, household furniture, an arrow, edge-tools of copper, with "store of red salmon." Here also several birds, unknown in Siberia, were noticed by the faithful Steller, among which was the blue jay, of a peculiar species, now called by his name.

Steering northward, Behring found himself constrained by the elbow in the coast to turn westward, and then in a southerly direction. Hugging the shore, his voyage was constantly arrested by islands without number, among which he zigzagged to find his way ; several times he landed. On one of these occasions he saw natives, who wore "upper garments of whale's guts, breeches of seal-skins, caps of the skins of sea-lions, adorned with various feathers, especially those of hawks." These "Americans," as they are called, were fishermen, without bows and arrows. They regaled the Russians with "whale's flesh," but declined strong drink. One of them, on receiving a cup of brandy, "spit it out again as soon as he tasted it, and cried aloud, as if complaining to his countrymen how ill he had been used." This was on one of the Shumagin Islands, near the southern coast of the Peninsula of Alaska.

Meanwhile, the other solitary ship proceeding on its way, had sighted the same coast on the 15th July, 1741, in the latitude of 56°. Anchoring at some distance from the steep and rocky cliffs before him, Tschirikow sent his mate with the long boat and ten of his best men, provided with small-arms and a brass cannon, to inquire into the nature of the country and to obtain fresh water. The long boat disappeared in a small wooded bay, and was never seen again. Thinking it might have been damaged in landing, the Captain sent his boatswain with the small boat and carpenters well armed to furnish necessary assistance. The small boat disappeared also, and was never seen again. At the same time great smoke was observed continually ascending from the shore.

Shortly afterwards two boats filled with natives sallied forth and lay at some distance from the vessel, when, crying "Agai, Agai," they put back to the shore. Sorrowfully the Russian navigator turned away, not knowing the fate of his comrades, and unable to help them. This was not far from Sitka.

Such was the first discovery of these north-western coasts, and such are the first recorded glimpses of the aboriginal inhabitants. The two navigators had different fortunes. Tschirikow, deprived of his boats, and therefore unable to land, hurried home. Adverse winds and storms interfered. He supplied himself with fresh water only by distilling the ocean or pressing rain from the sails. But at last on the 9th October he reached Kamtchatka, with his ship's company of seventy diminished to forty-nine.

During this time Behring was driven, like Ulysses, on the uncertain waves. A single tempest raged for seventeen days, so that Andrew Hosselberg, the ancient pilot, who had known the sea for fifty years, declared that he had seen nothing like it in his life. Scurvy came with its disheartening horrors. The Commodore himself was a sufferer. Rigging broke; cables snapped; anchors were lost. At last the tempest-tossed vessel was cast upon a desert island, then without a name, where the Commodore, sheltered in a ditch and half covered with sand as a protection against cold, died on the 8th December, 1741. His body after his decease was "scraped out of the ground" and buried on this island, which is called by his name, and constitutes an outpost of the Asiatic Continent. Thus the Russian navigator, after the discovery of America, died in Asia. Russia, by the recent demarcation, does not fail to retain his last resting-place among her possessions.

Title of Russia.

For some time after these expeditions, by which Russia achieved the palm of discovery, Imperial enterprise slumbered in those seas. The knowledge already acquired was continued and confirmed only by private individuals, who were led there in quest of furs. In 1745 the Aleutian Islands were discovered by an adventurer in search of sea-otters. In successive voyages all these islands were visited for similar purposes. Among these was Ounalaska, the principal of the group of Fox Islands, constituting a continuation of the Aleutian Islands, whose inhabitants and productions were minutely described.

In 1768 private enterprise was superseded by an expedition ordered by the Empress Catharine, which, leaving Kamtchatka, explored this whole archipelago and the Peninsula of Alaska, which to the islanders stood for the whole continent. Shortly afterwards all these discoveries, beginning with those of Behring and Tschirikow, were verified by the great English navigator Captain Cook. In 1778 he sailed along the north-western coast, "near where Tschirikow anchored in 1741;" then again in sight of mountains "wholly covered with snow from the highest summit down to the sea-coast," "with the summit of an elevated mountain above the horizon," which he supposed to be the Mount St. Elias of Behring; then by the very anchorage of Behring; then among the islands through which Behring zigzagged, and along the coast by the Island of St. Lawrence until arrested by ice. If any doubt existed with regard to Russian discoveries it was removed by the authentic Report of this navigator, who shed such a flood of light upon the geography of this region.

Such from the beginning is the title of Russia, dating at least from 1741. The coast of British Columbia, next below, was discovered by Vancouver in 1790, and that of Oregon, still further down, by Gray, who, sailing from Boston in 1789, entered the Columbia River

N

in 1790, so that the title of Russia is the earliest on the north-western coast. I have not stopped to quote volume and page, but I beg to be understood as following approved authorities, and I refer especially to the Russian work of Müller, already cited, on the "Voyages from Asia to America;" the volume of Coxe on "Russian Discoveries," with its supplement on the "Comparative View of Russian Discoveries;" the volume of Sir John Barrow, on "Arctic Voyages;" Burney's "Russian and North-eastern Voyages;" and the third voyage of Captain Cook, unhappily interrupted by his tragical death from the natives of the Sandwich Islands, but not until after his exploration of this coast.

There were at least four other Russian expeditions by which this title was confirmed, if it needed any confirmation. The first was ordered by the Empress Catharine in 1785. It was under the command of Commodore Billings, an Englishman in the service of Russia, and was narrated from the original papers by Martin Sauer, Secretary of the expedition. In the instructions from the Admiralty at St. Petersburgh the Commodore was directed to take possession of "such coasts and islands as he shall first discover, whether inhabited or not, that cannot be disputed, and are not yet subject to any European Power, with consent of the inhabitants, if any," and this was to be accomplished by setting up "posts marked with the Arms of Russia, with letters indicating the time of sovereignty, a short account of the people, their voluntary submission to the Russian sovereignty, and that this was done under the glorious reign of the great Catharine II."— (Billings' "Northern Russia," Appendix.)

The next was in 1803, in the interest of the Russian-American Company. There were two ships, one under the command of Captain Lisiansky, and the other of Captain Krusenstern, of the Russian navy. It was the first voyage round the world by the Russian Government, and lasted three years. During its progress these ships visited separately the north-west coast of America, and especially Sitka and the Island of Kodiak.

Still another enterprise organized by the celebrated Minister Count Romanzoff, at his expense, left Russia in 1815, under the command of Lieutenant Kotzebue, an officer of the Russian navy, and son of the German dramatist whose assassination darkened the return of the son from his long voyage. It is enough for the present to say of this expedition that it has left its honourable traces on the coast even as far as the Frozen Ocean.

There remains the enterprise of Lütke, at the time Captain, and afterwards Admiral, in the Russian navy, which was a voyage round the world, embracing especially the Russian possessions, commenced in 1826, and described in French with instructive fulness. With him sailed the German naturalist Kittlitz, who has done so much to illustrate the natural history of this region.

A French Aspiration on this Coast.

So little was the Russian title recognized for some time, that when the unfortunate expedition of La Pérouse, with the frigates "Boussole" and "Astrolabe," stopped on this coast in 1787, he did not hesitate to consider the friendly harbour, in latitude 58° 36', where he was moored, as open to permanent occupation. Describing this harbour, which he named "Port des Français," as sheltered behind a breakwater of rocks, with a calm sea, and with a mouth sufficiently large, he says that Nature seemed to have created at this extremity of the world a port like that of Toulon, but vaster in plan and accommodation; and then, considering that it had never been discovered before, that it was situated 33 leagues north-west of Remedios, the limit of Spanish navigation, about 284 leagues from Nootka, and 100 leagues from Prince William Sound, the mariner records his judgment that "if the French Government had any project of a factory on this coast, no nation could have the slightest right to oppose it."—(La Pérouse, "Voyage," Tom. 2, p. 147.)

Thus quietly was Russia dislodged. The frigates sailed further on their voyage, and never returned to France. Their fate was unknown, until, after fruitless search and the lapse of a generation, their shipwrecked hulls were accidentally found on a desert island of the Southern Pacific. The unfinished journal of La Pérouse recording his visit to this coast had been sent overland by way of Kamtchatka and Siberia to France, where it was published by a Decree of the National Assembly, thus making known his supposed discovery and his aspiration.

Early Spanish Claim.

Spain also has been a claimant. In 1775 Bodega, a Spanish navigator, seeking new opportunities to plant the Spanish flag, reached the parallel of 58° on this coast, not far from Sitka, but this supposed discovery was not followed by any immediate assertion of dominion. The universal aspiration of Spain had embraced this whole region even at an early day, and shortly after the return of Bodega another enterprise was equipped to verify the larger claim, being nothing less than the original title as discoverer of the straits between America and Asia, and of the conterminous continent under the name of Anian. This curious episode is not out of place in this brief history. It has two branches: one concerning early maps on which straits are represented between America and Asia under the name of Anian; the other concerning a pretended attempt by a Spanish navigator at an early day to find these straits.

There can be no doubt that early maps exist with north-western straits marked "Anian." There are two in the Congressional Library in atlases of the years 1717 and 1680; but these are of a date comparatively modern. Engel, in his "Mémoires

Géographiques," mentions several earlier, which he believes to be genuine. There is one purporting to be by Zaltieri, and bearing date 1566, an authentic pen-and-ink copy of which is now before me from the collection of our own Coast Survey. On this very interesting map, which is without latitude or longitude, the western coast of the continent is delineated with straits separating it from Asia not unlike the Behring Straits in outline and with the name in Italian "Stretto di Anian." Southward the coast has a certain conformity with what is now known to exist. Below the straits is an indentation corresponding to Bristol Bay; then a peninsula somewhat broader than that of Alaska; then comes the elbow of the coast; then lower down three islands, not unlike Sitka, Queen Charlotte, and Vancouver; and then, further south, is the peninsula of Lower California. Sometimes the story of Anian is explained by the voyage of the Portuguese navigator Caspar de Cortereal in 1500-1505, when, on reaching Hudson Bay in quest of a passage round America, he imagined that he had found it, and proceeded to name his discovery "in honour of two brothers who accompanied him." Very soon maps began to record the Straits of Anian; but this does not explain the substantial conformity of the early delineation with the reality, which seems truly remarkable.

The other branch of inquiry is more easily disposed of. This turns on a Spanish document entitled "Relation of the Discovery of the Strait of Anian, made by me, Captain Lorenzo Ferren Maldonado," purporting to be written at the time, although it did not see the light till 1781, when it was published in Spain, and shortly afterward became the subject of a Memoir before the French Academy. If this early account of a north-west passage from the Atlantic to the Pacific were authentic the whole question would be settled, but recent geographers indignantly discarded it as a barefaced imposture. Clearly Spain once regarded it otherwise; for her Government in 1789 sent out an expedition "to discover the strait by which Maldonado was supposed to have passed in 1588 from the coast of Labrador to the Great Ocean." The expedition was not successful, and nothing more has been heard of any claim from this pretended discovery. The story of Maldonado has taken its place in the same category with that of Munchausen.

Reasons for this Cession by Russia.

Turning from this question of title, which time and testimony have already settled, I meet the inquiry, Why does Russia part with possessions thus associated with the reign of her greatest Emperor and filling an important chapter of geographical history? On this head I have no information which is not open to others. But I do not forget that the first Napoleon in parting with Louisiana was controlled by three several considerations: first, he needed the purchase-money for his Treasury; secondly, he was unwilling to leave this distant unguarded territory a prey to Great Britain in the event of hostilities which seemed at hand; and thirdly, he was glad, according to his own remarkable language, "to establish for ever the power of the United States and give to England a maritime rival destined to humble her pride." Such is the record of history. Perhaps a similar record may be made hereafter with regard to the present cession. It is sometimes imagined that Russia, with all her great Empire, is financially poor, so that these few millions may not be unimportant to her. It is by foreign loans that her railroads have been built and her wars have been aided. All, too, must see that in those "coming events," which now more than ever "cast their shadows before," it will be for her advantage not to hold outlying possessions from which thus far she has obtained no income commensurate with the possible expense for their protection. Perhaps, like a wrestler, she now strips for the contest, which I trust sincerely may be averted. Besides, I cannot doubt that her enlightened Emperor, who who has given pledges to civilization by an unsurpassed act of emancipation, would join the first Napoleon in a desire to enhance the maritime power of the United States.

These general considerations are reinforced when we call to mind the little influence which Russia has thus far been able to exercise in this region. Though possessing dominion over it for more than a century this gigantic Power has not been more genial or productive there than the soil itself. Her Government there is little more than a name or a shadow. It is not even a skeleton. It is hardly visible. Its only representative is a Fur Company, to which has been added latterly an Ice Company. The immense country is without form and without light; without activity and without progress. Distant from the Imperial capital, and separated from the huge bulk of Russian Empire, it does not share the vitality of a common country. Its life is solitary and feeble. Its Settlements are only encampments or lodges. Its fisheries are only a petty perquisite, belonging to local or personal adventurers rather than to the commerce of nations.

In these statements I follow the record. So little were these possessions regarded during the last century that they were scarcely recognized as a component part of the Empire. I have now before me an authentic map, published by the Academy of Sciences at St. Petersburgh in 1776, and reproduced at London in 1787, entitled "General Map of the Russian Empire," where you will look in vain for Russian America, unless we accept that link of the Aleutian chain nearest to Asia, which appears to have been incorporated under the Empress Anna at the same time with Siberia. (See Coxe's "Russian Discoveries.") Alexander Humboldt, whose insight into geography was unerring, in his great work on "New Spain," published in 1811, after stating that he is able from official documents to give the position of the Russian factories on the American Continent, says that they are "nothing but sheds and cabins employed as magazines of furs." He remarks further that " the larger part of these small Russian Colonies do not communicate with each other except by sea," and then, putting us on our guard not to expect too much from a name, he proceeds to say that " the new denomination of *Russian America* or *Russian possessions* on the new continent must not make us think that the coasts of Behring's Basin, the Peninsula of Alaska, or the country of Tchuktchi have become *Russian provinces* in the sense given to this word, when we speak of the Spanish Provinces of Sonora or New Biscay." (Humboldt, " Essai Politique sur La Nouvelle-Espagne." Tom. 1, pp. 344. 345.) Here is a distinction between the foothold of Spain in California and the foothold of Russia in North America, which will at least illustrate the slender power of the latter in this region.

In ceding possessions so little within the sphere of her Empire, embracing more than 100 nations or tribes, Russia gives up no part of herself, and even if she did the considerable price paid, the alarm of war which begins to fill our ears, and the sentiments of friendship declared for the United States, would explain the transaction.

The Negotiation, in its Origin and Completion.

I am not able to say when the idea of this cession first took shape. 1 have heard that it was as long ago as the Administration of Mr. Polk. It is within my knowledge that the Russian Government was sounded on the subject during the Administration of Mr. Buchanan. This was done through Mr. Gwin, at the time Senator of California, and Mr. Appleton, Assistant Secretary of State. For this purpose the former had more than one interview with the Russian Minister at Washington some time in December 1859, in which, while professing to speak for the President unofficially, he represented " that Russia was too far off to make the most of these possessions; and that as we are near, we can derive more from them." In reply to an inquiry of the Russian Minister Mr. Gwin said that " the United States could go as high as 5,000,000 dollars for the purchase," on which the former made no comment. Mr. Appleton, on another occasion, said to the Minister that " the President thought that the acquisition would be very profitable to the States on the Pacific ; that he was ready to follow it up, but wished to know in advance if Russia was ready to cede ; that if she were, he would confer with his Cabinet and influential Members of Congress." All this was unofficial; but it was promptly communicated to the Russian Government, who seem to have taken it into careful consideration. Prince Gortschakow, in a despatch which reached here early in the summer of 1860, said that " the offer was not what might have been expected : but that it merited mature reflection ; that the Minister of Finance was about to inquire into the condition of these possessions, after which Russia would be in a condition to treat." The Prince added for himself that " he was by no means satisfied personally that it would be for the interest of Russia politically to alienate these possessions; that the only consideration which could make the scales incline that way would be the prospect of great financial advantages ; but that the sum of 5,000,000 dollars does not seem in any way to represent the real value of these possessions." and he concluded by asking the Minister to tell Mr. Appleton and Senator Gwin that the sum offered was not considered " an equitable equivalent." The subject was submerged by the Presidential election which was approaching, and then by the rebellion. It will be observed that this attempt was at a time when politicians who believed in the perpetuity of slavery still had power. Mr. Buchanan was President, and he employed as his intermediary a known sympathizer with slavery, who shortly afterward became a rebel. Had Russia been willing, it is doubtful if this controlling interest would have sanctioned any acquisition too far north for slavery.

Meanwhile, the rebellion was brought to an end, and peaceful enterprise was renewed, which on the Pacific coast was directed toward the Russian possessions. Our people there, wishing new facilities to obtain fish, fur, and ice, sought the intervention of the National Government. The Legislature of Washington Territory, in the winter of 1866, adopted a Memorial to the President of the United States, entitled " in reference to the co and other fisheries," as follows :—

" To his Excellency Andrew Johnson, President of the United States,

" Your memorialists, the Legislative Assembly of Washington Territory, beg leave to show that abundance of codfish, halibut, and salmon of excellent quality have been found along the shores of the Russian possessions. Your memorialists respectfully request your Excellency to obtain such rights and privileges of the Government of Russia as will enable our fishing-vessels to visit the ports and harbours of its possessions to the end that fuel, water, and provisions may be easily obtained, that our sick and disabled fishermen may obtain sanitary assistance, together with the privilege of curing fish and repairing vessels in need of repairs. Your memorialists further request that the Treasury Department be instructed to forward to the Collector of Customs of this Puget Sound district such fishing licences, abstract journals, and log-books as will enable our hardy fishermen to obtain the bounties now provided and paid to the fishermen in the Atlantic States. Your memorialists finally pray your Excellency to employ such ships as may be spared from the Pacific Naval Fleet in exploring and surveying the fishing banks known to navigators to exist along the Pacific coast from the Cortes Bank to Behring Straits, and as in duty bound your memorialists will ever pray."

"Passed the House of Representatives, the 10th January, 1866.
(Signed) "EDWARD ELDRIDGE, *Speaker,*
House of Representatives.
" Passed the Council, the 13th January, 1866.
(Signed) "HARVEY K. HINES, *President of the Council.*"

This Memorial on its presentation to the President in February 1866 was referred to the Secretary of State, by whom it was communicated to M. de Stoeckl, the Russian Minister, with remarks on the importance of some early and comprehensive arrangement between the two Powers in order to prevent the growth of difficulties, especially from the fisheries in that region.

Shortly afterwards another influence was felt. Mr. Cole, who had been recently elected to the Senate from California, acting in behalf of certain persons in that State, sought to obtain from the Russian Government a licence or franchise to gather furs in a portion of its American possessions. The Charter of the Russian-American Company was about to expire. This Company had already underlet to the Hudson Bay Company all its franchise on the mainland between 54° 40′ and Mount St. Elias; and now it was proposed that an American Company, holding direct from the Russian Government, should be substituted for the latter. The mighty Hudson Bay Company, with its head-quarters in London, was to give way to an American Company, with its head-quarters in California. Among the letters on this subject addressed to Mr. Cole, and now before me, is one dated at San Francisco, the 10th April, 1866, in which this scheme is developed as follows :—

"There is at the present time a good chance to organize a Fur Trading Company to trade between the United States and the Russian possessions in America, and as the Charter formerly granted to the Hudson Bay Company has expired this would be the opportune moment to start in.

    *   *   *   *   *   *

" I should think that by a little management this Charter could be obtained from the Russian Government for ourselves, as I do not think they are very willing to renew the Charter of the Hudson Bay Company, and I think they would give the preference to an American Company, especially if the Company should pay to the Russian Government 5 per cent. on the gross proceeds of their transactions, and also aid in civilizing and ameliorating the condition of the Indians by employing missionaries, if required by the Russian Government. For the faithful performance of the above we ask a Charter for the term of twenty-five years, to be renewed for the same length of time if the Russian Government finds the Company deserving. The Charter to invest us with the right of trading in all the country between the British-American line and the Russian archipelago.

" Remember, we wish for the same Charter as was formerly granted to the Hudson Bay Company, and we offer in return more than they did."

Another correspondent of Mr. Cole, under date of San Francisco, the 17th September, 1866, wrote as follows :—

" I have talked with a man who has been on the coast and in the trade for ten years past, and he says it is much more valuable than I have supposed, and I think it very important to obtain it if possible."

The Russian Minister at Washington, whom Mr. Cole saw repeatedly upon this subject, was not authorized to act, and the latter, after conference with the Department of State, was induced to address Mr. Clay, Minister of the United States at St. Petersburgh, who laid the application before the Russian Government. This was an important step. A letter from Mr. Clay, dated at St. Petersburgh as late as the 1st February, 1867, makes the following revelation :—

" The Russian Government has already ceded away its rights in Russian America for a term of years, and the Russo-American Company has also ceded the same to the Hudson Bay Company. This lease expires in June next, and the President of the Russo-American Company tells me that they have been in correspondence with the Hudson Bay Company about a renewal of the lease for another term of twenty-five or thirty years. Until he receives a definite answer he cannot enter into negotiations with us or your California Company. My opinion is that if he can get off with the Hudson Bay Company he will do so, when we can make some arrangements with the Russo-American Company."

Some time had elapsed since the original attempt of Mr. Gwin, also a Senator from California, and it is probable that the Russian Government had obtained information which enabled it to see its way more clearly. It will be remembered that Prince Gortschakow had promised an inquiry, and it is known that in 1861 Captain-Lieutenant Golowin, of the Russian navy, made a detailed Report on these possessions. Mr. Cole had the advantage of his predecessor. There is reason to believe, also, that the administration of the Fur Company had not been entirely satisfactory, so that there were well-founded hesitations with regard to the renewal of its franchise. Meanwhile, in October 1866, M. de Stoeckl, who had long been the Russian Minister at Washington, and enjoyed in a high degree the confidence of our Government, returned home on a leave of absence, promising his best exertions to promote good relations between the two countries. While he was at St. Petersburgh the applications from the United States were under consideration; but the Russian Government was disinclined to any minor arrangement of the character proposed. Obviously something like a crisis was at hand with regard to these possessions. The existing government was not adequate. The franchises granted there were about to terminate. Something must be done. As M. de Stoeckl was leaving in February to return to his post the Archduke Constantine, the brother and chief adviser of the Emperor, handed him a map with the lines in our Treaty marked upon it, and told him he might treat for this cession. The Minister arrived in Washington early in March. A negotiation was opened at once with our Government. Final instructions were received by the Atlantic cable from St. Petersburgh on the 29th March, and at 4 o'clock on the morning of the 30th March this important Treaty was signed by Mr. Seward on the part of the United States, and by M. de Stoeckl on the part of Russia.

Few Treaties have been conceived, initiated, prosecuted, and completed in so simple a manner without Protocols or despatches. The whole negotiation will be seen in its result, unless we accept two brief notes, which constitute all that passed between the negotiators. These have an interest general and special, and I conclude the history of this transaction by reading them :—

"Sir,   "*Department of State, Washington, March* 23, 1867.

"With reference to the proposed Convention between our respective Governments for a cession by Russia of her American territory to the United States, I have the honour to acquaint you that I must insist upon that clause in the 6th Article of the draft which declares the cession to be free and unincumbered by any reservations, privileges, franchises, grants, or possessions by any associated Companies, whether corporate or incorporate, Russian or any other, &c., and must regard it as an ultimatum. With the President's approval, however, I will add 200,000 dollars to the consideration money on that account.

         "I avail, &c.
      (Signed) "WILLIAM H. SEWARD.

"M. Edward de Stoeckl, &c."

"(Translation.)
"Mr. Secretary of State,   *Washington, March* 17 (29), 1867.

"I have the honour to inform you that, by a telegram dated the 16th (28th) of this month from St. Petersburgh, Prince Gortschakow informs me that His Majesty the Emperor of All the Russias gives his consent to the cession of the Russian possessions on the American Continent to the United States for the stipulated sum of 7,200,000 dollars in gold, and that His Majesty the Emperor invests me with full powers to negotiate and sign the Treaty.

         "Please accept, &c.
      (Signed) "STOECKL.

"To Honourable William H. Seward,
 "Secretary of State of the United States."

The Treaty.

The Treaty begins with the declaration that "the United States of America and His Majesty the Emperor of All the Russias, being desirous of strengthening, if possible, the good understanding which exists between them," have appointed Plenipotentiaries, who have proceeded to sign Articles, wherein it is stipulated on behalf of Russia that "His Majesty the Emperor of All the Russias agrees to cede to the United States by this Convention, immediately upon the exchange of the ratifications thereof, all the territory and dominion now possessed by His said Majesty on the Continent of America and in the adjacent islands, the same being contained within the geographical limits herein set forth;" and it is stipulated on behalf of the United States that, "in consideration of the cession aforesaid, the United States agree to pay at the Treasury in Washington, within ten months after the ratification of this Convention, to the Diplomatic Representative or other Agent of His Majesty the Emperor of All the Russias duly authorized to receive the same, 7,200,000 dollars in gold." The ratifications are to be exchanged within three months from the date of the Treaty, or sooner, if possible.

Beyond the consideration founded on the desire of "strengthening the good understanding" between the two countries, there is the pecuniary consideration already mentioned, which underwent a change in the progress of the negotiation. The sum of

7,000,000 dollars was originally agreed upon; but when it was understood that there was a Fur Company and also an Ice Company enjoying monopolies under the existing Government, it was thought best that these should be extinguished, in consideration of which our Government added 200,000 dollars to the purchase-money, and the Russian Government in formal terms declared " the cession of territory and dominion to be free and unincumbered by any reservations, privileges, franchises, grants, or possessions, by any associated Companies, whether corporate or incorporate, or by any parties, except merely private individual property-holders." Thus the United States receive this cession free of all incumbrances, so far at least as Russia is in a condition to make it. The Treaty proceeds to say that " the cession hereby made conveys all the rights, franchises, and privileges now belonging to Russia in the said territory or dominion and appurtenances thereto." In other words, Russia conveys all that she has to convey.

Questions arising under the Treaty.

There are questions not unworthy of attention, which arise under the Treaty between Russia and Great Britain, fixing the eastern limits of these possessions, and conceding certain privileges to the latter Power. By this Treaty, signed at St. Petersburgh on the 28th February, 1825, after fixing the boundaries between the Russian and British possessions, it is provided that " for the space of ten years the vessels of the two Powers, or those belonging to their respective subjects, shall mutually be at liberty to frequent, without any hindrance whatever, all the inland seas, gulfs, havens, and creeks on the coast for the space of fishing and of trading with the natives;" and also that " for the space of ten years the port of Sitka or Novo-Archangelsk shall be open to the commerce and vessels of British subjects."—(Hertslet's " Commercial Treaties," vol. ii, p. 365.)

In the same Treaty it is also provided that " the subjects of His Britannic Majesty, from whatever quarter they may arrive, whether from the ocean or from the interior of the continent, shall for ever enjoy the right of navigating freely and without any hindrance whatever all the rivers and streams which, in their course toward the Pacific Ocean, may cross the line of demarcation."—(Ibid.)

Afterwards a Treaty of Commerce and Navigation between Russia and Great Britain was signed at St. Petersburgh on the 11th January, 1843, subject to be terminated on notice from either party at the expiration of ten years, in which it is provided that " in regard to commerce and navigation in the Russian possessions on the north-west coast of America the Convention of the 28th February, 1825, continues in force."—(Ibid., vol. vi, p. 767.)

Then ensued the Crimean war between Russia and Great Britain, effacing or suspending Treaties. Afterwards another Treaty of Commerce and Navigation was signed at St. Petersburgh on the 12th January, 1859, subject to be terminated on notice from either party at the expiration of ten years, which repeats the last provision.—(Ibid., vol. x, p. 1063.)

Thus we have three different stipulations on the part of Russia: one opening seas, gulfs, and havens on the Russian coast to British subjects for fishing and trading with the natives; the second making Sitka a free port to British subjects; and the third making British rivers which flow through the Russian possessions for ever free to British navigation. Do the United States succeed to these stipulations?

Among these I make a distinction in favour of the last, which by its language is declared to be " for ever," and may have been in the nature of an equivalent at the settlement of the boundaries between the two Powers. But whatever may be its terms or its origin it is obvious that it is nothing but a declaration of public law as it has always been expounded by the United States and is now recognized on the Continent of Europe. While pleading with Great Britain in 1826 for the free navigation of the St. Lawrence, Mr. Clay, who was at the time Secretary of State, said that " the American Government did not mean to contend for any principle the benefit of which, in analogous circumstances, it would deny to Great Britain." (Wheaton's " Elements of International Law," Part II, cap. 4.) During the same year Mr. Gallatin, our Minister in London, when negotiating with Great Britain for the adjustment of our boundaries on the Pacific, proposed that " if the line should cross any of the branches of the Columbia at points from which they are navigable by boats to the main stream the navigation of both branches and of the main stream should be perpetually free and common to the people of both nations." At an earlier day the United States made the same claim with regard to the Mississippi, and asserted as a general principle that " if the right of the upper inhabitants to descend the stream was in any case obstructed it was an act by a stronger society against a weaker, condemned by the judgment of mankind." (Ibid.) By these admissions our country is estopped, even if the public law of the European Continent, first declared at Vienna with regard to the Rhine, did not offer an example which we cannot afford to reject. I rejoice to believe that on this occasion we shall apply to Great Britain the generous rule which from the beginning we have claimed for ourselves.

The two other stipulations are different in character. They are not declared to be " for ever," and do not stand on any principle of public law. Even if subsisting now they cannot be onerous. I doubt much if they are subsisting now. In succeeding to the Russian possessions it does not follow that the United States succeed to ancient obligations assumed by Russia, as if, according to a phrase of the common law, they are " covenants running with the land." If these stipulations are in the nature of *servitudes* they depend for their duration on the sovereignty of Russia, and are *personal* or *national* rather than *territorial*. So at least I am inclined to believe. But it is hardly profitable to speculate on a point of so little practical value. Even if " running with the land " these *servitudes* can be terminated at the expiration of ten years from the last Treaty by a notice, which equitably the United States may give, so as to take effect on the 12th January, 1869. Meanwhile, during this brief period, it will be easy by Act of Congress in advance to limit importations at Sitka, so that this " free port " shall not be made the channel or doorway by which British goods may be introduced into the United States free of duty.

General Considerations on the Treaty.

From this survey of the Treaty, as seen in its origin and the questions under it, I might pass at once to a survey of the possessions which have been conveyed; but there are other matters of a more general character which present themselves at this stage and challenge the judgment. These concern nothing less than the unity, power, and grandeur of the Republic, with the extension of its dominion and its institutions. Such considerations, where not entirely inapplicable, are apt to be controlling. I do not doubt that they will in a great measure determine the fate of this Treaty with the American people. They are patent, and do not depend on research or statistics. To state them is enough.

Advantages to the Pacific Coast.

1. Foremost in order, if not in importance, I put the desires of our fellow-citizens on the Pacific coast, and the special advantages which they will derive from this enlargement of boundary. They were the first to ask for it, and will be the first to profit by it. While others knew the Russian possessions only on the map they knew them practically in their resources. While others were still indifferent they were planning how to appropriate Russian peltries and fisheries. This is attested by the Resolutions of the Legislature of Washington Territory; also by the exertions at different times of two Senators from California, who, differing in political sentiments and in party relations, took the initial steps which ended in this Treaty.

These well-known desires were founded, of course, on supposed advantages; and here experience and neighbourhood were prompters. Since 1854 the people of California have received their ice from the fresh-water lakes in the Island of Kodiak, not far westward from Mount St. Elias. Later still their fishermen have searched the waters about the Aleutians and the Shumagins, commencing a promising fishery. Others have proposed to substitute themselves to the Hudson Bay Company in their franchise on the coast. But all are looking to the Orient, as in the time of Columbus, although like him they sail to the West. To them China and Japan, those ancient realms of fabulous wealth, are the Indies. To draw this commerce to the Pacific coast is no new idea. It haunted the early navigators. Meares, the Englishman, whose voyage in the intervening seas was in 1789, closes his volumes with an essay, entitled " The Trade between the North-West Coast of America and China," in the course of which he dwells on the " great and very valuable source of commerce " afforded by China as " forming a chain of trade between Hudson Bay, Canada, and the north-west coast," and then he exhibits on the American side the costly furs of the sea-otter, which are still so much prized in China ; " mines which are known to lie between the latitudes 40° and 60° north ;" and also an " inexhaustible supply " of ginseng, for which there is still such a demand in China that even Minnesota, at the head-waters of the Mississippi, supplies her contribution. His catalogue might be extended now.

As a practical illustration of this idea, it may be mentioned that for a long time most if not all the sea-otter skins of this coast found their way to China, excluding even Russia herself. China was the best customer, and therefore Englishmen and Americans followed the Russian Company in carrying these furs to her market, so that Pennant, the English naturalist, impressed by the peculiar advantages of this coast, exclaimed, " What a profitable trade with China might not a Colony carry on were it possible to penetrate to that part of the country by means of rivers and lakes !" But under the present Treaty this coast is ours.

The absence of harbours at present belonging to the United States on the Pacific limits the outlets of the country. On that whole extent, from Panamá to Puget Sound, the only harbour of any considerable value is San Francisco. Further north the harbours are abundant, and they are all nearer to the great marts of Japan and China. But San Francisco itself will be nearer by the way of the Aleutians than by Honolulu. The projection of maps is not always calculated to present an accurate idea of distances. From measurement on a globe it appears that a voyage from San Francisco to Hong Kong by the common way of the Sandwich Islands is 7,140 miles, but by way of the Aleutian Islands it is only 6,00 0 miles, being a saving of more than 1,000 miles, with the enormous additional advantage of being obliged to carry much less coal. Of course a voyage from Sitka, or from Puget Sound, the terminus of the Northern Pacific Railroad, would be shorter still.

The advantages to the Pacific coast have two aspects, one domestic and the other foreign. Not only does the Treaty extend the coasting trade of California, Oregon, and

Washington Territory northward, but it also extends the base of commerce with China and Japan.

To unite the east of Asia with the west of America is the aspiration of commerce now as when the English navigator recorded his voyage. Of course whatever helps this result is an advantage. The Pacific Railroad is such an advantage, for, though running westward, it will be, when completed, a new highway to the East. This Treaty is another advantage, for nothing than be clearer than that the western coast must exercise an attraction which will be felt in China and Japan just in proportion as it is occupied by a commercial people communicating readily with the Atlantic and with Europe. This cannot be done without consequences not less important politically than commercially. Owing so much to the Union, the people there there will be bound to it anew, and the national unity will receive another confirmation. Thus the whole country will be a gainer. So are we knit together that the advantages to the Pacific coast will contribute to the general welfare.

Extension of Dominion.

2. The extension of dominion is another consideration, calculated to captivate the the public mind. Few are so cold or philosophical as to regard with insensibility a widening of the bounds of country. Wars have been regarded as successful when they have given a new territory. The discoverer who had planted the flag of his Sovereign on a distant coast has been received as a conqueror. The ingratitude which was shown to Columbus during his later days was compensated by the epitaph that he had given a new world to Castile and Leon. His discoveries were continued by other navigators, and Spain girdled the earth with her possessions. Portugal, France, Holland, England, each followed the example of Spain and rejoiced in extended Empire.

Our territorial acquisitions are among the landmarks of our history. In 1803 Louisiana, embracing the valley of the Mississippi, was acquired from the Mississippi for 15,000,000 dollars. In 1819 Florida was acquired from Spain for 3,000,000 dollars. In 1845 Texas was annexed without any purchase, but subsequently her debt was assumed to the amount of 7,500,000 dollars. In 1848 California, New Mexico, and Utah were acquired from Mexico after war, and on payment of 15,000,000 dollars. In 1854 Arizona was acquired from Mexico for 10,000,000 dollars. And now it is proposed to acquire Russian America.

The passion for acquisition, which is so strong in the individual, is not less strong in the community. A nation seeks an outlying territory as an individual seeks an outlying farm. The passion shows itself constantly. France, passing into Africa, has annexed Algeria. Spain set her face in the same direction, but without the same success. There are two Great Powers with which annexation has become a habit. One is Russia, which from the time of Peter the Great has been moving her flag forward in every direction, so that on every side her limits have been extended. Even now the report comes that she is lifting her southern landmarks in Asia, so as to carry her boundary to India. The other annexationist is Great Britain, which from time to time adds another province to her Indian dominion. If the United States have from time to time added to their dominion they have only yielded to the universal passion, although I do not forget that the late Theodore Parker was accustomed to say that among all people the Anglo-Saxons were remarkable for "a greed of land." It was land, not gold, that aroused the Anglo-Saxon phlegm. I doubt, however, if this passion be stronger with us than with others, except, perhaps, that in a community where all participate in government the national sentiments are more active. It is common to the human family. There are few anywhere who could hear of a considerable accession of territory, obtained peacefully and honestly, without a pride of country, even if at certain moments the judgment hesitated. With an increased size on the map there is an increased consciousness of strength, and the citizen throbs anew as he traces the extending line.

Extension of Republican Institutions.

3. More than the extension of dominion is the extension of Republican institutions, which is a traditional aspiration. It was in this spirit that independence was achieved. In the name of human rights our fathers overthrew the kingly power, whose Representative was George III. They set themselves openly against this form of government. They were against it for themselves, and offered their example to mankind. They were Roman in character, and turned to Roman lessons. With a cynical austerity the early Cato said that Kings were "carnivorous animals," and at his instance the Roman Senate decreed that no King should be allowed within the gates of the city. A kindred sentiment, with less austerity of form, has been received from our fathers; but our city can be nothing less than the North American Continent with its gates on all the surrounding seas.

John Adams, in the preface to his "Defence of the American Constitution," written in London, where he resided at the time as Minister, and dated the 1st January, 1787, at Grosvenor Square, the central seat of aristocratic fashion, after exposing the fabulous origin of the kingly power in contrast with the simple origin of our Republican Constitutions, thus for a moment lifts the curtain of the future: "Thirteen Governments," he says plainly, "thus founded on the natural authority of the people alone, and without any

P

pretence of miracle or mystery, and *which are destined to spread over the northern part of that whole quarter of the globe*, is a great point gained in favour of the rights of mankind." (John Adams' Works, vol. iv, p. 293). Thus, according to this prophetic Minister, even at that early day was the destiny of the Republic manifest. It was to spread over the northern part of the American quarter of the globe; and it was to be a support to the rights of mankind.

By the text of our Constitution the United States are bound to guarantee a " Republican form of government" to every State in this Union; but this obligation, which is only applicable at home, is an unquestionable indication of the national aspiration everywhere. The Republic is something more than a local policy; it is a general principle, not to be forgotten at any time, especially when the opportunity is presented of bringing an immense region within its influence. Elsewhere it has for the present failed; but on this account our example is more important. Who can forget the generous lament of Lord Byron, whose passion for freedom was not mitigated by his rank as an hereditary legislator of England, when he exclaims in memorable verse?—

> "The name of commonwealth is past and gone
> O'er the three fractions of the groaning globe!"

Who can forget the salutation which the poet sends to the "one great clime," which, nursed in freedom, enjoys what he calls "the proud distinction" of not being confounded with other lands?—

> " Whose sons must bow them at a Monarch's motion, —
> As if his senseless sceptre were a wand !"

The present Treaty is a visible step in the occupation of the whole North American Continent. As such it will be recognized by the world and accepted by the American people. But the Treaty involves something more. By it we dismiss one more Monarch from this Continent. One by one they have retired; first France; then Spain; then France again; and now Russia; all giving way to that absorbing Unity which is declared in the national motto "*E pluribus unum.*"

Anticipation of Great Britain.

4. Another motive to this acquisition may be found in a desire to anticipate the imagined schemes or necessities of Great Britain. With regard to all these I confess my doubts, and yet, if we may credit report, it would seem as if there was already a British movement in this direction. Sometimes it is said that Great Britain desires to buy if Russia will sell. Sir George Simpson, Governor-in-chief of the Hudson Bay Company, declared that without the strip on the coast underlet to the former by the Russian Company the interior would be "comparatively useless to England." Here, then, is a provocation to buy. Sometimes report assumes a graver character. A German scientific journal, in an elaborate paper, entitled, "The Russian Colonies on the North-west Coast of America," after referring to the constant "pressure" upon Russia, proceeds to say that there are already crowds of adventurers from British Columbia and California now at the gold mines on the Stikine, which flows from British territory through the Russian possessions, who openly declare their purpose of driving the Russians out of this region. I refer to the "Archiv für Wissenschaftliche Kunde von Russland," edited at Berlin as late as 1863, by A. Erman, vol. xxii, pp. 47-70, and unquestionably the leading authority on Russian questions. At the same time it presents a curious passage bearing directly on British policy from the "British Colonist," a newspaper of Victoria, on Vancouver's Island. As this was regarded of sufficient importance to be translated into German for the instruction of the readers of a scientific journal, I shall be justified in laying it before you restored from the German to English. It is as follows:—

"The information which we daily publish from the Stikine River very naturally excites public attention to a great extent. Whether the territory through which the river flows be considered in a political, commercial, or industrial light, there is a probability that in a short time there will be a still more general interest in the claim. Not only will the intervention of the Royal jurisdiction be demanded in order to give to it a complete form of government, but if the land proves to be as rich as there is now reason to believe it to be, it is not improbable that it will result in negotiations between England and Russia for the transfer of the sea-coast to the British Crown. It certainly is not acceptable that a stream like the Stikine, which for 170 to 190 miles is navigable for steamers, which waters a territory so rich in gold that it will allure thousands of men—certainly it is not desirable that the business of such a highway should reach the interior through a Russian door of 30 miles of coast. The English population which occupies the interior cannot be so easily managed by the Russians as the Stikine Indians of the coast manage the Indians of the interior. Our business must be in British hands. Our resources, our energies, our undertakings cannot be fully developed in building up a Russian emporium at the mouth of the Stikine. We must have for our productions a depôt over which the British flag waves. By the Treaty of 1825 the navigation of the river is secured to us. The navigation of the Mississippi was also open to the United States before the Louisiana purchase, but the growing strength of the North made the attainment of that territory either by purchase or by might an evident necessity. We look upon the sea-coast of Stikine-land in the same light. The strip of land which stretches along from Portland Canal to Mount St. Elias, with a breadth of 30 miles, and which according to the Treaty of 1825 forms a part of Russian America, *must eventually become the property of Great Britain*, either as the direct result of the development of gold, or for reasons which are now yet in the beginning, but whose results are certain. For it is clearly undesirable that the strip 300 miles long and 30 miles wide, which is only used by the Russians for the collection of furs and walrus teeth, shall for ever control the entrance to our very extensive northern territory. It is a principle of England to acquire territory only as a point of defence. Canada, Nova Scotia, Malta, the Cape of Good Hope, and the great part of our Indian possessions were all acquired as defensive points. In Africa, India, and China the same rule is to-day followed by the Government. With a Power like Russia it would perhaps be more difficult to get ready, but if we need the sea-coast to help us in our business in the precious metals with the interior and for defence, then we must have it. The United States needed Florida and Louisiana, and they took them. We need the shore of New Norfolk and New Cornwall.

"It is just as much the destiny of our Anglo-Norman race to possess the whole of Russian America, however wild and inhospitable it may be, as it has been the destiny of the Russian Northmen to prevail over Northern Europe and Asia. As the Wandering Jew and his phantom in the tale of Eugène Sue, so will the Anglo-Norman and the Russian yet look upon each other from the opposite side of Behring Straits. Between the two races the northern half of the Old and New World must be divided. America must be ours.

"The present development of the precious metals in our hyperborean Eldorado will most probably hasten the annexation of the territory in question. It can hardly be doubted that the gold region of the Stikine extends away to the western source of the Mackenzie. In this case the increase of the business and of the population will exceed our most sanguine expectations. Who shall reap the profit of this? The mouths of rivers have as well before as since the time of railroads controlled the business of the interior. For our national pride the thought, however, is unbearable that the Russian Eagle should possess a point which owes its importance to the British Lion. The mouth of the Stikine must be ours, or at least an outer harbour must be established on British soil from which our steamers can pass the Russian girdle. Fort Simpson, Dundas Land, Portland Canal, or some other convenient point, must be selected for this purpose. The necessity of speedy action in order to secure the control of the Stikine is apparent. If we let slip the opportunity, so shall we permit a Russian State to arrive at the door of a British Colony."

Thus, if we may credit this colonial ejaculation, caught up and preserved by German science, the Russian possessions were destined to round and complete the domain of Great Britain on this continent. The Russian "Eagle" will give way to the British "Lion." The Anglo-Norman was to be master as far as Behring Straits, across which he might survey his Russian neighbour. How this was to be accomplished is not precisely explained. The promises of gold on the Stikine failed, and it is not improbable that this colonial plan was as unsubstantial. Colonists become excited easily. This is not the first time in which Russian America has been menaced in a similar way. During the Crimean war there seemed to be in Canada a spirit not unlike that of the Vancouver journalist, unless we are misled by the able pamphlet of Mr. A. K. Roche, of Quebec, where, after describing Russian America as "richer in resources and capabilities than it has hitherto been allowed to be either by the English who shamefully gave it up, or by the Russians who cunningly obtained it," the author urges an expedition for its conquest and annexation. His proposition fell on the happy termination of the war, but it exists as a warning, with a notice also of a former English title "shamefully" abandoned.

This region is distant enough from Great Britain; but there is an incident of past history which shows that distance from the Metropolitan Government has not excluded the idea of war. Great Britain could hardly be more jealous of Russia on these coasts than was Spain in a former day, if we may credit the Report of Humboldt. I quote again his authoritative work, "Essai Politique sur la Nouvelle-Espagne" (Tom. 1 p. 345). where it is recorded that as early as 1788, even while peace was still unbroken, the Spaniards could not bear the idea of Russians in this region, and when in 1790 the Emperor Paul declared war on Spain the hardy project was formed of an expedition from the Mexican ports of Monterey and San Blas against the Russian Colonies, on which the philosophic traveller remarks, in words which are recalled by the Vancouver manifesto, that "if this project had been executed the world would have witnessed two nations in conflict, which, occupying the opposite extremities of Europe, found themselves neighbours in another hemisphere on the eastern and western boundaries of their vast Empires." Thus, notwithstanding an intervening circuit of half the globe, two Great Powers were about to encounter each other on these coasts. But I hesitate to believe that the British of our day in any considerable numbers have adopted the early Spanish disquietude at the presence of Russia on this continent.

The Amity of Russia.

5. There is still another consideration concerning this Treaty which must not be disregarded. It attests and assures the amity of Russia. Even if you doubt the value of

these possessions, the Treaty is a sign of friendship. It is a new expression of that *entente cordiale* between the two Powers which is a phenomenon of history. Though unlike in institutions, they are not unlike in recent experience. Sharers of a common glory in a great act of emancipation, they also share together the opposition or antipathy of other nations. Perhaps this experience has not been without its effect in bringing them together. At all events, no coldness or unkindness has interfered at any time with their good relations.

The archives of the State Department show an uninterrupted cordiality between the two Governments dating far back in our history. More than once Russia has offered her good offices between the United States and Great Britain; once also she was a recognized arbitrator. She offered her mediation to prevent war in 1812, and again by her mediation in 1815 brought about peace. Afterwards it was under her arbitration that questions with Great Britain arising under the Treaty of Ghent were amicably settled in 1822. But it was during our recent troubles that we felt more than ever her friendly sentiments, although it is not improbable that the accident of position and of distance had its influence in preserving these undisturbed. The Rebellion, which tempted so many other Powers into its embrace, could not draw Russia from her habitual good-will. Her solicitude for the Union was early declared. She made no unjustifiable concession of *ocean belligerency*, with all its immunities and powers, to rebels in arms against the Union. She furnished no hospitality to rebel cruizers; nor was any rebel agent ever received, entertained, or encouraged at St. Petersburgh; while, on the other hand, there was an understanding that the United States should be at liberty to carry prizes into Russian ports. So natural and easy were the relations between the two Governments that such complaints as incidentally arose on either side were amicably adjusted by verbal explanations without any written controversy.

Positive acts occurred to strengthen these relations. As early as 1861 the two Governments came to an agreement to act together for the establishment of a connection between San Francisco and St. Petersburgh by an interoceanic telegraph across Behring Straits; and this agreement was subsequently sanctioned by Congress. Meanwhile occurred the visit of the Russian fleet in the winter of 1863, which was intended by the Emperor and accepted by the United States as a friendly demonstration. This was followed by a communication of the Secretary of State, dated 26th December, 1864, in the name of the President, inviting the Archduke Constantine to visit the United States, in which it was suggested that such a visit would be "beneficial to us and by no means unprofitable to Russia," but forbearing "to specify reasons," and assuring him that coming as a national guest he would receive a cordial and most demonstrative welcome. Affairs in Russia prevented the acceptance of this invitation. Afterwards, in the spring of 1866, Congress by solemn resolution declared the sympathies of the people of the United States with the Emperor on his escape from the madness of an assassin, and Mr. Fox, at the time Assistant Secretary of the Navy, was appointed to take the Resolution of Congress to the Emperor, and, in discharge of this trust, to declare the friendly sentiments of our country for Russia. He was conveyed to Cronstadt in the monitor "Miantonomah," the most formidable ship of our navy; and thus this agent of war became a messenger of peace. The monitor and the Minister were received in Russia with unbounded hospitality.

In relations such as I have described the cession of territory seems a natural transaction entirely in harmony with the past. It remains to hope that it may be a new link in an amity which, without effort, has overcome differences of institutions and intervening space on the globe.

Shall the Treaty be ratified?

Such are some of the obvious considerations of a general character bearing on the Treaty. The interests of the Pacific States; the extension of the national domain; the extension of Republican institutions; the foreclosure of adverse British possessions and the amity of Russia; these are the points which we have passed in review. Most of these, if not all, are calculated to impress the public mind; but I can readily understand a difference of opinion with regard to the urgency of negotiation at this hour. Some may think that the purchase-money and the annual outlay which must follow might have been postponed for another decade, while Russia continued in possession as a trustee for our benefit. And yet some of the reasons for the Treaty do not seem to allow delay.

At all events, now that the Treaty has been signed by Plenipotentiaries on each side duly empowered, it is difficult to see how we can refuse to complete the purchase without putting to hazard the friendly relations which happily subsist between the United States and Russia. The overtures originally proceeded from us. After a delay of years, and other intervening propositions, the bargain was at length concluded. It is with nations as with individuals. A bargain once made must be kept. Even if still open to consideration it must not be lightly abandoned. I am satisfied that the dishonour of this Treaty, after what has passed, would be a serious responsibility for our country. As an international question, it would be tried by the public opinion of the world, and there are many who, not appreciating the requirement of our Constitution by which a Treaty must have "the advice and consent of the Senate," would regard its rejection as bad faith. There would be jeers at us and jeers at Russia also; at us for levity in making overtures, and at Russia for levity in yielding to them. Had the Senate been consulted in advance, before the Treaty was signed or either Power publicly committed, as is often done on important

57

occasions, it would now be under less constraint. On such a consultation there would have been an opportunity for all possible objections, and a large latitude to a reasonable discretion. Let me add that, while forbearing objection now, I hope that this Treaty may not be drawn into a precedent at least in the independent manner of its negotiation. I would save to the Senate an important power that justly belongs to it.

A Caveat.

But there is one other point on which I file my *caveat*. This Treaty must not be a precedent for a system of indiscriminate and costly annexation. Sincerely believing that Republican institutions under the primacy of the United States must embrace this whole continent, I cannot adopt the sentiment of Jefferson, who, while confessing satisfaction in settlements on the Pacific coast, saw there in the future nothing but "free and independent Americans," bound to the United States only by "ties of blood and interest" without political unity. Nor am I willing to restrain myself to the principle so tersely expressed by Andrew Jackson in his letter to President Monroe, "Concentrate our population, confine our frontier to proper limits, until our country, to those limits, is filled with a dense population." But I cannot disguise my anxiety that every stage in our predestined future shall be by natural processes without war, and I would add even without purchase. There is no territorial aggrandizement which is worth the price of blood. Only under peculiar circumstances can it become the subject of pecuniary contract. Our triumph should be by growth and organic expansion in obedience to "pre-established harmony," recognizing always the will of those who are to become our fellow-citizens. All this must be easy if we are only true to ourselves. Our motto may be that of Goethe, "Without haste, without rest." Let the Republic be assured in tranquil liberty with all equal before the law, and it will conquer by its sublime example. More happy than Austria, who acquired possessions by marriage, we shall acquire them by the attraction of Republican institutions;

"Bella gerant alii ; tu, felix Austria, nube ;
Nam quæ Mars aliis, dat tibi regna Venus."

The famous epigram will be just as applicable to us, inasmuch as our acquisitions will be under the sanction of wedlock to the Republic. There may be wedlock of a people as well as of a Prince. Meanwhile, our first care should be to improve and elevate the Republic, whose sway will be so comprehensive. Plant it with schools ; cover it with churches ; fill it with libraries ; make it abundant with comfort so that poverty shall disappear ; keep it constant in the assertion of Human Rights. And here we may fitly recall those words of antiquity, which Cicero quoted from the Greek, and which Webster in our day quoted from Cicero, "You have a Sparta ; adorn it."

Sources of Information upon Russian America.

I am now brought to consider the character of these possessions and their probable value. Here I am obliged to confess a dearth of authentic information easily accessible. There are few among us who read Russian, so that works in this language are locked up from the world. One of these, in two large and showy volumes, is now before me, entitled "A Historical Survey of the Formation of the Russian-American Company, and its Progress to the Present Time," by P. Teshmenew, St. Petersburgh. The first volume appeared in 1860, and the second in 1863. Here, among other things, is a tempting engraving of Sitka, wrapped in mists, with the sea before and the snow-capped mountains darkened with forest behind. Judging from the table of contents, which has been translated for me by a Russian, the book ought to be instructive. There is also another Russian work of an official character, which appeared in 1861 at St. Petersburgh in the "Morskoi Sbornich," or "Naval Review," and is entitled, "Materials for the History of the Russian Colonies on the Coasts of the Pacific." The Report of Captain-Lieutenant Golowin made to the Grand Duke Constantine in 1861, with which we have become acquainted through a scientific German journal, appeared originally in the same review. These are recent productions. After the early voyages of Behring, first ordered by Peter the Great and supervised by the Imperial Academy at St. Petersburgh, the spirit of geographical research seems to have subsided at St. Petersburgh. Other enterprises absorbed the attention. And yet I would not do injustice to the voyages of Billings, recounted by Sauer, or of Lisiansky, Krusenstern, and Langsdorf, or of Kotzebue, all under the auspices of Russia, the last of which may compare with any as a contribution to science. I may add Lütke also ; but Kotzebue was a worthy successor to Behring and Cook.

Beside these official contributions, most of which are by no means fresh, there are materials derived from casual navigators, who, scudding these seas, rested in the harbours there as the water-fowl on its flight ; from whalemen, who were there merely as Nimrods of the ocean ; or from adventurers in quest of the rich furs which it furnished. There are also the gazetteers and geographies, but they are less instructive on this head than usual, being founded on information now many years old.

Perhaps no region of equal extent on the globe, unless we except the interior of Africa

[607]   Q

or possibly Greenland, is as little known. Here I do not speak for myself alone. A learned German, whom I have already quoted, after saying that the explorations have been limited to the coast, testifies that "the interior, not only of the continent, but even of the Island of Sitka, is to-day unexplored, and is in every respect *terra incognita*." The same has been repeated of the islands also. Admiral Lütke, whose circumnavigation of the globe began in 1825, and whose work bears date in 1835, says of the Aleutian Archipelago that, "although frequented for more than a century by Russian vessels and those of other nations, it is to-day almost as little known as in the time of Cook." Another writer of authority, the compiler of the official work on the "People of Russia," published as late as 1862, speaks of the interior as "a mystery." And yet another says that our ignorance with regard to this region would make it a proper scene for a chapter of "Gulliver's Travels."

Where so little was known there was scope for invention. Imagination was made to supply the place of knowledge, and poetry pictured the savage desolation in much-admired verse. Campbell, in the "Pleasures of Hope," while exploring "earth's loneliest bounds and ocean's wildest shore," reaches this region, which he portrays:—

> "Lo! to the wintry winds the pilot yields,
> His bark careering o'er unfathomed fields.
> Now far he sweeps, where scarce a summer smiles,
> On Behring's rocks, or Greenland's naked isles;
> Cold on his midnight watch the breezes blow,
> From wastes that slumber in eternal snow,
> And waft across the wave's tumultuous roar
> *The wolf's long howl from Ounalaska's shore.*"

All of which, so far, at least, as it describes this region, is inconsistent with the truth. The poet ignores the isothermal line, which plays such a conspicuous part on the Pacific coast. Here the evidence is positive. Portlock, the navigator, who was there toward the close of the last century, after describing Cook's Inlet, which is several degrees north of Ounalaska, records his belief "that the climate here is not so severe as has been generally supposed; for in the course of traffic with the natives they frequently brought berries of several sorts, and in particular black berries equally fine with those met with in England." ("Voyage," p. 118.) Kotzebue, who was here later, records that he found the weather "pretty warm at Ounalaska." ("Voyage," vol. i, p. 275.) South of the Aleutians the climate is warmer still. The poet ignores natural history also as regards the distribution of animals. Curiously enough, it does not appear that there are "wolves" on any of the Aleutians. Coxe, in his work on Russian discoveries (p. 174), records that "reindeer, bears, *wolves,* and ice-foxes are not to be found on these islands." But he was never there. Meares, who was in those seas, says "the *only animals* on these islands are foxes, some of which are black." ("Voyage," vol. i, p. 16.) Cook, who was at Ounalaska twice, and once made a prolonged stay, expressly says, "foxes and weasels were the *only quadrupeds* that we saw; they told us that they had hares also." ("Voyage," vol. ii, p. 518.) But quadrupeds like these hardly sustain the exciting picture. The same experienced navigator furnishes a glimpse of the inhabitants as they appeared to him, which would make us tremble if the "wolves" of the poet were numerous. He says that "to all appearance they are the most peaceable, inoffensive people he ever met with;" and Cook had been at Otaheite. "No such thing as an offensive or defensive weapon was seen amongst the natives of Ounalaska." (*Ibid.*, pp. 509, 515.) Then, at least, the inhabitants did not share the ferocity of the "wolves" and of the climate. Another navigator fascinates us by a description of the boats of Ounalaska, which struck him "with amazement beyond expression;" and he goes on to say, "if perfect symmetry, smoothness, and proportion constitute beauty, they are beautiful beyond anything that I ever beheld. I have seen some of them as transparent as oiled paper." ("Billing's Voyages," p. 15.) But these are the very boats that buffet "the wave's tumultuous roar," while "the breezes" waft the "wolf's long howl." This same navigator introduces another feature. According to him the Russians sojourning there "seem to have no desire to leave this place, where they enjoy that indolence so pleasing to their minds." (Page 161.) The lotus-eaters of Homer were no better off. The picture is completed by another touch from Lütke. Admitting the want of trees on the island, the Admiral suggests that their place is supplied not only by luxuriant grass, but by wood thrown upon the coast, including trunks of camphor from Chinese and Japanese waters, and "a tree which gives forth the odour of the rose." ("Voyage," Tom. 1, p. 132.) Such is a small portion of the testimony, most of which was in print before the poet wrote.

Nothing has been written about this region, whether the coast or the islands, more authentic or interesting than the narrative of Captain Cook on his third and last voyage. He saw with intelligence, and described with clearness almost elegant. The record of Captain Portlock's voyage from London to the north-west coast in 1786, 1787, and 1788 seems to be honest and is instructive. Captain Meares, whose voyage was contemporaneous, saw and exposed the importance of trade between the north-west coast and China. Vancouver, who came a little later, has described some parts of this coast. La Pérouse, the unfortunate French navigator, has afforded another picture of the coast painted with French colours. Before him was La Maurelle, a Frenchman sailing in the service of Spain, who was on the coast in 1779, a portion of whose journal is preserved in the Appendix to the volumes of La Pérouse. After him was Marchand, also a Frenchman, who, during a voyage round the world, stopped here in 1791. The voyage of the latter, published in three quartos, is accompanied by an "Historical Introduction," which is a mine of information on all the voyages to this coast. Then came the several successive Russian voyages already mentioned. Later came the "Voyage round the World" by Captain Belcher, with a familiar sketch of life at Sitka, where he stopped in 1837, and an engraving representing the arsenal and lighthouse there. Then came the "Journey round the World" in 1841 and 1842 by Sir George Simpson, Governor-in chief of the Hudson Bay Company, containing an account of a visit to Sitka and the hospitality of its Governor. To these I may add "The Nautical Magazine" for 1849, vol. xviii, which contains a few excellent pages about Sitka; the "Journal of the London Geographical Society" for 1841, vol. xi, and for 1852, vol. xii, where this region is treated under the head of Arctic languages and animal life; Burney's "Russian and North-eastern Voyages;" the magnificent work entitled "Les Peuples de la Russie," which appeared at St. Petersburgh in 1862, on the Tenth Centennial Anniversary of the foundation of the Russian Empire, a copy of which is in the Astor Library; the very recent work of Murray on the "Geographical Distribution of Mammals;" the work of Sir John Richardson, "Fauna Boreali-Americana;" "Latham on Nationalities" in the chapters of which treat of the population of Russian America; the "Encyclopædia Britannica;" and the admirable "Atlas of Physical Geography" by Keith Johnston. I mention also an elaborate article by Holmberg, in the Transactions of the Finland Society of Sciences at Helsingfors, said to be replete with information on the ethnography of the north-west coast.

Perhaps the most precise and valuable information has been contributed by Germany. The Germans are the best geographers; besides many Russian contributions are in German. Müller, who recorded the discoveries of Behring, was a German. Nothing more important on this subject has ever appeared than the German work of the Russian Admiral von Wrangel, "Statistische und Ethnographische Nachrichten über die Russischen Besitzungen an der Nordwestküste von America," first published by Baer in his Russian "Beiträge" in 1839. There is also the "Verhandlungen der Russisch-Kaiserlichen Mineralogischen Gesellschaft zu St. Petersburg," 1848 and 1849, which contains an elaborate article, in itself a volume, on the orography and geology of the north-west coast and the adjoining islands, at the end of which is a bibliographical list of the works and materials illustrating the discovery and history of the west half of North America and the neighbouring seas. I may also refer generally to the "Archiv für Wissenschaftliche Kunde von Russland," edited by Erman, but especially the volume for 1863, containing the abstract of Golowin's Report on the Russian Colonies in North America as it appeared originally in the "Morskoi Shornich." Besides these there are Wappäus' "Handbuch von Geographie und Statistik von Nord Amerika," published at Leipsic in 1855; Peterman in his "Mittheilungen über wichtige neue Erforschungen auf dem gesammtgebiete der Geographie" for 1856, vol. ii, p. 486; for 1859, vol. v, p. 41; and for 1863, vol. ix, pp. 70, 236, 277, 278; Kittlitz "Denkwürdigkeiten einer Reise nach dem Russischen America durch Kamtschatka," published at Gotha in 1858; also by the same author, "The Vegetation of the Coasts and Islands of the Pacific," translated from the German and published at London in 1861.

Much recent information has been derived from the great Companies possessing the monopoly of trade here. Latterly there has been an unexpected purveyor in the Russian-American Telegraph Company, under the direction of Colonel Charles L. Bulkley, and here our own countrymen come to help us. To this expedition we are indebted for authentic evidence with regard to the character of the country and the great rivers which traverse it. The Smithsonian Institution and the Chicago Academy of Sciences co-operated with the Telegraph Company in the investigation of the natural history of the region. Major Kennicott, a young naturalist, originally in the service of the Institution, and Director of the Museum of the Chicago Academy, was the enterprising chief of the Youkon division of the expedition. While in the midst of his valuable labours he died suddenly in the month of May last at Nulato, on the banks of the great river, the Kwichpak, which may be called the Mississippi of the north, far away in the interior and on the confines of the Arctic Circle, where the sun was visible all night. Even after death he was still an explorer. From this remote outpost his remains, after descending the unknown river in an Esquimaux boat of seal-skins, steered by the faithful companion of his labours, were transported by way of Panama to his home at Chicago, where he now lies buried. Such an incident cannot be forgotten, and his name will always remind us of courageous enterprise, before which distance and difficulty disappeared. He was not a beginner when he entered into the service of the Telegraph Company. Already he had visited the Youkon country by the way of the Mackenzie River, and contributed to the Smithsonian Institution important information with regard to its geography and natural history, some of which will be found in their Reports. Nature in novel forms was open to him. The birds here maintained their kingdom. All about him was the mysterious breeding place of the canvas-back duck, whose eggs, never before seen by a naturalist, covered acres.

If we look to maps for information, here again we find ourselves disappointed. Latterly the coast is outlined and described with reasonable completeness; so also are the islands. This is the contribution of navigators and of recent Russian charts. But the interior is little more than a blank, calling to mind "the pathless downs," where, according to Prior, the old geographers "place elephants instead of towns." I have already referred to what purports to be a "General Map of the Russian Empire," published by the

Academy of Sciences at St. Petersburgh in 1776, and republished at London in 1787, where Russian America does not appear. I might mention also that Captain Cook complained in his day of the Russian maps as "wonderfully erroneous." On his return English maps recorded his explorations and the names he assigned to different parts of the coast. These were reproduced in St. Petersburgh, and the Russian copy was then reproduced in London, so that geographical knowledge was very little advanced. Some of the best maps of this region are by Germans, who always excel in maps. Here, for instance, is an excellent Map of the Aleutian Islands and the neighbouring coasts, especially to illustrate their orography and geography, which will be found at the end of the volume of " Transactions of the Imperial Mineralogical Society " at St. Petersburgh, to which I have already referred.

Late maps attest the tardiness of information. Here, for instance, is an excellent Map of North America, purporting to be published by the Geographical Institute of Weimar as late as 1859, on which we have the Youkon pictured, very much like the Niger, in Africa, as a large river meandering in the interior without any outlet to the sea. Here, also, is a Russian map of this very region, as late as 1861, in which the course of the Youkon is left in doubt. On other maps, as in the Atlas of Keith Johnston, it is pictured under another name as entering into the Frozen Ocean. But the secret is penetrated at last. Recent discovery by the enterprise of our citizens in the service of the Telegraph Company fixes that this river is an affluent of the Kwichpak, as the Missouri is an affluent of the Mississippi, and enters into Behring Sea, by many mouths, between the parallels of 64° and 65°. After the death of Major Kennicott a division of his party, with nothing but a skin boat, ascended the river to Fort Youkon, where it bifurcates, and descended it again to Nulato, thus establishing the entire course from its sources in the Rocky Mountains for a distance exceeding 1,000 miles. I have before me now an outline map just prepared by our Coast Survey, where this correction is made. But this is only the harbinger of the maturer labours of our accomplished Bureau when the coasts of this region are under the jurisdiction of the United States.

In closing this abstract of authorities, being the chief sources of original information on this subject, I cannot forbear expressing my satisfaction that, with the exception of a single work, all these may be found in the Congressional Library, now so happily enriched by the rare collection of the Smithsonian Institution. Sometimes individuals are like libraries; and this seems to be illustrated in the case of Professor Baird, of the Smithsonian Institution, who is thoroughly informed on all questions connected with the natural history of Russian America, and also of George Gibbs, Esq., now of Washington, who is the depositary of valuable knowledge, the result of his own personal studies and observations, with regard to the native races.

Character and Value of Russian America.

I pass now to a consideration of the character and value of these possessions, as seen under these different heads: (1) government; (2) population; (3) climate; (4) vegetable products; (5) mineral products; (6) furs; and (7) fisheries. Of these I shall speak briefly in their order. There are certain words of a general character, which I introduce by way of preface. I quote from Blodgett on the " Climatology of the United States and of the Temperate Latitudes of the North American Continent ":—

" It is most surprising that so little is known of the great islands and the long line of coast from Puget's Sound to Sitka, ample as its resources must be even for recruiting the transient commerce of the Pacific, independent of its immense intrinsic value. To the region bordering the Northern Pacific the finest maritime positions belong throughout its entire extent; and no part of the west of Europe exceeds it in the advantages of equable climate, fertile soil, and commercial accessibility of the coast. The western slope of the Rocky Mountain system may be included as a part of this maritime region, embracing an immense area from the 45th to the 60th parallel, and 5 degrees of longitude in width. The cultivable surface of this district cannot be much less than 300,000 square miles."

From this sketch, which is in the nature of a picture, I pass to the different heads.

Government.

I. The Russian Settlements were for a long time without any regular Government. They were little more than temporary lodgments for purposes of trade, where the will of the stronger prevailed. The natives, who had enslaved each other, became in turn the slaves of these mercenary adventurers. Captain Cook records " the great subjection " of the natives at Ounalaska when he was there in 1778, and a Russian navigator, twenty years later, describes the islands generally as " under the sway of roving hunters more savage than any tribes he had hitherto met with." (" Billings' Voyage," p. 274.) At Ounalaska the Russians for a long time employed all the men in the chase, " taking the fruits of their labour to themselves."

The first trace of government which I find was in 1790, at the important Island of Kodiak, or the Great Island, as it was called, where a Russian Company was established, under the direction of a Greek by the name of Delareff, who, according to the partial report of a Russian navigator, "governed with the strictest justice, as well natives as Russians, and established a school, where the young natives were taught the Russian language, reading, and writing." (" Billings," p. 171.) Here were about fifty Russians, including officers of the Company, and another person described as there "on the part of Government to collect tribute." The establishment consisted of five houses after the Russian fashion; barracks laid out on either side somewhat like the boxes at a coffee-house, with different offices, which are represented as follows: "An office of appeal to settle disputes, levy fines, and punish offenders by a regular trial; here Delareff presides; and I believe that few Courts of Justice pass a sentence with more impartiality; an office of receival and delivery, both for the Company and for tribute; the Commissary's department; counting-house; all in this building, at one end of which is Delareff's habitation." (*Ibid.*, p. 173.) If this picture is not overdrawn, and it surely is, affairs here did not improve with time.

It seems that there were various small Companies, of which that at Kodiak was the most considerable, all of which were finally fused into one large trading Company, known as the Russian-American Company. which was organized in 1799, under a Charter from the Emperor Paul, with the power of administration throughout the whole region, including the coasts and the islands. In this respect it was not unlike the East India Company, which has played such a part in English history; but it may be more properly compared to the Hudson Bay Company, of which it was a Russian counterpart. The Charter was for a term of years, but it has been from time to time extended, and, as I understand, is now on the point of expiring. The powers of the Company are sententiously described by the "Almanach de Gotha" for 1867, where, under the head of Russia, it says that "to the present time Russian America has been the *property of a Company.*"

I know no limitation upon the Company, except that latterly it has been bound to appoint its chief functionary, called "Administrator-General," from the higher officers of the Imperial Navy, when he becomes invested with what are declared the prerogatives of a Governor in Siberia. This requirement has doubtless secured the superior order of Magistrates which the country has latterly enjoyed. Among these have been Baron Wrangel, an Admiral, who was there at the time of the Treaty with Great Britain in 1825; Captain Konpreanoff, who had commanded the "Azof," a ship of the line, in the Black Sea, and spoke English well; Captain Etholine; Admiral Fujarelm, who, after being there five years, was made Governor of the Province of the Amoor; Admiral Wodski; and Prince Macksoutoff, an Admiral also, who is the present Administrator-General. The term of service is ordinarily five years.

The seat of Government is the town of New Archangel, better known by its aboriginal name of Sitka, with a harbour as smooth and safe as a pond. Its present population cannot be far from 1,000 souls, although even this is changeable. In the spring, when sailors leave for the sea and trappers for the chase, it has been reduced to as few as 180. It was not without a question that Sitka at last prevailed as the metropolis. Lütke sets forth reasons elaborately urged in favour of St. Paul, on the Island of Kodiak. ("Voyage," Tom. 1, p. 153.)

The first Settlement there was in 1800 by Baranow, the Superintendent of the Company, whose life was passed in this country, and whose name has been given to the island. But the Settlement made slow progress. Lisiansky, who was there in 1804, records that "from his entrance into Sitka Sound there was not to be seen on the shore the least vestige of habitation" (p. 145.) The natives had set themselves against a Settlement there. Meanwhile, the seat of Government was at Kodiak, of which we have an early and friendly glimpse. I quote what Lisiansky says, as exhibiting in a favourable light the beginning of that Government which has been transferred to the United States:—

"The Island of Kodiak, with the rest of the Russian Settlements along the north-west coast of America, are superintended by a kind of Governor-General or Commander-in-chief, who has agents under him, appointed, like himself, by the Company at Petersburgh. The smaller Settlements have each a Russian overseer. These overseers are chosen by the Governor, and are selected for the office in consequence of their long services and orderly conduct. They have the power of punishing, to a certain extent, those whom they superintend; but are themselves amenable to the Governor if they abuse their power by acts of injustice. The seat of Government is on the harbour of St. Paul, which has a barrack, different store-houses, several respectable wooden habitations, and a church, the only one to be found on the coast."—(*Ibid.*, p. 214.)

From this time the Company seems to have established itself on the coast. Lisiansky speaks of "a single hunting party of 900 men, gathered from different places, as Alaska, Kodiak, Kenay, Cook's Inlet, and commanded by thirty-six 'toyons,' who are subordinate to the Russians in the service of the American Company, and receive from them their orders." (*Ibid.*, p. 153.) From another source I learn that the inhabitants of Kodiak and of the Aleutian Islands were regarded as "immediate subjects of the Company," the males from 18 to 50 being bound to serve it for a term of three years each. They were employed in the chase. The population of Alaska and of the two great bays, Cook's Inlet and Prince William Sound, were also subject to the Company; but they were held to a yearly tax in furs without any regular service, and they could trade only with the Company; otherwise they were independent. This seems to have been before the division of the whole into

R

districts, all under the Company, which, though primarily for the business of the Company, may be regarded as so many distinct jurisdictions, each with local powers of government.

Among these were two districts which I mention only to put aside, as not included in the present cession : (1) The Kurile Islands, being the group nestling near the coast of Japan, on the Asiatic side of the dividing line between the two continents. (2) The Ross Settlement in California, now abandoned.

There remain five other districts : (1) The District of Atcha, with the Bureau at this island, embracing the two western groups of the Aleutians known as the Andreauowsky Islands and the Rat Islands. and also the group about Behring's Island, which is not embraced in the present cession. (2) The District of Ounalaska, with the Bureau at this island, embracing the Fox Islands, the Peninsula of Alaska to the meridian of the Shumagin Islands, including these and also the Prybilov Islands to the north of the Peninsula. (3) The District of Kodiak, embracing the Peninsula of Alaska east of the meridian of the Shumagin Islands, and the coast westward to Mount St. Elias, with the adjacent islands, including Kodiak, Cook's Inlet, and Prince William Sound. then northward along the coast of Bristol Bay, and the country watered by the Nushagak and Kuskokwim Rivers, all of which is governed from Kodiak, with redoubts or palisaded stations at Nushagak, Cook's Inlet, and Prince William Sound. (4) The Northern District, embracing the country of the Kwichpak and of Norton's Sound, under the direction of the commander of the redoubt at St. Michael's ; leaving the country northward, with the Islands St. Lawrence and St. Mathews, not embraced in this district, but visited direct from Sitka. (5) The District of Sitka, embracing the coast from Mount St. Elias, where the Kodiak district ends, southward to the latitude of 54° 40', with the adjacent islands. But this district has been curtailed by a lease of the Russian-American Company in 1839, for the space of ten years, and subsequently renewed, in which this Company, in consideration of the annual payment of 2,000 otter-skins of Columbia River, underlets to the Hudson Bay Company all its franchise for the strip of continent between Cape Spencer at the north and the latitude of 54° 40', excluding the adjacent islands.

The Central Government of all these districts is at Sitka, from which emanates all orders and instructions. Here also is the chief factory, from which supplies are forwarded to different places, and where the proceeds of the trade are collected.

The operations of the Government may be seen in its receipts and expenditures, including its salaries and allowances. In the absence of a complete series of such statistics to the present time, I mass together what I have been able to glean in different fields, relating to particular years, knowing well its unsatisfactory character. But each item has its instruction for us.

The capital of the Company in buildings, wares, and vessels in 1833 was said to be 3,658,577 roubles. In 1838 the Company possessed 12 vessels, amounting together to 1,556 tons, most of which were built at Sitka. According to Wappäus, who follows Wrangel, the salaries of the officers and workmen of the Company in 1832 amounted to 442,877 roubles. At that time the persons in its service numbered 1,025, of whom 556 were Russians, 152 Creoles, and 317 Aleutians. In 1851 there were in the service of the Company 1 Staff officer, 3 officers of the Imperial Navy, 1 officer of engineers, 4 civil officers, 30 religious officers, and 686 servants. The expenses of the Company from 1826 to 1833, a period of 7 years, were 6,608,077 roubles. These become interesting to us when it is considered that, besides what was paid on account of furs, and the support of the persons in the service of the Company, were other items incident to government, such as ship-building, navigation, fortifications, hospitals, schools, and churches. From a later authority it appears that the receipts of the Company, reported at St. Petersburgh for the year ended 1855, were 832,749 roubles, against expenses, 683,892 roubles, incurred for "administration in Russia and the Colonies," insurance, transportation, and duties. The relative proportion of these different expenses does not appear. I have another Report for 1857, where the revenue was 832,749 roubles, with expenditures of 683,892 roubles, leaving the difference for dividends, which were fixed at 18 roubles a share.

These are explained by other statistics, which I am able to give from the Report of Golowin, who furnishes the receipts and expenditures of the Company from 1850 to 1859 inclusive. The silver rouble, which is the money employed in the Table, is taken at our Mint for 75 cents.

RECEIPTS from 1850 to 1859, inclusive.

				Silver Roubles.
Tea traffic	..	..	..	4,145,869·79
Sale of furs	..	..	..	1,709,149·00
Commercial licences	..	..	..	2,493,296·61
Other traffics	..	..	..	170,235·76
Total	..		..	8,528,551·13

EXPENDITURES from 1850 to 1859, inclusive.

					Silver Roubles.
Sustenance of the Colony	..	..	..	..	2,298,207·20
Colonies' churches	..	..	..	..	71,723·18
Benevolent institutions..	..	..	..	..	143,366·23
Principal administrative officers ..	..	..	..	..	1,536,436·49
Ten duty	..	..	..	..	1,761,559·85
Transportation and packing of tea	..	..	..	..	586,901·72
Purch.se and transportation of merchandize	..	..	..	213,696·29
Insurance of tea and merchandize	..	..	..	..	217,026·55
Loss during war and by shipwreck	..	..	..	..	132,620·20
Reconstruction of the Company's house in St. Petersburgh	..	..	76,976·00
Capital for the use of the poor	..	..	..	..	6,773·02
Revenue fund capital	..	..	..	..	135,460·40
Dividends	..	..	..	..	1,354,604·00
Total	..	..	..	..	8,528,551·13

Analyzing this Table we shall arrive at a clearer insight into the affairs of the Company. If its receipts have been considerable they have been subject to serious deductions. From the expenditures we may also learn something of the obligations which we are about to assume.

From another Table I learn that during this same period 122,006 roubles were received for ice, mostly sent to California, 26,399 roubles for timber, and 6,250 roubles for coal. I think it not improbable that these items are included in the list of "receipts" under the term "other traffics."

In Russia the churches belong to the Government, and this rule prevails in these districts, where there are four Greek churches and five Greek chapels. There is also a Protestant church at Sitka. I am glad to add that at the latter place there is a public library, which some years ago contained 1,700 volumes, together with journals, maps, atlases, and mathematical instruments. In Atcha, Ounalaska, Kodiak, and Sitka schools are said to have been maintained at the expense of the Company, though not on a very comprehensive scale, for Admiral Wrangel mentions only ninety boys as enjoying these advantages in 1839. In Ounalaska and Kodiak there were at the same time orphan asylums for girls, where there were in all about thirty. But the Admiral adds that "these useful institutions will, without doubt, be improved to the utmost." Besides these, which are confined to particular localities, there is said to be a hospital near every factory in all the districts.

I have no means of knowing if these territorial subdivisions have undergone any recent modifications. They will be found in the "Russichen Besitzungen" of Wrangel, published in 1839, in the "Geographic" of Wappäus in 1856, and in the "Archiv von Russland" of 1863, containing the article on the Report of Golowin. I am thus particular with regard to them from a double motive. Besides helping to an understanding of the existing government, they may afford suggestions of practical importance in any future organization.

The Company has not been without criticism. Some of the pictures of it are by no means rose-colour. These, too, may furnish instruction for the future. Early in the century its administration was the occasion of open and repeated complaint. It was pronounced harsh and despotic. Langsdorf is indignant that "a free-trading Company should exist independent of the Government, not confined within any definite regulations, but who can exercise their authority free and uncontrolled, nay, even unpunished, over so vast an extent of country." In stating the case he adds that "the Russian subject here enjoys no protection of his property, lives in no security, and if oppressed has no one to whom he can apply for justice. The agents of the factories and their subordinates, influenced by humour or interest, decide everything arbitrarily." ("Voyages," vol. ii, p. 70.) And this arbitrary power seemed to prevail wherever a factory was established; "the stewardship in each single establishment is entirely despotic; though nominally depending upon the principal factory these stewards do just what they please, without the possibility of being called to account." (Ibid., vol. ii, p. 69.) If such was the condition of Russians, what must have been that of the natives? Here the witness answers: "I have seen the Russian fur-hunters dispose of the lives of the natives solely according to their own arbitrary will, and put these defenceless creatures to death in the most horrible manner." (Page 70.) Krusenstern concurs in this testimony, and, if possible, darkens the colours. According to him, "every one must obey the iron rule of the agent of the American Company; nor can there be either personal property or individual security where there are no laws. The chief agent of the American Company is the boundless despot over an extent of country which, comprising the Aleutian Islands, stretches from 57° to 60° of latitude, and from 130° to 190° of east longitude;" and he adds, in a note, "there are no Courts of Justice in Kodiak, nor any of the Company's possessions." ("Voyages," vol. ii, p. 107.) Kotzebue, who came later, while confessing his incompetency to speak on the treatment of the natives by the Company, declares his "wounded feelings and commiseration." ("Voyage," vol. iii, p. 314.) It is too probable that the melancholy story of our own aborigines has been repeated here. As these criticisms were by Russian officers they must have had a certain effect. I cannot believe that the recent government, administered by the enlightened Magistrates of whom we have heard, has been obnoxious to such terrible accusations; nor must it be forgotten that the report of Lisiansky, the other Russian officer who was there at the same time, is much less painful.

Baranow, who had been so long Superintendent, retired in 1818. He is praised much by Langsdorf, who saw him in 1806, and by Lütke, who was at Sitka in 1828. Both attribute to him a genius for his place and a disinterested devotion to the interests of the Company, whose confidence he enjoyed to the end. Although administering affairs here for more than a generation without rendering any accounts, he died poor. He was succeeded by Captain Haguemeister. Since then, according to Lütke, an infinity of reforms has taken place by which order and system have been introduced into the Government.

The Russian officer, Captain Golowin, who visited these possessions in 1860, has recommended certain institutional reforms, which are not without interest to us at this time. His recommendations concern the Governor and the people. According to him the Governor should be appointed by the Crown with the concurrence of the Company, removable only when his continuance is plainly injurious to the Colony; he should be subject only to the Crown, and his powers should be limited, especially in regard to the natives: he should provide protection for the colonists by means of cruizers, and should personally visit every district annually; the colonists, Creoles, and subject natives, such as the Aleutians, should be governed by Magistrates of their own selection; the name of "free Creole" should cease; all disputes should be settled by the local Magistrates unless the parties desire an appeal to the Governor; schools should be encouraged, and, if necessary, provided at the public expense. Surely these suggestions, which are in the nature of a Reform Bill, foreshadow a condition of self-government in harmony with Republican institutions.

It is evident that these Russian Settlements, distributed through an immense region and far from any civilized neighbourhood, have little in common with those of European nations elsewhere, unless we except those of Denmark on the west coast of Greenland. Nearly all are on the coast or the islands. They are nothing but "villages" or "factories," under the protection of palisades. Sitka is an exception, due unquestionably to its selection as the head-quarters of the Government, and also to the eminent character of the Governors who have made it their home. The Executive Mansion and the social life there have been described by recent visitors, who acknowledged the charms of politeness on this distant north-western coast. Lütke describes life among its fogs, and especially the attractions of the Governor's house. This was in the time of Admiral Wrangel, whose wife, possessing a high education, embellished this wilderness by her presence, and exhibited the example of a refined and happy household. His account of Sitkan hospitality differs in some respects from that of the English writers who succeeded. He records that fish was the staple dish at the tables of functionaries as well as of the poor, and that the chief functionary himself was rarely able to have meat for dinner. During the winter a species of wild sheep, the "musimon" or "argalis," also known in Siberia and hunted in the forests, furnished an occasional supply. But a fish diet did not prevent his house from being delightful.

Sir Edward Belcher, the English circumnavigator, while on his voyage round the world, stopped there. From him we have an account of the Executive Mansion and fortifications, which will not be out of place in this attempt to portray the existing Government. The house is of wood, described as "solid," 140 feet in length by 70 feet wide, of two stories, with lofts, capped by a lighthouse in the centre of the roof which is covered with sheet iron. It is about 60 feet above the sea-level, and completely commands all the anchorages in the neighbourhood. Behind is a line of picketed logs 25 feet in height, flanked at the angles by block-houses, loop-holed and furnished with small guns and swivels. The fortifications when complete "will comprise five sides, upon which forty pieces of cannon will be mounted, principally old ship guns, varying from 12- to 24-pounders." The arsenal is praised for the best of cordage in ample stores, and for the best of officers in every department. The interior of the Greek church was found to be "splendid, quite beyond conception in such a place as this." The school and hospital had "a comparative cleanliness and much to admire, although a man-of-war's man's ideas of cleanliness are occasionally acute." But it is the social life which seems to have most surprised the gallant Captain. After telling us that "on Sunday all the officers, civil and military, dine at the Governor's," he introduces us to an evening party and dance, which the latter gave to show his English guest "the female society of Sitka," and records that everything "passed delightfully," especially that "the ladies, although self-taught, acquitted themselves with all the ease and elegance communicated by European instruction." Sir Edward adds that "the society is indebted principally to the Governor's elegant and accomplished lady, who is of one of the first Russian families, for much of this polish." And he describes sympathetically her long journey through Siberia with her husband, "on horseback or mules, enduring great hardships in a most critical moment, in order to share with him the privations of this barbarous region." But according to him barbarism is disappearing; and he concludes by declaring that "the whole establishment appears to be rapidly on the advance, and at no distant period we may hear of a trip to Norfolk Sound through America as little more than a summer excursion." (Belcher's "Voyage," vol. i, p. 107.) Is not this time near at hand?

Shortly afterwards, Sir George Simpson, Governor-in-chief of the Hudson Bay

Company, on his overland journey round the world, stopped at Sitka. He had just crossed the continent by way of the Red River Settlements to Vancouver. He, too, seems to have been pleased. He shows us in the harbour "five sailing-vessels, ranging between 200 and 350 tons, besides a large bark in the offing in tow of a steamer," and he carries us to the Executive Mansion, already described, which reappears as "a suite of apartments, communicating, according to the Russian fashion, with each other, all of the public rooms being handsomely decorated and richly furnished; commanding a view of the whole establishment, which was in fact a little village, while about half way down the rock two batteries on terraces frowned respectively over land and water." There was another Administrator-General since the visit of Sir Edward Belcher; but again the wife plays her charming part. After portraying her as a native of Helsingfors, in Finland, the visitor adds: "So this pretty and ladylike woman had come to this secluded home from the farthest extremity of the Empire." Evidently in a mood beyond contentment, he says: "We sat down to a good dinner in the French style, the party, in addition to our host and hostess and ourselves, comprising twelve of the Company's officers;" and his final judgment seems to be given when he says: "The good folks appear to live well. The surrounding country abounds in the chevreuil [roebuck], the finest meat that I ever ate, with the single exception of moose, while in a little stream within a mile of the fort salmon are so plentiful that, when ascending the river, they have been known literally to embarrass the movements of a canoe." (Simpson's "Journey," vol. i, p. 227.) Such is the testimony.

With these concluding pictures I turn from the Government.

Population.

II. I come now to the *Population*, which may be considered in its numbers and in its character. In neither respect, perhaps, can it add much to the value of the country, except so far as native hunters and trappers are needed for the supply of furs. Professor Agassiz touches this point in a letter which I have just received from him, where he says: "To me the fact that there is as yet hardly any population would have great weight, as this secures the Settlement to our race." But we ought to know something at least of the people about to become the subjects of our jurisdiction, if not our fellow-citizens.

(1.) In trying to arrive at an idea of their *numbers*, I begin with Lippincott's "Gazetteer," as it is the most accessible, according to which the whole population in 1855, aboriginal, Russian, and Creole, was 61,000. The same estimate appears also in the "London Imperial Gazetteer" and in the "Geographic" of Wappäus. Keith Johnston, in his "Atlas," calls the population in 1852, 66,000. McCulloch, in the last edition of his "Geographical Dictionary," puts it as high as 72,375. On the other hand, the "Almanach de Gotha" for the present year, received only a few weeks ago, calls it in round numbers 50,000. This estimate seems to have been adopted substantially from the great work entitled "Les Peuples de la Russie," which from its character I am disposed to consider as the best authority.

Exaggerations are common with regard to the inhabitants of newly-acquired possessions, and this distant region has been no exception. An enthusiastic estimate once placed its population as high as 400,000. Long ago Schelekoff, an early Russian adventurer, reported that he had subjected to the Crown of Russia 50,000 "men" in the Island of Kodiak alone. But Lisiansky, who followed him there in 1805, says "the population of this island, when compared with its size, is very small." ("Voyage," p. 193.) After the "minutest research" at that time he found that it amounted only to 4,000 souls. It is much less now; probably not more than 1,500.

Of course, it is easy to know the number of those within the immediate jurisdiction of the Company. This is determined by a census from time to time. Even here the aborigines are the most numerous. Then come the Creoles, and last the Russians. But here you must bear in mind a distinction with regard to the former persons. In Spanish America all born there of European parentage are "Creoles;" in Russian America this term is applicable only to those whose parents are European and native, in other words, "half-breeds." According to Wrangel, in 1839, the census of dependents of the Company in all its districts was 246 Russians, 684 Creoles, and 8,882 Aleutians and Kodiaks, being in all 9,812. Of these, 4,918 were men, and 4,804 were women. Here the number of Russians is small. There is another Report a little later preserved by Wappäus, which is not materially different. In 1851, according to the Report of the Company, there was an increase of Russians and Creoles, with a corresponding diminution of aborigines: being 505 Russians, 1,703 Creoles, and 7,055 aborigines; in all, 9,283. In 1857 there were 644 Russians, 1,903 Creoles, and 7,245 aborigines; in all, 9,792, of whom 5,733 were men, and 4,659 were women. The increase from 1851 to 1857 was only 500, or about 1 per cent. annually. In 1860 there were "some 100" Russians, 2,000 Creoles, and 8,000 aborigines, amounting in all to 10,540, of whom 5,382 were men, and 5,158 were women. I am thus particular with these details that you may see how stationary population has been even within the sphere of the Company.

The number of Russians and Creoles in the whole Colony at the present time cannot be more than 2,500. The number of aborigines under the direct government of the Company may be 8,000. There remain also the mass of aborigines outside the jurisdiction of the Company, and having only a temporary or casual contact with it for purposes of

S

trade. In this respect they are not unlike the aborigines of the United States while in their tribal condition, described so often as "Indians not taxed." For the number of these outside aborigines I prefer to follow the authority of the recent work already quoted, "Les Peuples de la Russie," according to which they are estimated at between 40,000 and 50,000.

2. In speaking of *character* I turn to a different class of materials. The early Russians here were not pilgrims. They were mostly runaways, fleeing from justice. Langsdorf says that "the greater part of the inferior officers of the different Settlements were Siberian criminals, malefactors, and adventurers of various kinds." ("Voyages," vol. ii, p. 67.) Their single and exclusive business was the collection of furs, from which they obtained the name of "Promüschleniks," or fur collectors. But the name very early acquired a bad odour. Here again we have the same Russian authority, who, after saying that the inhabitants of the distant islands are under the superintendence of a Promüschlenik, adds, "which is, in other words, under that of a rascal, by whom they are oppressed, tormented, and plundered in every possible way." (*Ibid.*, p. 70.) It must not be forgotten that this authentic portrait is not of our day.

The aborigines are all in common language called Esquimaux; but they differ essentially from the Esquimaux of Greenland, and they also differ among themselves. Though popularly known by this family name, they have as many divisions and subdivisions, with as many languages and idioms, as France once had. There are large groups, each with its own nationality and language, and there are smaller groups, each with its tribal idiom. In short, the great problem of language is repeated here. Its forms seem to be infinite. Scientific inquiry traces many to a single root, but practically they are different. Here is that confusion of tongues which yields only to the presence of civilization, and it becomes more remarkable, as the idiom is often confined to so small a circle.

If we look at them ethnographically we shall find two principal groups or races, the first scientifically known as Esquimaux, and the second as Indians. By another nomenclature, which has the sanction of authority and of usage, they are divided into Esquimaux, Aleutians, Kenaians, and Koloschians, being four distinct groups. The Esquimaux and Aleutians are said to be Mongolian in origin. According to a doubtful theory they passed from Asia to America by the succession of islands beginning on the coast of Japan and extending to Alaska, which for this purpose became a bridge between the two continents. The Kenaians and Koloschians are Indians, belonging to known American races; so that these four groups are ethnographically resolved into two, and the two are resolved popularly into one.

There are general influences more or less applicable to all these races. The climate is peculiar, and the natural features of the country are commanding. Cool summers and mild winters are favourable to the huntsman and fisherman. Lofty mountains, volcanic forms, large rivers, numerous islands, and an extensive sea-coast constitute the great book of Nature for all to read. None are dull. Generally they are quick, intelligent, and ingenious, excelling in the chase and in navigation, managing a boat as the rider his horse, until the man and the boat seem to be one. Some are very skilful with tools, and exhibit remarkable taste. The sea is bountiful, and the land has its supplies. From these they are satisfied. Better still, there is something in their nature which does not altogether reject the improvements of civilization. Unlike our Indians, they are willing to learn. By a strange superstition, which still continues, these races derive their descent from different animals. Some are gentle and pacific, others are warlike. All, I fear, are slave-holders; some are cruel task-masters, others in the interior are reputed to be cannibals. But the country back from the sea-coast is still an undiscovered secret.

(1.) Looking at them in their ethnographical groups I begin with the *Esquimaux*, who popularly give their name to the whole. They number about 17,000, and stretch along the indented coast from its eastern limit on the Frozen Ocean to the mouth of the Copper River in 60° north latitude, excluding the Peninsula of Alaska, occupied by the Aleutians, and the Peninsula of Kenay, occupied by the Kenaians. More powerful races of Indian origin, following the courses of the great rivers northward and westward, have gradually crowded the Esquimaux from the interior, until they constitute a belt on the salt water, including the islands of the coast, and especially Kodiak. Their various dialects are traced to a common root, while the prevailing language betrays an affinity with the Esquimaux of Greenland, and the intervening country watered by the Mackenzie. They share the characteristics of that extensive family, which, besides spreading across the continent, occupies an extent of sea-coast greater than any other people of the globe, from which their simple navigation has sallied forth so as to give them the name of Phœnicians of the North. Words exclusively belonging to the Esquimaux are found in the dialects of other races completely strangers to them, as Phœnician sounds are observed in the Celtic speech of Ireland.

The most known of the Russian Esquimaux is the small tribe now remaining on the Island of Kodiak, which from the beginning has been a centre of trade. Although by various intermixture they already approach the Indians of the coast, losing the Asiatic type, their speech remains as a distinctive sign of their race. They are Esquimaux, and I describe them in order to give an idea of this people.

The men are tall, with copper skins, small black eyes, flat faces, and teeth of dazzling whiteness. Once the women pierced the nostrils, the lower lip, and the ears for ornaments; but now only the nostrils are pierced. The aboriginal costume is still preserved, especially out of doors. Their food is mostly from the sea, without the roots or berries which the island supplies. The flesh and oil of the whale are a special luxury. The oil is drunk pure or to season other food. Accustomed to prolonged abstinence, they exhibit at times an appetite amounting to prodigy. In one night six men were able to devour the whole of a large bear. A strong drink made from the strawberry and myrtle, producing the effect of opium, has yielded to brandy. Sugar and tea are highly esteemed; but snuff is a delight. Lisiansky records that they would go out of their way 20 miles merely for a pinch of snuff. They have tools of their own, which they use with skill. Their baidars, or canoes, are distinguished for completeness of finish and beauty of form. Unlike those of the Koloschians, lower down on the coast, which are hollowed from the trunks of trees, they are of seal-skins stretched on frames, with a single aperture in the covering to receive the person of the master. The same skill appears in the carving of wood, whalebone, and walrus ivory. Their general mode of life is said to be like that of other tribes on the coast. To all else they add a knowledge of the healing art and a passion for gaming.

Opposite to Kodiak, on the mainland to the east, are the Tshugatchi, a kindred tribe, speaking the same language, but a different dialect. To the north is a succession of kindred tribes, differing in speech, and each with local peculiarities, but all are represented as kind, courteous, hospitable, and merry. It is a good sign that merriment should prevail. Their tribal names are derived from a neighbouring river or some climatic circumstance. Thus, for instance, those on the mighty Kwichpak have the name of Kwichpaknutes, or "inhabitants of the great river." Those on Bristol Bay are called by their cousins of Norton Sound Akhkonghnutes, or "inhabitants of the warm country;" and the same designation is applied to the Kodiaks. Warmth, like other things in this world, is comparative, and to an Esquimaux at 64° north latitude another five degrees further south is in a "warm country." These northern tribes have been visited lately by our Telegraphic Exploring Expedition, who report especially their geographical knowledge and good disposition. As the remains of Major Kennicott descended the Kwichpak they were not without sympathy from the natives. Curiosity also had its part. At a village where the boat rested for the night the Chief announced that it was the first time white men had ever been seen there.

(2.) The *Aleutians*, sometimes called Western Esquimaux, number about 3,000. By a plain exaggeration, Knight, in his "Cyclopædia of Geography," puts them at 20,000. Their home is the archipelago of volcanic islands whose name they bear, and also a portion of the contiguous Peninsula of Alaska. The well-defined type has already disappeared, but the national dress continues still. This is a long shirt with tight sleeves, made from the skins of birds, either the sea-parrot or the diver. This dress, which is called the "parka," is indispensable as clothing, blanket, and even as habitation during a voyage, being a complete shelter against wind and cold. They, too, are fishermen and huntsmen, but they seem to excel as artificers. Their instruments and utensils have been noted for beauty, and their baidars were pronounced by Sauer "infinitely superior to those of any other island." Still another navigator declares them to be "the best means yet discovered to go from place to place, either upon the deepest or shallowest water, in the quickest, easiest, and safest manner possible." (Langsdorf's "Voyage," vol. i, p. 43.) These illustrate their nature, which is finer than that of their neighbours. They are at home on the water, and excite admiration by the skill with which they manage their elegant craft, so that Admiral Lütke recognized them as Cossacks of the sea.

Ounalaska is the principal of these islands, and, from the time they were first visited, seems to have excited a peculiar interest. Captain Cook painted it kindly; so have succeeding navigators. And here have lived the highlanders who seem to have given to navigators a new experience. Alluding especially to them, the reporter of Billings' voyage says: "The capacity of the natives of these islands infinitely surpasses every idea that I had formed of the abilities of savages" (p. 273). There is another remark of this authority which shows how they had yielded, even in their favourite dress, to the demands of commerce. After saying that formerly they had worn garments of sea-otter, he pathetically adds, "but not since the Russians have had any intercourse with them" (p. 155). Poor islanders! Exchanging choice furs, once their daily wear, for meaner skins.

(3.) The *Kenaians*, numbering as many as 25,000, take their common name from the Peninsula of Kenay, with Cook's Inlet on the north and Prince William Sound on the south. Numerous beyond any other family in Russian America, they belong to a widespread and teeming Indian race, which occupies all the northern interior of the continent, stretching from Hudson Bay in the east to the Esquimaux in the west. This is the great nation called sometimes Athabascan, or from the native name of the Rocky Mountains, on whose flanks they live, Chepewyan, but more properly designated as Tinneh, with branches in Southern Oregon and Northern California, and then again with other offshoots, known as the Apaches and Navajoes, in Arizona, New Mexico, and Chihuahua, more than thirty parallels of latitude from the parent stem. Of this extended race, the north-western branch, known to travellers as Loucheux, and in their own tongue as Kutchin, after occupying the inner portion of Russian America on the Youkon and the Porcupine, reached the sea-coast at Cook's Inlet, where it appears under the name of Kenaians. The latter are said to bear about the same relation in language and intellectual development to the entire group as the islanders of Kodiak bear to the Esquimaux.

The Kenaians call themselves in their own dialect by yet another name, Thnainas, meaning men, thus by a somewhat boastful designation asserting manhood. Their features and complexion associate them with the red men of America, as does their speech. The first to visit them was Cook, and he was struck by the largeness of their heads, which seemed to him disproportioned to the rest of the body. They were strong-chested also, with thick short necks, spreading faces, eyes inclined to be small, white teeth, black hair, and thin beard. Their persons seemed to be clean and decent without grease or dirt. In dress they were thought to resemble the people of Greenland. Their boats had a similar affinity. But in these particulars they were not unlike the other races I have already described. They were clothed in the skins of animals with the fur outward, or sometimes in the skins of birds, over which, as a protection against rain, was worn a frock made from the intestines of the whale, and resembling the gold-beater leaf, as was observed by Behring in his early voyage. Their boats were of seal-skin stretched on frames, and were of different sizes. In one of these Cook counted twenty women and one man, besides children. At that time, though thievish in propensity, they were not unamiable. Shortly afterwards they were reported by Russian traders, who had much to do with them, as "good people," who behaved "in a very friendly manner." (Billings' "Voyage," p. 197.) I do not know that they have lost this character since.

Here, too, is the accustomed multiplicity of tribes, each with its idiom, and sometimes differing in religious superstition, especially on the grave question of descent from the dog or the crow. There is also a prevailing usage for the men of one tribe to choose their wives from another tribe, when the tribal character of the mother attaches to the offspring, which is another illustration of the law of slavery *partus sequitur ventrem*. The late departure from this usage is quoted by the old men as a sufficient reason for the mortality which has afflicted the Kenaians, although a better reason may be found in the ravages of the small-pox, unhappily introduced by the Russians. In 1838, 10,000 persons on the coast are reported to have fallen victims to this disease.

(4.) Last of the four races are the *Koloschians*, numbering about 4,000, who occupy the coast and islands from the mouth of the Copper River to the southern boundary of Russian America, making about sixteen Settlements. They belong to an Indian group, extending as far south as the Straits of Fuca, and estimated to contain 25,000 souls. La Pérouse, after considerable experience of the aborigines on the Atlantic coast, asserts that those whom he saw here are not Esquimaux. ("Voyage," Tom. 2, p. 205.) The name seems to be of Russian origin, and is equivalent to Indian. Here again is another variety of languages and as many separate nations. Near Mount St. Elias are the Jacoutats, who are the least known: then come the Thlinkitts, who occupy the islands and coast near Sitka, and are known in Oregon under the name of Stikines; and then again we have the Kaigans, who, beginning on Russian territory, overlap Queen Charlotte's Island, beneath the British flag. All these, with their subdivisions, are Koloschians, but every tribe or nation has four different divisions, derived from four different animals, the whale, the eagle, the crow, and the wolf, which are so many heraldic devices, marking distinct groups.

There are points already noticed in the more northern groups which are repeated here. As among the Kenaians, husband and wife are of different animal devices. A crow cannot marry a crow. There is the same skill in the construction of canoes, but the stretched seal-skin gives place here to the trunk of a tree shaped and hollowed so that it will sometimes hold forty persons. There are good qualities among the Aleutians which the Koloschians do not possess, but they have perhaps a stronger sense. They are of constant courage. As daring navigators they are unsurpassed, sailing 600 or 700 miles in their open canoes. Some are thrifty, and show a sense of property. Some have developed an aptitude for trade unknown to their northern neighbours or to the Indians of the United States, and will work for wages, whether in tilling the ground or other employment. Their superior nature discards corporal punishment, even for boys, as an ignominy not to be endured. They believe in a Creator and in the immortality of the soul; but here a mystic fable is woven into their faith. The spirits of heroes dead in battle are placed in the sky and appear in the Aurora Borealis. Long ago a deluge occured, when the human family was saved in a floating vessel, which, after the subsidence of the waters, struck on a rock and broke in halves. The Koloschians represent one-half of the vessel, and the rest of the world the other half. Such is that pride of race which civilization does not always efface.

For generations they have been warriors, prompt to take offence and vindictive, as is the nature of the Indian race; always ready to exact an eye for an eye and a tooth for a tooth. This character has not changed. As was the case once in Italy, the dagger is an inseparable companion. Private quarrels are common; the duel is an institution. So is slavery still, having a triple origin in war, purchase, or birth. The slave is only a dog, and must obey his master in all things, even to taking the life of another. He is without civil rights; he cannot marry or possess anything; he can eat only the offal of another, and his body, when released by death, is thrown into the sea. A Chief sometimes sacrifices his slaves, and then another Chief seeks to outdo him in this inhumanity. All this is indignantly described by Sir Edward Belcher and Sir George Simpson. But a slave once a freed man has all the rights of a Koloschian. Here, too, are the distinctions of wealth. The rich paint their faces daily; the poor renew the paint only when the colours begin to disappear.

These are the same people who for more than a century have been a terror on this coast. It was Koloschians who received the two boats' crews of the Russian discoverer in 1741, as they landed in one of its wooded coves, and no survivor returned to tell their fate. They were the actors in another tragedy at the beginning of the century, when the Russian fort at Sitka was stormed and its defenders put to death, some with excruciating torture.

69

Lisiansky, whose visit was shortly afterward, found them "a shrewd, bold, though perfidious people," whose Chiefs used "very sublime expressions," and swore oaths, like that of Demosthenes, by their ancestors living and dead, "calling heaven, earth, sun, moon, and stars to witness, particularly when they want to deceive." ("Voyage," p. 16.)

Since then the fort has been repeatedly threatened by these warriors, who multiply by reinforcements from the interior, so that the Governor in 1837 said, "Although 700 only are now in the neighbourhood, 7,000 may arrive in a few hours." (Belcher's "Voyage," vol. i, p. 94.)

A little later their constant character was recognized by Sir George Simpson, when he pronounced them "numerous, treacherous, and fierce," in contrast with Aleutians, whom he describes as "peaceful even to cowardice." And yet this fighting race is not entirely indocile, if we may credit recent report, that its warriors are changing to traders.

Climate.

III. From population I pass to *Climate*, which is more important, as it is a constant force. Climate is the key to this whole region. It is the governing power which rules production and life, for Nature and man each must conform to its laws. Here at last the observations of science give to our inquiry a solid support.

Montesquieu has a famous chapter on the influence of climate over the customs and institutions of a people. Conclusions which in his day were regarded as visionary or far-fetched are now unquestioned truth. Climate is a universal master. But nowhere, perhaps, does it appear more eccentric than in the southern portion of Russian America. Without a knowledge of climatic laws the weather here would seem like a freak of Nature. But a brief explanation shows how all its peculiarities are the result of natural causes, which operate with a force as unerring as gravitation. Heat and cold, rain and fog, to say nothing of snow and ice, which play such a part in this region, are not abnormal, but according to law.

This law has been known only of late years. Even so ingenious an inquirer as Captain Cook notices the mildness of the climate without attempting to account for it. He records that, in his opinion, "cattle might exist in Ounalaska all the year round without being housed" ("Voyages," vol. ii, p. 520); and this was in latitude 53° 52', on the same parallel with Labrador, and several degrees north of Quebec; but he stops with a simple statement of the suggestive fact. This, however, was inconsistent with the received idea at the time.

A geographer, who wrote just before Cook sailed, has a chapter to show that the climate of Quebec continues across the continent, and, by a natural consequence, that America is colder than Asia. I refer to the "Mémoires Géographiques" of Engel (p. 196). He would have been astonished had he seen the revelations of an isothermal map, showing that precisely the reverse is true; that the climate of Quebec does not continue across the continent; that the Pacific coast of our continent is warmer than the corresponding Atlantic coast, and that America is warmer than Asia, so far at least as can be determined by the two opposite coasts. Such is the unquestionable truth, of which there are plentiful signs. The flora on the American side, even in Behring Straits, is more vigorous than that on the Asiatic side; the American mountains have less snow than their Asiatic neighbours.

Among many illustrations of the temperature I know none more direct than that furnished by the late Honourable William Sturgis, of Boston, who was familiar with the north-west coast at the beginning of the century, in a lecture on the Oregon question in 1845. After remarking that the climate there is "altogether milder, and the winter less severe, than in corresponding latitudes on this side of the continent," he proceeds to testify that, "as a proof of its mildness, he had passed seven winters between the latitudes of 51° and 57°, frequently lying so near the shore as to have a small cable fast to the trees, and only once was his ship surrounded by ice sufficiently firm to bear the weight of a man." But this intelligent navigator assigns no reason. To the common observer it seemed as if the temperature grew milder, travelling with the sun until it dipped in the ocean.

Among the authorities open before me I quote two, which show that this difference of temperature between the Atlantic and Pacific coasts was imagined, if not actually recognized, during the last century. Portlock, the Englishman, who was on this coast in 1787, after saying that during stormy and unsettled weather the air had been mild and temperate, remarks that he is "inclined to think that the climate here is not so severe as has been generally supposed." ("Voyage," p. 188.) La Pérouse, the Frenchman, who was here the same year, and had been before in Hudson Bay, on the other side of the continent, says still more explicitly that "the climate of this coast appeared to him infinitely milder than that of Hudson Bay in the same latitude, and that the pines which he had measured here were much larger." ("Voyage," vol. ii, p. 187.) Langsdorf, when at Sitka in 1806, records that Mr. John D. Wolff, a citizen of the United States, who had passed the winter at the Settlement, "is much surprised at finding the cold less severe than at Boston, Rhode Island, and other provinces of the United States which lie more to the south." ("Voyages," vol. ii, p. 101.)

All this is now explained by certain known forces in Nature. Of these, the most important is a thermal current in the Pacific, corresponding to the Gulf Stream in the

[607]   T

Atlantic. The latter, having its origin in the heated waters of the Gulf of Mexico, flows as a river through the ocean northward, encircling England, bathing Norway, and warming all within its influence. A similar stream in the Pacific, sometimes called the Japanese current, having its origin under the Equator near the Philippines and the Malaccas, amid no common heats, after washing the ancient Empire of Japan sweeps northward until, forming two branches, one moves onward to Behring Straits and the other bends eastward along the Aleutian Islands, and then southward along the coast of Sitka, Oregon, and California. Geographers have described this "heater," which in the lower latitudes is as high as 81 degrees of Fahrenheit, and even far to the north it is as high as 50 degrees. A chart now before me in Findlay's "Pacific Ocean Directory" portrays its course as it warms so many islands and such an extent of coast. An officer of the United States' navy, Lieutenant Bent, in a paper before the Geographical Society of New York, while exhibiting the influence of this current in mitigating the climate of the north-west coast, mentions that vessels on the Asiatic side, becoming unwieldly with accumulations of ice on the hull and rigging, run over to the higher latitude on the American side and "thaw out." But the tepid waters which melt the ice on a vessel must change the atmosphere wherever they flow.

I hope you will not regard the illustration as too familiar if I remind you that in the economy of a household pipes of hot water are sometimes employed in tempering the atmosphere by heat carried from below to rooms above. In the economy of Nature these thermal currents are only pipes of hot water, modifying the climate of continents by carrying heat from the warm cisterns of the south into the most distant places of the north. So also there are sometimes pipes of hot air, having a similar purpose; and these, too, are found in this region. Every ocean wind, from every quarter, as it traverses the stream of heat, takes up the warmth and carries it to the coast, so that the oceanic current is reinforced by an aerial current of constant influence.

But these forces are aided essentially by the configuration of the north-west coast, with a lofty and impenetrable barricade of mountains, by which its islands and harbours are protected from the cold of the north. Occupying the Aleutian Islands, traversing the Peninsula of Alaska, and running along the margin of the ocean to the latitude of 54° 40', this mountain ridge is a climatic division, or, according to a German geographer, a "climatic shed," such as perhaps exists nowhere else in the world. Here are Alps, some of them volcanic, with Mount St. Elias higher than Mont Blanc, standing on guard against the Arctic Circle. So it seems even without the aid of science. Here is a dyke between the icy waters of Behring Sea and the milder Southern Ocean. Here is a partition between the treeless northern coast and the wooded coast of the Kenaians and Koloschians. Here is a fence which separates the animal kingdom of this region, leaving on one side the walrus and ice-fox from the Frozen Ocean, and on the other side the humming bird from the tropics. I simply repeat the statements of geography. And now you will not fail to observe how by this configuration the thermal currents of ocean and air are left to exercise all their climatic power.

There is one other climatic incident here, which is now easily explained. Early navigators record the prevailing moisture. All are enveloped in the fog. Behring names an island Foggy. Another gives the same designation to a cape at the southern extremity of Russian America. Cook records fog. La Pérouse speaks of continued rain and fog in the month of August. And now visitors, whether for science or business, make the same report. The forests testify also. According to physical geography it could not be otherwise. The warm air from the ocean encountering the snow-capped mountains would naturally produce this result. Rain is nothing but atmosphere condensed and falling in drops to the earth. Fog is atmosphere still held in solution, but so far condensed as to become visible. This condensation occurs when the air is chilled by contact with a colder atmosphere. Now these very conditions occur on the north-west coast. The ocean air, as it comes in contact with the elevated range, is chilled until its moisture is set free.

Add to these influences, especially as regards Sitka, the presence of mountain masses and of dense forests, all tending to make this coast warmer in winter and colder in summer than it would otherwise be.

Practical observation has verified these conclusions of science. Any isothermal map is enough for our purpose; but there others which show the relative conditions generally of different portions of the globe. I ask attention to those of Keith Johnston, in his admirable Atlas. But I am glad to present a climatic table of the Pacific coast in comparison with the Atlantic coast, which has been recently compiled, at my request, from the archives of the Smithsonian Institution with permission of its learned Secretary, by a collaborator of the Institution, who visited Russian America under the auspices of the Telegraph Company. In studying this Table we shall be able to comprehend the relative position of this region in the physical geography of the world:—

	Mean Temperature in Degrees Fahrenheit.					Precipitation in Rain or Snow: Depth in Inches.				
	Spring.	Summer.	Autumn.	Winter.	Year.	Spring.	Summer.	Autumn.	Winter.	Year.
St. Michael's, Russian America Lat. 63° 28′ 45″ north.	28·75	52·25	27·00	7·00	27·48	..	..	..	..	..
Fort Youkon, Russian America Lat. (near) 67°.	14·22	59·67	17·37	23·80	16·92	..	..	..	..	..
Ikoniut, Russian America Lat. 61° 47′.	19·62	49·32	36·05	0·95	21·57	..	..	..	..	..
Sitka, Russian America Lat. 57° 3′.	39·65	53·37	43·50	32·30	42·12	18·32	15·75	32·10	23·77	89·94
Puget Sound, Washington Territory Lat. 47° 7′.	48·88	63·44	51·30	39·38	50·75	7·52	3·68	15·13	20·65	46·98
Astoria, Oregon Lat. 46° 11′.	51·16	61·36	53·55	42·43	52·13	16·43	4·85	21·77	44·15	87·20
San Francisco, California Lat. 37° 48′.	55·39	58·98	58·29	50·25	55·73	6·65	0·09	2·69	13·49	22·92
Nain, Labrador Lat. 57° 10′.	23·67	48·57	33·65	0·40	26·40	..	..	..	..	..
Montreal, Canada East Lat. 45° 30′.	41·20	68·53	44·93	16·40	42·77	7·66	11·20	7·42	0·72	27·00
Portland, Maine Lat. 43° 39′.	40·12	63·75	45·75	21·52	42·78	..	..	..	..	..
Fort Hamilton, New York Lat. 40° 37′.	47·84	71·35	55·79	32·32	51·82	11·69	11·64	9·88	10·31	43·22
Washington, District of Columbia	54·19	73·07	53·91	33·57	53·69	10·48	10·53	10·16	10·06	41·21

It will be seen from this Table that the winters of Sitka are relatively warm, not differing much from those of Washington, and several degrees warmer than those of New York; but the summers are colder. The mean temperature of winter is 32° 30′, while that of summer is 53° 37′. The Washington winter is 38° 57′; the Washington summer is 73° 7′. These points exhibit the peculiarities of this coast—warm winters and cool summers.

The winter of Sitka is milder than that of many European capitals. It is much milder than that of St. Petersburgh, Moscow, Stockholm, Copenhagen, Berne, or Berlin. It is milder even than that of Manheim, Stuttgard, Vienna, Sebastopol in the Crimea, or Turin. It is not much colder than that of Padua. According to observations at Sitka in 1831, it froze for only two days in December and seven days in January. In February the longest frost lasted five days; in March it did not freeze during the day at all, and rarely in the night. During the next winter the thermometer did not fall below 21 degrees Fahrenheit; in January 1834 it reached 11 degrees. On the other hand a temperature of 50 degrees has been noted in January. The roadstead is open throughout the year, and only a few land-locked bays are frozen.

The prevailing dampness at Sitka makes a residence there far from agreeable, although it does not appear to be injurious to health. England is also damp, but Englishmen boast that theirs is the best climate of the world. At Sitka the annual fall of rain is 89 inches. The mean annual fall in all England is 40 inches, although in mountainous districts of Cumberland and Westmoreland the fall amounts to 90 and even 140 inches. In Washington it is 41 inches. The forests at Sitka are so wet that they will not burn, although frequent attempts have been made to set them on fire. The houses, which are of wood, suffer from the constant moisture. In 1828 there were 20 days when it rained or snowed continuously; 120 when it rained or snowed part of the day, and only 66 days of clear weather. Some years only 40 bright days have been counted. Hinds, the naturalist, records only 37 "really clear and fine days." A scientific observer who was there last year counted 60. A visitor for 14 days found only 2 when nautical observations could be made; but these were as fine as he had ever known in any country.

The whole coast from Sitka to the Peninsula of Alaska seems to have the same continuous climate, whether as regards temperature or moisture. The Island of Kodiak and the recess of Cook's Inlet are outside of this climatic curve, so as to be comparatively dry. Langsdorf reports the winters "frequently so mild in the lower parts of Kodiak that the snow does not lie upon the ground for any length of time, nor is anything like severe cold felt." The Aleutian Islands, further west, are somewhat colder than Sitka, although the difference is not great. The summer temperature is seldom above 66 degrees; the winter temperature is more seldom as low as 2 degrees below zero. The snow falls about the beginning of October, and is seen sometimes as late as the end of April; but it does not remain long on the surface. The mean temperature of Ounalaska is about 40 degrees. Chamisso found the temperature of spring water at the beginning of the year to be 38 degrees 50 minutes. There are some years when it rains on this island the whole winter. The fog prevails from April till the middle of July, when they seem for the time to be driven further north. The islands north ward toward Behring Straits are proportionately colder, but you will not forget that the American coast is milder than the opposite coast of Asia.

From Mr. Bannister I have an authentic statement with regard to the temperature north of the Aleutians, as observed by himself in the autumn of 1865 and the months following. Even here the winter does not seem so terrible as is sometimes imagined. During most of the time work could be done with comfort in the open air. It was only when it stormed that the men were kept within doors. In transporting supplies from St. Michael's to Nulato, a distance of 250 miles, they found no hardship, even when obliged to bivouac in the open air.

On Norton Sound and the Kwichpak River winter may be said to commence at the end of September, although the weather is not severe till the end of October. The first snow falls about the 20th or 25th September. All the small ponds and lakes were frozen early in October. The Kwichpak was frozen solid about the 20th or 25th of this month. On the 1st November the harbour at St. Michael's was still open, but on the morning of the 4th it was frozen solid enough for sledges to cross on the ice. In December there were two thaws, one of them accompanied by rain for a day. The snow was about 2 feet deep at the end of the month. January was uniformly cold, and it was said that at one place 65 miles north-east of St. Michael's the thermometer descended to 58 degrees below zero. February was unusually mild all over the country. In the middle of the month there was an extensive thaw, with showers of rain. About half of the snow disappeared, leaving much of the ground bare. March was pleasant, without very cold weather. Its mean temperature was 20 degrees; its minimum was 3 degrees below zero.

Spring commences on the Kwichpak on the 1st May, or a few days later, when the birds return and vegetation begins to appear. The ice did not entirely disappear from the river till after the 20th May. The sea ice continued in the Bay of St. Michael's as late as the 1st June. The summer temperature is much higher in the interior of the country than on the coast. Parties travelling on the Kwichpak in June complained sometimes from the heat.

The River Youkon, which, flowing into the Kwichpak, helps to swell that stream, is navigable for at least four, if not five, months in the year. The thermometer at Fort Youkon is sometimes at 65 degrees below zero of Fahrenheit, and for three months of a recent winter it stood at 50 degrees below zero without variation. In summer it rises above 80 degrees in the shade; but a hard frost occurs at times in August. The south-west wind brings warmth; the north-east wind brings cold. Some years there is no rain for months, and then again showers alternate with sunshine. The snow packs hard at an average of 2½ feet deep. The ice is 4 or 5 feet thick; in a severe winter it is 6 feet thick. Life at Fort Youkon under these rigours of Nature, although not inviting, is not intolerable.

Such is the climate of this extensive region, so far as is known, along its coast, among its islands, and on its great rivers, from its southern limits to its most northern ice, with contrasts and varieties such as Milton describes—

"For hot, cold, moist and dry, four champions fierce
Strive here for mastery."

Vegetable Products.

IV. *Vegetable Products* depend upon climate. They are determined by its laws. Therefore what has been already said upon the one prepares the way for the consideration of the other; and here we have the reports of navigators and the suggestions of science.

From the time this coast was first visited navigators reported the aspects which Nature assumed. But their opportunities were casual, and they were obliged to confine themselves to what was most obvious. As civilization did not exist, the only vegetable products were indigenous to the soil. These were trees, berries, and plants. At the first landing, on the discovery of the coast by Behring, Steller found among the provisions in one of the Indian cabins "a sweet herb dressed for food in the same manner as in Kamtchatka." That "sweet herb" is the first vegetable production of which we have any record on this coast. At the same time, although ashore only six hours, this naturalist "gathered herbs and brought such a quantity to the ship that the describing of them took him a considerable time." This description it is said was adopted afterwards in the *Flora Siberica*.

Trees were noticed even before landing. They enter into descriptions, and are often introduced to increase the savage wildness of the scene. La Pérouse doubts "if the deep valleys of the Alps and the Pyrenees present a picture so frightful and at the same time so picturesque, which would deserve to be visited by the curious if it were not at one of the extremities of the earth." (Tom. 2, p. 191.) Lisiansky, as he approached the coast of Sitka, records that "nothing presented itself to the view but impenetrable woods reaching from the waterside to the very tops of the highest mountains, so wild and gloomy that they appeared more adapted for the residence of wild beasts than of men" (p. 143). Lütke portrays the "savage and picturesque aspect" of the whole north-west coast. (Tom. 1, p. 101.)

As navigators landed they saw Nature in detail; and here they were impressed by the size of the trees. Cook finds at Prince William Sound "Canada and spruce pine, some of them tolerably large." La Pérouse alludes to trees more than once. He describes pines measuring 6 feet in diameter and 140 feet in height, and then again introduces us to "those superb pines fit for the masts of our largest vessels." Portlock notices in Cook's

Inlet "wood of different kinds in great abundance, such as pine, black birch, witch hazel, and poplar; many of the pines large enough for lower masts to a ship of 400 tons burden;" and then again at Port Etches he noticed "trees of the pine kind, some very large, a good quantity of alder, a kind of hazel, but not larger than will do for making handspikes." Meares reports "woods thick," also "the black pine in great plenty, capable of making excellent spars." Vancouver reports in latitude 60° 1' "a woodland country." Sauer, who was there a little later, in the expedition of Billings, saw trees 6 feet in diameter, and 150 feet in height, "excellent wood for ship-building." In Prince William Sound the ship "took in a variety of fine spars," and he proceeds to say, "the timber comprised a variety of pines of immense thickness and height, some entirely tough and fibrous, and of these we made our best oars." Lisiansky says that at Kodiak, "for want of fir he made a new bowsprit of one of the pine trees, which answered admirably." Lütke testifies to the "magnificent pine and fir" at Sitka, adding what seems an inconsistent judgment with regard to its durability. Belcher notices Garden Island, in latitude 60° 21', as "covered with pine trees;" and then again at Sitka speaks of a "very fine-grained bright yellow cypress as the most valuable wood, which, besides being used in boats, was exported to the Sandwich Islands in return especially for Chinese goods."

Turning westward from Cook's Inlet the forests on the sea-line are rarer until they entirely disappear. The first Settlement on the Island of Kodiak was on the south-western coast, but the want of timber there caused its transfer to the north-eastern coast, where there are "considerable forests of fine tall trees." But where trees are wanting grass seems to abound. This is the case with Kodiak, the Peninsula of Alaska, and the Aleutian Islands generally. Of these, Ounalaska, libelled by the immortal verse of Campbell, has been the most described. This well-known island is without trees; but it seems singularly adapted to the growth of grass, which is often so high as to impede the traveller, and to over-top even the willows. The mountains themselves are for a considerable distance clothed with rich turf. One of these scenes is represented in a print which you will find among the views of the vegetation of the Pacific in the London reproduction of the work of Kittlitz. This peculiarity was first noticed by Cook, who says, with a sailor sententious-ness, that he did not see there "a single stick of wood of any size," but "plenty of grass very thick and to a great length." Lütke records that after leaving Brazil he met nothing so agreeable as the grass of this island.

North of Alaska, on Behring Sea, the forests do not approach the coast, except at the heads of bays and sounds, although they abound in the interior, and extend even to within a short distance of the Frozen Ocean. Such is the personal testimony of a scientific observer who has recently returned from this region. In Norton's Sound, Cook, who was the first to visit it, reports "a coast covered with wood, an agreeable sight," and, on walking in the country, "small spruce trees, none more than 6 or 8 inches in diameter." The next day he sent men ashore "to cut brooms, which he needed, and the branches of spruce trees for brewing beer." On the Kwichpak and its affluent, the Youkon, trees are sometimes as high as 100 feet. The supply of timber at St. Michael's is from the drift wood of the river. Near Fort Youkon, at the junction of the Porcupine and the Youkon, are forests of pine, poplar, willow, and birch. The pine is the most plentiful; but the small islands in the great river are covered with poplar and willow. Immense trunks rolling under the fort show that there must be large trees nearer the head-waters.

But even in northern latitudes the American coast is not without vegetation. Grass here takes the place of trees. At Fort Youkon, in latitude 67°, there is "a thin, wiry grass." Navigators notice the contrast between the opposite coasts of the two continents. Kotzebue, while in Behring Straits, where the two approach each other, was struck by black, mossy rocks frowning with snow and icicles on the Asiatic side, while on the American side "even the summits of the highest mountains were free from snow, and the coast was covered with a green carpet. ("Voyage," vol. i, p. 249.) But the contrast with the Atlantic coast of the continent is hardly less. The northern limit of trees is full seven degrees higher in Russian America than in Labrador. In point of fact, on the Atlantic coast, in latitude 57° 58', which is that of Sitka, there are no trees. All this is most suggestive.

Next after trees early navigators speak oftenest of *berries*, which they found in profusion. Not a sailor lands who does not find them. Cook reports "berries" on Norton Sound, and "a great variety" at Ounalaska. Portlock finds at Port Etches "fruit bushes in great abundance, such as bilberry, raspberry, strawberry, and currant, red and black." At Prince William Sound "any quantity might be gathered for a winter stock." Meares saw there "a few black currant bushes." Billings finds at Kodiak "several species of berries, with currants and raspberries in abundance, the latter white, but extremely large, being bigger than a mulberry." Langsdorf finds all these at Ounalaska, with whortle-berries and cranberries besides. Belcher reports at Garden Island "strawberries, pigeon-berries, whortleberries, and a small cranberry in tolerable profusion, without going in search of them." All these I quote precisely, and in the order of time.

Next to berries were *plants* for food; and these were in constant abundance. Behring, on landing at the Shumagin Islands, observed the natives "to eat roots which they dug out of the ground, and scarce shaked off the earth before they ate them." Cook reports at Ounalaska "a great variety of plants, such as are found in Europe and other parts of America, particularly Newfoundland, one of which was like parsley and ate very well, either in soups or salads." La Pérouse, who landed in latitude 58° 37', finds a French bill of fare, including celery, chicory, sorrel, and "almost all that exists in the meadows and mountains of France," besides several grains for forage. Every day and each meal the ship's kettle was filled with these supplies, and all ate them in soups, ragouts, and salads, much to the benefit of their health. Portlock reports at Port Etches, besides water-cresses, "just above the beach, between the bay and the lake, a piece of wild wheat, about 200 yards long and 5 yards broad, growing at least 2 feet high, which with proper care might certainly be made a useful article of food;" at Cook's Inlet he reports "ginseng and snakeroot." Meares reports at Prince William Sound "snakeroot and ginseng, some of which the natives have always with them as a medicine." Billings finds at Kodiak "ginseng, wild onions, and the edible roots of Kamtchatka;" and then again in Prince William Sound he finds "plenty of ginseng and some snakeroot." Vancouver finds at Cape Phipps "wild vegetables in great abundance." Langsdorf adds to the list at Ounalaska "Siberian parsnip, or sweet plant." These, too, I quote precisely, and in the order of time.

Since the establishment of Europeans on this coast an attempt has been made to introduce the nutritious grains and vegetables known to the civilized world, but without very brilliant success. Against wheat and rye and against orchard fruits there are obstacles of climate, perhaps insuperable. All these require summer heat; but here the summer is comparatively cold. The northern limit of wheat is several degrees below the southern limit of these possessions, so that this friendly grain is out of the question. Rye flourishes further north, as do oats also. The supposed northern limit of these grains embraces Sitka and grazes the Aleutian Islands. But there are other climatic conditions which are wanting at least for rye. One of these is dry weather, which is required at the time of its bloom. Possibly the clearing of the forest may produce some modification of the weather. For the present barley grows better, and there is reason to believe that it may be cultivated successfully very far to the north. It has ripened at Kodiak. There are many garden vegetables which have become domesticated. Lütke reports that at Sitka potatoes flourish; so that all have enough. Langsdorf reports the same of Kodiak. There are also radishes, cabbages, cauliflowers, peas, and carrots—making a very respectable list. The same, perhaps, may be found at Ounalaska. On Norton Sound I hear of radishes, beets, and cabbages. Even as far north as Fort Youkon, on the parallel of 67°, potatoes, peas, turnips, and even barley have been grown; but the turnips were unfit for the table, being rotten at the heart. A recent resident reports that there are no fruit trees, and not even a raspberry bush, and that he lost all his potatoes during one season by a frost in the latter days of July; but do not forget that these potatoes were the wall-flowers of the Arctic Circle.

Thus it appears that the vegetable productions of the country are represented practically by trees. The forests which overshadow the coast from Sitka to Cook's Inlet are all that we can show under this head out of which a revenue can be derived, unless we add ginseng, which is so much prized by the Chinese, and perhaps also snakeroot. Other things may contribute to the scanty support of a household; but timber will in all probability be an article of commerce. It has been so already. Ships from the Sandwich Islands have come for it, and there is reason to believe that this trade may be extended indefinitely, so that Russian America may be on the Pacific like Maine on the Atlantic, and the lumbermen of Sitka may vie with their hardy brethren of the East.

Here a question occurs. These forests as described seem to afford all that can be desired. The trees are abundant, and they are perfect in size, not unlike

> "The tallest pine
> Hewn on Norwegian hills to be the mast
> Of some great Admiral."

But a doubt arises as to their commercial value. Here we have the inconsistent testimony of Lütke. According to him the pines and firs which he calls "magnificent" constitute an untried source of commercial wealth. Not only California, but other countries poor in trees, like Mexico, the Sandwich Islands, and even Chile, will need them. And yet he does not conceal an unfavourable judgment of the timber, which as seen in the houses of Sitka, suffering from constant moisture, did not seem to be durable. ("Voyage," Tom. 1, pp. 105, 151.) Sir Edward Belcher differs from the Russian Admiral, for he praises especially the timber of "the higher latitudes, either for spars or plank." ("Voyage," vol. i, p. 300.) Perhaps its durability may depend upon the climate where it is used, so that the timber of this region may be lasting enough when transported to another climate. In the rarity of trees on the islands and mainland of the Pacific the natural supply is in Russian America. One of the early navigators even imagined that China must look this way, and he expected that "the woods would yield a handsome revenue when the Russian commerce with China should be established." American commerce with China is established. Perhaps timber may become one of its staples.

A profitable commerce in timber has begun at Puget Sound. By the official Returns of 1866 it appears that it was exported to a long list of foreign countries and places, in which I find Victoria, Honolulu, Callao, Tahiti, Canton, Valparaiso, Adelaide, Hong Kong, Sydney, Monte Video, London, Melbourne, Shanghae, Peru, Coqnimbo, Calcutta, Hilo, Cape Town, Cork, Guaymas, and Siam; and that in this commerce were employed no less than 18 ships, 80 barks, 4 brigs, 28 schooners, and 10 steamers. The value of the lumber and spars exported abroad was over half a million dollars, while more than four times that amount was shipped coastwise. But the coasts of Russian America are darker with trees than those further south. The pines in which they abound do not flourish as low down as Puget Sound. Northward they are numerous and easily accessible.

In our day the flora of the coast has been explored with care. Kittlitz, who saw it as a naturalist, portrays it with the enthusiasm of an early navigator; but he speaks with knowledge. He, too, dwells on the "surprising power and luxuriance" of the pine forests, describing them with critical skill. The trees which he identifies are the *Pinus Canadensis*, distinguished for its delicate foliage; the *Pinus Mertensiana*, a new species, rival of the other in height; and *Pinus Palustris*, growing in swampy declivities, and not attaining height. In the clearings or on the outskirts of thickets are shrubs, being chiefly a species of *Rubus*, with flowers of carmine and aromatic fruit. About and over all are mosses and lichens invigorated by the constant moisture, while colossal trees, undermined or uprooted, crowd the surface, reminding the scientific observer of the accumulations of the coal measures. Two different prints in the London reproduction of the work of Kittlitz present pictures of these vegetable productions grouped for beauty and instruction. I refer to these, and also to the Essay of Hinds on the "Regions of Vegetation," the latter to be found at the end of the volumes containing Belcher's "Voyage."

In turning from the vegetable products of this region, it will not be out of place if I refer for one moment to its domestic animals, for these are necessarily associated with such products. Some time ago it was stated that cattle had not flourished at Sitka owing to the want of proper pasturage and the difficulty of making hay in a climate of such moisture. Hogs are more easily sustained, but feeding on fish, instead of vegetable products, their flesh acquires a fishy taste, which does not recommend it. Nor has there been greater success with poultry, for this becomes the prey of the crow, whose voracity here is absolutely fabulous. A Koloschian tribe traces its origin to this bird, which in this neighbourhood might be a fit progenitor. Not content with swooping upon hens and chickens, it descends upon hogs to nibble at their tails, and so successfully "that the hogs here are without tails," and then it scours the streets so well that it is called the scavenger of Sitka. But there are other places more favoured. The grass at Kodiak is well suited to cattle, and it is supposed that sheep would thrive there. The grass at Ounalaska is famous, and Cook thought the climate good for cattle, of which we have at least one illustration. Langsdorf reports that "a cow grazed there luxuriously for several years, and then was lost in the mountains." That grazing animal is a good witness. Perhaps also it is typical of the peaceful inhabitants.

Mineral Products.

V. In considering the *Mineral Products* I shall first ask attention to such indications as are afforded by the early navigators. They were not geologists. Indeed, geology was at that time unknown. They saw only what was exposed. And yet during the long interval that has elapsed not very much has been added to their conclusions. The existence of iron is hardly less uncertain now than then. The existence of copper is hardly more certain now than then. Gold, which is so often a dangerous *ignis fatuus*, did not appear to deceive them. But coal, which is much more desirable than gold, was reported by several, and once at least with reasonable certainty.

The boat that landed from Behring, when he discovered the coast, found among other things "a whetstone on which it appeared that copper knives had been sharpened." This was the first sign of that mineral wealth which already excites such an interest. At another point where Behring landed "one of the Americans had a knife hanging by his side, of which his people took notice on account of its unusual make." It has been supposed that this knife was of iron. Next came Cook, who, when in Prince William Sound, saw "copper and iron." In his judgment the iron came through the intervention of Indian tribes from Hudson Bay or the Settlements on the Canadian lakes, and his editor refers in a note to the knife seen by Behring as coming from the same quarter; but Cook thought that the copper was obtained near at home, as the natives, when engaged in barter, gave the idea "that having so much of this metal of their own, they wanted no more." Naturally enough, for they were not far from the Copper River. Maurelle, the French officer in the service of Spain, landed in sight of Mount St. Elias in 1779, and he reports Indians with arrow-heads of copper, "which made the Spaniards suspect mines of this metal there." La Pérouse, who was also in this neighbourhood, after mentioning that the naturalists of the expedition allowed no rock or stone to escape observation, reports ochre, schist, mica, very pure quartz, granite, pyrites of copper, plumbago, and coal, and then adds that some things announce that the mountains contain mines of iron and copper. He reports further that the natives had daggers of iron and sometimes of red copper; that the latter metal was common enough with them, serving for ornaments and for the points of their arrows; and he then states the very question of Cook with regard to the way in which they acquired these metals. He insists that "the natives know how to forge iron and work copper." Spears and arrows "pointed with bone or iron," and also "an iron dagger" for each man, appear in Vancouver's account of the natives on the parallel of 51° 59', just within the southern limits of Russian America. Lisiansky also saw at Sitka "a thin plate of virgin copper," found on Copper River, 3 feet in length, and at one end 20 inches in breadth, with figures painted on its sides, which had come from the possession of the natives. Meares reports "pure malleable lumps of copper in the possession of the natives," sometimes weighing as much as a pound, also necklaces, all obtained in barter with other natives further north. Portlock, while in Cook's Inlet, in latitude 59 26', at a place called Graham's Harbour, makes another discovery. Walking round the bay he saw "two veins of Kennel coal just above the beach, and with very little trouble several pieces were got out of the bank nearly as large as a man's hand." If the good captain did not report more than he saw, this would be most important, for from the time when the amusing biographer of Lord Keeper North described that clean flaky coal which he called "candle," because often used for its light, but which is generally called "Kennel," no coal has been more of a household favourite. He reports further that, "returning on board in the evening he tried some of the coal, and found it to burn clear and well." Add to these different reports the general testimony of Meares, who, when dwelling on the resources of this country, boldly includes "mines which are known to be between the latitudes of 40° and 60° north, and which may hereafter prove a most valuable source of commerce between America and China."

It is especially when we seek to estimate the mineral products that we feel the want of careful explorations. We know more of the roving aborigines than of these stationary citizens of the soil. We know more of the trees—a tree is conspicuous. A mineral is hidden in the earth to be found by chance or science. Thus far it seems as if chance only had ruled. The Russian Government handed over the country to a trading Company, whose exclusive interest was furs. The Company only followed its business when it looked to wild beasts with rich skins rather than to the soil. Its mines were above ground, and not below. There were also essential difficulties in the way of any explorations. The interior was practically inaccessible. The thick forest, saturated with rain and overgrown with wet mosses, presented obstacles which nothing but enlightened enterprise could overcome. Even at a short distance from the port of Sitka all effort had failed, and the inner recesses of the island, only 30 miles broad, were never penetrated.

The late Professor Henry D. Rogers, in his admirable paper on the "Physical Features of America," being a part of his contribution to Keith Johnston's Atlas, full of knowledge and of fine generalization, says of this north-west belt of country that it is "little known in its topography to any but the roving Indians and the thinly-scattered fur trappers." But there are certain general features which he proceeds to designate. According to him it belongs to what is known as the Tertiary Period of geology, intervening between the Cretaceous Period and that now in progress, but including also granite, gneiss, and ancient metamorphic rocks. It is not known if the true coal measures prevail in any part, although there is reason to believe that they may exist on the coast of the Arctic Ocean between Cape Lisburne and Point Barrow.

Beginning at the south, we have Sitka and its associate islands, composed chiefly of volcanic rocks, with limestone near. Little is known even of the coast between Sitka and Mount St. Elias, which, itself a volcano, is the beginning of a volcanic region occupying the Peninsula of Alaska and the Aleutian Islands, and having no less than thirty volcanoes, some extinct, but others still active. Most of the rocks here are volcanic, and the only fossiliferous beds are of the Tertiary Period North of Alaska, and near the mouth of the Kwichpak, the coast seems to be volcanic or metamorphic, and probably tertiary, with a vein of lignite near the head of Norton's Sound. At the head of Kotzebue's Sound the cliffs abound in the bones of elephants and other extinct mammals, together with those of the musk ox and animals now living in the same latitude. From Kotzebue's Sound northward the coast has a volcanic character. Then at Cape Thomson it is called sub-carboniferous, followed by rocks of the carboniferous age, being lime-stones, shales, and sand-stones, which extend from Cape Lisburne far round to Point Barrow. At Cape Beaufort, very near the 70th parallel of latitude, and north of the Arctic Circle, on a high ridge a quarter of a mile from the beach, is a seam of coal, which appears to be of the true coal measures.

From this general outline, which leaves much in uncertainty, I come now to what is more important.

It is not entirely certain that iron has been found in this region, although frequently reported. The evidence points to the south, and also to the north. Near Sitka it was reported by the Russian engineer Doroschin, although it does not appear that anything has been done to verify his report. A visitor there as late as last year saw excellent iron, reported to be from a bed in the neighbourhood, which was said to be inexhaustible, and with abundant wood for its reduction. Then again on Kotzebue's Sound specimens have been collected. At 66° 35' Kotzebue found a false return in his calculations, which he attributes to the disturbing influence of "iron." A resident on the Youkon thinks that there is iron in that neighbourhood.

Silver also has been reported at Sitka by the same Russian engineer who reported iron there; and, like the iron, in "sufficient quantity to pay for the working."

Lead was reported by the Russian explorer, Lieutenant Zagoyskin, on the lower part of the Kwichpak, but it is not known to what extent it exists.

Copper is found on the banks of the Copper River, called by the natives Mjedraja, meaning copper, and of its affluent, the Tshitachitna, in masses sometimes as large as 40 lbs. Of this there can be little doubt. It is mentioned by Golowin in the "Archiv" of Erman as late as 1863. It was undoubtedly from this neighbourhood that the copper was obtained which arrested the attention of the early navigators. Traces of copper are also found in other places on the coast, also in the mountains near the Youkon, where the Indians use it for arrow-heads.

Coal seems to exist all along the coast, according to Golowin "everywhere in greater

77

or less abundance." Traces of it are reported on the islands of the Sitkan Archipelago, and this is extremely probable, for it has been worked successfully on Vancouver's Island below. It is also found on the Kenaian Peninsula, Alaska, the Island of Unga, belonging to the Shumagin group, Ounalaska, and far to the north at Beaufort. At the latter place it is "slaty, burning with a pure flame and rapid consumption," and it is supposed that there are extensive beds in the neighbourhood better in quality. For an account of this coal I refer to the scientific illustrations of Beechey's "Voyage." The natives also report coal in the interior on the Kwichpak. The coal of Ounalaska, and probably of Alaska, is tertiary, and not adapted for steamers. With regard to that of Unga scientific authorities are divided. That of the Kenaian Peninsula is the best and the most extensive. It is found on the eastern side of Cook's Inlet, half-way between Cape Anchor and the Russian Settlement of St. Nicholas, in veins three-quarters of a yard or more in thickness, and ranging in quality from mere carboniferous wood to anthracite. According to one authority these coal veins extend and spread themselves far in the interior. It appears that this coal has been more than once sent to California for trial, and that it was there pronounced a good article. Since then it has been mined by the Company, not only for their own uses, but also for export to California. In making these statements I rely particularly upon Golowin in the "Archiv" of Erman, and also upon the elaborate work of Grewingk, in the "Transactions of the Mineralogical Society of Petersburgh" for 1848 and 1849 (p. 112), where will be found a special map of the Kenaian Peninsula.

Gold is less important than coal, but its discovery produces more excitement. The report of gold in any quarter stimulates the emigrant or the adventurer who hopes to obtain riches swiftly. Nor is this distant region without such experience. Only a few years ago the British Colony of Victoria was aroused by a rumour of gold in the mountains of the Stikine River, not far in the interior from Sitka. At once there was a race that way, and the solitudes of this river were penetrated by hunters in quest of the glittering ore. Discomfiture ensued. Gold had been found, but not in any sufficient quantities reasonably accessible. Nature for the present set up obstacles. But failure in one place will be no discouragement in another, especially as there is reason to believe that the mountains here contain a continuation of those auriferous deposits which have become so famous further south. The Sierra Nevada chain of California reaches here.

Traces of gold have been observed at other points. One report places a deposit not far from Sitka. The same writer, who reports iron there, also reports that during the last year he saw a piece of gold as large as a marble, which was shown by an Indian. But the Russian engineer, Doroschin, furnishes testimony more precise. He reports gold in at least three different localities, each of considerable extent. The first is the mountain range on the north of Cook's Inlet and extending into Alaska, consisting principally of clay slate with permeating veins of diorite, the latter being known as a gold-bearing rock. He observed this in the summer of 1851. About the same time certain Indians from the Bay of Jakutat, not far from Mount St. Elias, brought him specimens of diorite found in their neighbourhood, making, therefore, a second deposit. In the summer of 1855 the same engineer found gold on the southern side of Cook's Inlet, in the mountains of the Kenay Peninsula. Satisfying himself, first, that the bank occupied by the redoubt of St. Nicholas, at the mouth of the Kaknu River, is gold-bearing, he was induced to follow the development of diorite in the upper valley of the river, and as he ascended found a gold-bearing alluvion gradually increasing, with scales of gold becoming coarser and coarser, instead of being scarcely visible as at first.

It does not appear that the discoveries on Cook's Inlet were pursued, but it is reported that the Hudson Bay Company, holding the country about the Bay of Jakutat under a lease from the Russian Company, have found the diorite in that neighbourhood valuable. This incident has given rise to a recent controversy. Russian journals attacked the engineer for remissness in not exploring the Jakutat country. He has defended himself by setting out what he actually did in the way of discovery, and the essential difficulty at the time in doing more: all which will be found in a number just received of the work to which I have so often referred, the "Archiv von Russland," by Erman, for 1866, vol. xxv, p. 229.

Thus much for the mineral resources of this new-found country as they have been recognized at a few points on the extensive coast, leaving the vast unknown interior without a word.

Furs.

VI. I pass now to *Furs*, which at times have vied with minerals in value, although the supply is more limited and less permanent. Trappers are "miners" of the forest, seeking furs as others seek gold. The parallel continues also in the greed and oppression unhappily incident to the pursuit. A Russian officer who was one of the early visitors to this coast remarks that to his mind the only prospect of relief for the suffering natives "consists in the total extirpation of the animals of the chase," which he thought, from the daily havoc, must take place in a very few years. This was at the close of the last century. The trade still continues, though essentially diminished, an important branch of commerce.

Early in this commerce desirable furs were obtained in barter for a trifle, and when something of value was exchanged it was much out of proportion to the furs. This has been the case generally in dealing with the natives, until their eyes have been slowly

[607] X

opened. In Kamtchatka, at the beginning of the last century, half-a-dozen sables were obtained in exchange for a knife, and a dozen for a hatchet; and the Kamtchatkadales wondered that their Cossack conquerors were willing to pay so largely for what seemed worth so little. Similar incidents on the north-west coast are reported by the early navigators. Cook mentions that in exchange for "beads" the Indians at Prince William Sound "gave whatever they had, even their fine sea-otter skins," which they prized no more than other skins until it appeared how much they were prized by their visitors. Where there was no competition prices rose slowly, and many years after Cook, the Russians at Kodiak, "in return for trinkets and tobacco," received twelve sea-otter skins and fox-skins of different kinds to the number of near 600.

These instances will show in a general way the spirit of this trade even to our own day.

On the coast, and especially in the neighbourhood of the factories, the difference in the value of furs is recognized, and a proportionate price is obtained, which Sir Edward Belcher found in 1837 to be "for a moderately good sea-otter skin from six to seven blankets, increasing to thirteen for the best, together with sundry knickknacks." But in the interior it is otherwise. A recent resident in the region of the Youkon assures me that he has seen skins worth several hundred dollars bartered for goods worth only 50 cents.

Besides whalers and casual ships with which the Esquimaux are in the habit of dealing, the commerce in furs on both sides of the continent north of the United States has for a long time been in the hands of two Corporations, being the Hudson Bay Company, with its Directors in London, and the Russian-American Company, with its Directors in St. Petersburgh. The former is much the older of the two, and has been the most flourishing. Its original members were none other than Prince Rupert, the Duke of Albemarle, Earl Craven, Lord Ashley, and other eminent associates, who received a Charter from Charles II in 1670 to prosecute a search after a new passage to the South Sea, and to establish a trade in furs, minerals, and other considerable commodities in all those seas and in the British possessions north and west of Canada, with powers of government, the whole constituting a colossal monopoly, which stretched from Labrador and Baffin Bay to an undefined west. At present this great Corporation is known only as a Fur Company, to which all its powers are tributary. For some time its profits have been so considerable that it has been deemed advisable to hide them by nominal additions to the stock. With the extinction of the St. Petersburgh Corporation, under the present Treaty, the London Corporation will remain the only existing Fur Company on the continent, but necessarily restrained in its operation to British territory. It remains to be seen into whose hands the commerce on the Pacific side will fall now that this whole region will be open to the unchecked enterprise of our citizens.

This remarkable commerce began before the organization of the Company. Its profits may be inferred from a voyage in 1772, described by Coxe, between Kamtchatka and the Aleutians. The tenth part of the skins being handed to the custom-house, the remainder was distributed in fifty-five shares, containing each twenty sea-otters, sixteen black and brown foxes, ten red foxes, three sea-otter tails, and these shares were sold on the spot at from 800 to 1,000 roubles each, so that the whole lading brought about 50,000 roubles. The cost of these may be inferred from the articles given in exchange. A Russian outfit, of which I find a contemporary record, was, among other things, "7 cwt. of tobacco, 1 cwt. of glass beads, perhaps a dozen spare hatchets, and a few superfluous knives of very bad quality, an immense number of traps for foxes, a few hams, a little rancid butter." With such imports against such exports the profits must have been considerable.

From Langsdorf we have a general inventory of the furs at the beginning of the century in the principal magazine of the Russian Company on the Island of Kodiak, collected on the islands, the Peninsula of Alaska, Cook's Inlet, Prince William Sound, and the continent generally. Here were "a great variety of the rarest kinds of fox-skins," black, blackish, reddish, silver grey, and stone fox, the latter probably a species of the Arctic; brown and red bears, "the skins of which are of great value," and also "the valuable black bear;" the zizel marmot and the common marmot, the glutton; the lynx, chiefly of whitish grey; the reindeer; the beaver; the hairy hedgehog; the wool of a wild American sheep, whitish, fine, and very long, but he could never obtain sight of the animal that produced this wool; also "sea-otters, once the principal source of wealth to the Company, now nearly extirpated, a few hundreds only being annually collected." The same furs were reported by Cook as found on this coast in his day, including even the wild sheep. They still continue to be found, except that I hear nothing of any wild sheep save at a Sitkan dinner.

There has been much exaggeration with regard to the profits of the Russian Corporation. An English writer of authority calls them "immense," and adds that formerly they were much greater. I refer to the paper of Mr. Petermann, read before the Geographical Society of London in 1852 (Journal, vol. xxii, p. 120). The number of skins reported at times is prodigious, although this fails to reveal precisely the profits. For instance, Pribylow collected within two years on the islands north of Alaska which bear his name the skins of 2,000 sea-otters, 6,000 dark ice-foxes, 40,000 sea-bears, or ursine seals, together with 1,000 pouds of walrus ivory (the poud is a Russian weight of 36 lbs.). Liitke mentions that in 1803 no less than 800,000 skins of the ursine seal were accumulated in the factory at Ounalaska, of which 700,000 were thrown into the sea, partly because they were badly prepared, and partly in order to keep up the price, thus imitating the Dutch, who for the same reason burnt their spices. Another estimate masses the collection for a series of years :—

From 1787 to 1817, for only a part of which time the Company existed, the Ounalaska district yielded upwards of 2,500,000 seal-skins; and from 1817 to 1838, during all which time the Company was in power, the same district yielded 579,000 seal-skins. Assuming what is improbable, that these skins were sold at 25 roubles each, some calculating genius has cyphered out the sum-total of proceeds at more than 85,000,000 roubles; or, calling the rouble 75 cents, a sum-total of more than 63,000,000 dollars. Clearly the latter years can show no approximation to any such doubtful result.

Descending from these lofty figures, which, if not exaggerations, are at least generalities, and relate partly to the earlier periods, before the time of the Company, we shall have a better idea of the commerce if we look at authentic Reports for special periods of time.

Admiral von Wrangel, who was for so long Governor, must have been well informed. According to statements in his work, adopted also by Wappäus in his "Geographie," the Company from 1826 to 1833, a period of seven years, exported the skins of the following animals :—

9,853 sea-otters, with 8,751 sea-otter tails, 40,000 river beavers, 6,242 river- or land-otters, 5,243 black foxes, 7,759 black-bellied foxes, 1,633 red foxes, 24,000 Polar foxes, 1,093 lynxes, 559 wolverines, 2,976 sables, 4,335 swamp-otters, 69 wolves, 1,261 bears, 505 musk rats, 132,160 seals, 830 pouds of whalebone, 1,490 pouds of walrus ivory, and 7,122 sacks of castoreum. What was their value does not appear.

Sir George Simpson, the Governor-in-chief of the Hudson Bay Company, who was at Sitka in 1841, represents the returns of the Company for that year as follows :—

10,000 fur-seals, 1,000 sea-otters, 2,500 land-otters, and 20,000 walrus teeth, without including foxes and martens.

There is still one other Report for the year 1852, as follows :—

1,291 sea-otters, 129 young sea-otters, 2,948 common otters, 14,486 fur-seals, 107 bears, 13,300 beavers, 2 wolves, 458 sables, 243 lynxes, 163 mole-skins, 1,504 bags of castoreum, 684 black foxes, 1,590 cross foxes, 5,174 red foxes, 2,359 blue Arctic foxes, 355 white Arctic foxes, and also 31 foxes called white, perhaps albinos.

Besides these Reports for special years, I am enabled to present from the Russian Tables of Captain Golowin another, covering the period from 1842 to 1860, inclusive, being as follows :—

25,602 sea-otters, 63,826 "otters," probably river-otters, 161,042 beavers, 73,944 foxes, 55,540 Arctic foxes, 2,283 bears, 6,445 lynxes, 26,384 sables, 19,076 musk rats, 2,536 ursine seals, 338,604 marsh-otters, 712 "pairs of hare," 451 martens, 104 wolves, 46,274 castoreums, 7,309 beavers' tails.

Here is an inexplicable absence of seal-skins. On the other hand, sables, which belong to Asia and not to America, are mentioned. The list is Russian, and perhaps embraces furs from the Asiatic islands of the Company.

From a competent source I learn that the value of skins at Sitka during the last year was substantially as follows :—

Sea-otter, 50 dollars; marten, 4 dollars; beaver, 2 dol. 50 c.; bear, 4 dol. 50 c.; black fox, 50 dollars; silver fox, 40 dollars; cross fox, 25 dollars; red fox, 2 dollars.

A recent price current in New York gives the prices there, in currency, as follows :—

Silver fox, 10 to 50 dollars; cross fox, 3 to 5 dollars; red fox, 1 dollar to 1 dol. 50 c.; otter, 3 to 6 dollars; mink, 3 to 6 dollars; beaver, 1 to 4 dollars; musk rat, 20 to 50 cents; lynx, 2 to 4 dollars; black bear, 6 to 12 dollars; dark marten, 5 to 20 dollars.

These New York prices vary from those of Sitka. The latter will be the better guide to a comprehension of the proceeds at Sitka, which, of course, must be subject to deduction for the expenses of the Company. Of the latter I say nothing now, as I have considered them in speaking of the existing Government.

The skins, it appears, are obtained in three different ways : first, through the hunters employed by the Company; secondly, in payment of taxes imposed by the Company; and thirdly, by barter or purchase from independent natives. But with all these sources it is certain that the Russian Company has enjoyed no success comparable to that of its British rival; and still more, there is reason to believe that latterly its profits have not been large.

Amid all the concealment or obscurity which prevails with regard to the revenues of the Company, it is easy to see that for some time there must be a large amount of valuable furs on this coast. The bountiful solitudes of the forest and of the adjoining waters have not yet been exhausted; nor will they be until civilization has supplied substitutes. Such, indeed, is a part of that humane law of compensation which contributes so much to the general harmony. For the present there will be trappers on the land, who will turn aside only a little from its prizes there to obtain from the sea its otter, seal, and walrus. It cannot be irrelevant, and may not be without interest, if I call your attention briefly to those fur-bearing animals which are about to be brought within the sphere of Republican government. If we cannot find their exact census we may at least learn something of their character and value.

The comparative poverty of vegetation in the more northern parts of the continent contrasts with the abundance of animal life, especially if we embrace those tenants of the sea who seek the land for rest. These northern parallels are hardly less productive than the Tropics. The lion, the elephant, and the hippopotamus find their counterpart in the bear, the walrus, and the seal, without including the sables and the foxes. Here again Nature by an unerring law adapts the animal to the climate, and in providing him with needful protection creates also a needful supply for the protection of man; and this is the secret of rich furs. Under the sun of the Tropics such provision is as little needed by man as by beast, and therefore Nature, which does nothing inconsistent with a wise economy, reserves it for other places.

Among the furs most abundant in this commerce are those of the *fox*, in its different species and under its different names. Its numbers were noticed very early, and gave the name to the eastern group of the Aleutians, which were called Lyssie Ostrowa, or Fox Islands. Some of its furs are among the very precious. The most plentiful is the red, or as it is sometimes called American; but this fur is not highly prized. Then comes the Arctic, of little value, and of different colours, sometimes blue, and in full winter dress pure white, whose circumpolar home is indicated by his name. The cross fox is less known, but much more sought from the fineness of its fur and its colour. Its name is derived from dark cruciform stripes, extending from the head to the back and at right angles over the shoulders. It is now recognized to be a variety of the red, from which it differs more in commercial value than in general character. The black fox, which is sometimes entirely of shining black with silver white at the tip of the tail, is called also the silver fox, when the black hairs of the body are tipped with white. They are of the same name in science, sometimes called *Argentatus*, although there seem to be two different names, if not different values, in commerce. This variety is more rare than the cross fox. Not more than four or five are taken during a season at any one post in the fur countries, although the hunters use every art for this purpose. The temptation is great, as we are told that "its fur fetches six times the price of any other fur produced in North America." Sir John Richardson, who is the authority for this statement, forgot the sea-otter, of which he seems to have known little. Without doubt the black fox is admired for its rarity and beaty. La Hontan, the French Commander in Canada under Louis XIV, speaks of its fur in his time as worth its weight in gold.

Among the animals whose furs are less regarded are the *wolverine*, known in science as *Gulo* or *Glutton*, and called by Buffon the quadruped vulture, with a dark-brown fur, which becomes black in winter, and resembles that of the bear, but is not so long nor of so much value. There is also the *lynx*, belonging to the feline race, living north of the great lakes and eastward of the Rocky Mountains, with a fur moderately prized in commerce. There is also the *musk rat*, which is abundant in Russian America, as it is common on this continent, whose fur enters largely into the cheaper peltries of the United States in so many different ways, and with such various artificial colours, that the animal would not know his own skin.

Among inferior furs I may include that very respectable animal, the *black bear*, reported by Cook "in great numbers and of a shiny black colour." The grizzly bear is less frequent and is inferior in quality of fur to all the varieties of the bear. The brown bear is supposed to be a variety of the black bear. The Polar bear, which at times is a formidable animal, leaving a foot-print in the snow 9 inches long, was once said not to make an appearance west of the Mackenzie River, but he has been latterly found on Behring Straits, so that he, too, is included among our new population. The black bear, in himself a whole population, inhabits every wooded district from the Atlantic to the Pacific, and from Carolina to the ice of the Arctic, becoming more numerous inland than on the coast. Langsdorf early remarked that he did not appear on the Aleutians, but on the continent, near Cook's Inlet and Prince William Sound, which are well wooded. He has been found even on the Isthmus of Panamá. Next to the dog he is the most cosmopolitan and perhaps the most intelligent of animals, and among those of the forest he is the most known, even to the nursery. His showy fur once enjoyed great vogue in hammercloths and muffs, and it is still used in military caps and pistol holsters; so that he is sometimes called the army bear. Latterly the fur has fallen in value. Once it brought in London from 20 to 40 guineas. It will now hardly bring more than that same number of shillings.

The *beaver*, amphibious and intelligent, has a considerable place in commerce, and also a notoriety of its own as the familiar synonym for the common covering of a man's head, and here the animal becomes historic. By Royal Proclamation in 1638 Charles I of England prohibited the use of any material in the manufacture of hats "except beaver stuff or beaver wool." This Proclamation was the death-warrant of beavers innumerable, sacrificed to the demands of the trade. Wherever they existed over a wide extent of country, in the shelter of forests or in lodges built by their extraordinary instinct, they were pursued and arrested in their busy work. The importation of their skins into Europe during the last century was enormous, and it continued until one year it is said to have reached the unaccountable number of 600,000. I give these figures as I find them. Latterly other materials have been obtained for hats, so that this fur has become less valuable. But the animal is still hunted. A medicine supplied by him, and known as the *Castoreum*, has a fixed place in the *Materia Medica*.

The *marten* is perhaps the most popular of all the fur-bearing animals that belong to our new possessions. An inhabitant of the whole wooded region of the continent, he finds a favourite home in the cold forests of the Youkon, where he needs his beautiful fur, which is not much inferior to that of his near relative, the far-famed Russian sable. In the trade of the Hudson Bay Company the marten occupies the largest place, his skins for a single district amounting to more than 50,000 annually and being sometimes sold as sable. The ermine, which is of the same weasel family, is of little value except for its captivating name, although its fur finds its way to the English market in enormous quantities. The mink, also of the same general family, was once little regarded, but now, by a freak of fashion in our country, this animal has ascended in value above the beaver, and almost to the level of the marten. His fur is plentiful on the Youkon and along the coast. Specimens in the Museum of the Smithsonian Institution attest its occurrence at Sitka.

The *seal*, amphibious, polygamous, and intelligent as the beaver, has always supplied the largest multitude of furs to the Russian Company. The early navigators describe its appearance and numbers. Cook encountered them constantly. Excellent swimmers, ready divers, they seek rocks and recesses for repose, where, though watchful and never sleeping long without moving, they become the prey of the hunter. Early in the century there was a wasteful destruction of them. Young and old, male and female, were indiscriminately knocked on the head for the sake of their skins. Sir George Simpson, who saw this improvidence with an experienced eye, says that it was hurtful in two ways: first, the race was almost exterminated; and secondly, the market was glutted sometimes with as many as 200,000 a-year, so that prices did not pay the expense of carriage. The Russians were led to adopt the plan of the Hudson Bay Company, killing only a limited number of males who have attained their full growth, which can be done easily, from the known and systematic habits of the animal. Under this economy seals have multiplied again, vastly increasing the supply.

Besides the common seal there are various species, differing in appearance, so as to justify different names, and yet all with a family character, including the sea-leopard, so named from his spots; the elephant seal, from his tusks and proboscis; the sea-lion, with teeth, mane, and a think cylindrical body. These are of little value, although their skins are occasionally employed. The skin of the elephant seal is strong, so as to justify its use in the harness of horses. There is also the sea-bear, or *ursine seal*, very numerous in these waters, whose skin, especially if young, is prized for clothing. Steller speaks with grateful remembrance of a garment which he made from one while on the desert island after the shipwreck of Behring.

Associated with the seal, and belonging to the same family, is the *walrus*, called by the British the sea-horse, the morse, or the sea-cow, and by the French *bête à la grande dent*. His two tusks, rather than his skin, are the prize of the hunter. Unlike the rest of the seal family, he is monogamous and not polygamous. Cook vividly describes an immense herd asleep on the ice, with one of their number on guard, and when aroused roaring and baying aloud, while they huddled and tumbled together like swine. At times their multitude is so great that before being aroused several hundreds are slaughtered, as game in a park. Their hide is excellent for carriage braces, and is useful about ship. But it is exclusively for their ivory that these hecatombs are sacrificed. A single tooth weighs sometimes several pounds. Twenty thousand teeth reported as an annual harvest of the Russian Company must cost the lives of 10,000 walruses. The ivory compares with that of the elephant, and is for some purposes superior. Long ago, in the days of Saxon history, a Norwegian at the Court of Alfred exhibited to the King "teeth of price and excellency" from what he called a horse whale. Unquestionably these were teeth of walrus.

I mention the *sea-otter* last: but in beauty and value it is the first. In these respects it far surpasses the river or land otter, which, though beautiful and valuable, must yield the palm. It has also more the manners of the seal, with its fondness for sea-washed rocks, and with a maternal affection almost human. The sea-otter seems to belong exclusively to the North Pacific. Its haunts once extended as far as the Bay of San Francisco; but long ago it ceased to appear in that southern region. Cook saw it at Nootka Sound. Vancouver reports it at Chatham Strait "in immense numbers, so that it was easily in the power of the natives to procure as many as they chose to be at the trouble of taking." But these navigators, could they revisit this coast, would not find it in these places now. Its present zone is between the parallels of 60° and 65° north latitude on the American and Asiatic coasts, so that its range is very limited. Evidently it was Cook who first revealed the sea-otter to Englishmen. In the Table of Contents of his third voyage are the words, "Description of the Sea-Otter;" and in the pages that follow there is a minute account of this animal, and especially of its incomparable fur, which is pronounced "certainly softer and finer than that of any other we know of." Not content with description, the famous navigator adds in remarkable words, "therefore, the discovery of this part of North America, where so valuable an article of commerce may be met with, cannot be a matter of indifference." These words stimulated the commercial enterprise of that day. Other witnesses followed. Meares, describing his voyage to this coast, placed this fur high above all other furs: "the finest in the world, and of exceeding beauty;" and La Pérouse made it known in France as "peltry the most precious and common in those seas." Shortly afterwards all existing information with regard to it was elaborately set forth in the "Historical Introduction to the Voyages of Marchand," published at Paris under the auspices of the Institute.

The sea-otter was known originally to the Russians in Kamtchatka, where it was called the sea-beaver; but the discoveries of Behring constitute an epoch in the commerce. His shipwrecked crew, compelled to winter on the desert island which now bears his name, found this animal in flocks, ignorant of men and innocent as sheep, so that they were

Y

slaughtered without resistance to the number of more than 800. Their value became known. Fabulous prices were paid by the Chinese, sometimes, according to Coxe, as high as 140 roubles. At such a price a single sea-otter was more than an ounce of gold, and a flock was a gold mine. The pursuit of gold was renewed. It was the sea-otter that tempted the navigator, and subsequent discovery was under the incentive of obtaining the precious fur. Müller, calling him a beaver, says, in his "History of Russian Discovery," "the catching of beavers enticed many people to go to these parts, and they never returned without great quantities, which always produced large prices." All that could be obtained were sent to China, which was the objective point commercially for this whole coast. The trade became a fury. Wherever the animal with exquisite purple-black fur appeared he was killed; not always without effort, for he had learned something of his huntsman, and was now coy and watchful, so that his pursuit was often an effort, but his capture was always a triumph. The natives, who had been accustomed to his furs as clothing, surrendered them. Sometimes a few beads were their only pay. All the navigators speak of the unequal barter. "Any sort of beads" were enough, according to Cook. The story is best told by Meares, who says "such as were dressed in furs instantly stripped themselves, and in return for a moderate quantity of spike nails we received sixty-five sea-otter skins." Vancouver describes the "humble fashion" of the natives in poor skins as a substitute for the beautiful furs appropriated by their "Russian friends." The picture is completed by the Russian navigator when he confesses that "after the Russians had any intercourse with them" the natives ceased to wear sea-otter skins. In the growing rage the sea-otter nearly disappeared. Langsdorf reports them as "nearly extirpated, since the high prices for them induce the Russians for a momentary advantage to kill all they meet with, both old and young. Nor can they see that by such a procedure they must soon be deprived of the trade entirely." This was in 1804. Since then the indiscriminate massacre has been arrested.

Meanwhile, our countrymen entered into this commerce, so that Russians, Englishmen, and Americans were all engaged in slaughtering sea-otters and selling their furs to the Chinese until the market of Canton was glutted. Lisiansky, on his arrival there, found "immense quantities in American ships." By-and-by the commerce was engrossed by the Russians and English. And now it passes into the hands of the United States with all the other prerogatives belonging to this territory.

Fisheries.

VII. I come now to the *Fisheries*, the last head of this inquiry, and not inferior to any other in importance; perhaps the most important of all. What even are sea-otter skins by the side of that product of the sea, incalculable in amount, which contributes to the sustenance of the human family?

Here, as elsewhere, in the endeavour to estimate the resources of this region, there is vagueness and uncertainty. Information at least is wanting; and yet we are not entirely ignorant. Nothing is clearer than that fish in great abundance are taken everywhere on the coast, around the islands, in the bays, and throughout the adjacent seas. On this head the evidence is constant and complete. There are oysters, clams, crabs, and a dainty little fish of the herring tribe called the "oolachan," contributing to the luxury of the table, and so rich in its oily nature that the natives are said to use it sometimes as a "candle." Besides these, which I name now only to put aside, are those great staples of commerce and mainstays of daily subsistence, the salmon, the herring, the halibut, the cod, and, behind all, the whale. This short list is enough, for it offers a constant feast, with the whale at hand for light. Here is the best that the sea affords for the poor or the rich; for daily use or for the fast days of the Church. Here also is a sure support at least to the inhabitants of the coast.

But in order to determine the value of this supply we must go further and ascertain if these various tribes of fish, reputed to be in such numbers, are found under such conditions and in such places as to constitute a permanent and profitable fishery. This is the practical question, which is still undecided. It will not be enough to show that the whole coast may be subsisted by its fish. It should be shown further that the fish of this coast can be made to subsist other places, so as to become a valuable article of commerce. And here uncertainty begins. The proper conditions of an extensive fishery are not yet understood. It is known that certain fisheries exist in certain waters and on certain soundings, but the spaces of ocean are obscure, even to the penetrating eye of science. Fishing banks known for ages are still in many respects a mystery, which is increased where the fishery is recent or only coastwise. There are other banks, which fail from local incidents. Thus very lately a cod fishery was commenced on Rochdale Bank, 65 miles north-west of the Hebrides; but the deep rolling of the Atlantic and the intolerable weather compelled its abandonment.

Before proceeding to consider the capacity of this region for an extensive fishery it is important to know such evidence as exists with regard to the supply, and here again we must resort to the early navigators and visitors. Their evidence, reinforced by modern reports, is an essential element, even if it does not entirely determine the question.

Down to the arrival of Europeans on this coast the natives lived on fish. This had been their constant food, with small additions from the wild vegetation of the country. In summer it was fish freshly caught; in winter it was fish dried or preserved. At the first landing on the discovery Steller found in the deserted cellar which he visited "store of *red* salmon," and the sailors brought away "smoked fishes that appeared like carp, and tasted very well." This is the earliest notice of fish on this coast, which are thus directly associated with its discovery. The next of interest which appears is the account of a Russian navigator in 1765, who reports on the Fox Islands, and especially Ounalaska, "cod, perch, pilchards, smelts." Thus early cod appears.

If we repair to "Cook's Voyages" we shall find the accustomed instruction, and here I sha'l quote with all possible brevity. At Nootka Sound he reports fish "more plentiful than birds," of which the principal sorts in great numbers were "the common herring, but scarcely exceeding 7 inches in length, and a smaller sort, the same with the anchovy or sardine," and now and then "a small brownish cod, spotted with white." Then, again, he reports at the same place "herrings and sardines and small cod," the former "not only eaten fresh, but likewise dried and smoked." In Prince William Sound he reports that "the only fish got were some torsk and halibut, chiefly brought by the natives to sell." Near Kodiak he reports that, "having three hours' calm, his people caught upward of a hundred halibuts, some of which weighed 100 lbs., and none less than 20 lbs.," and he adds, naturally enough, "a very seasonable refreshment." In Bristol Bay, on the northern side of Alaska, he reports "tolerable success in fishing, catching cod, and now and then a few flat-fish." In Norton Sound, still further north, he reports that in exchange for four knives made from an old iron hoop he obtained of the natives "near 400 lbs. weight of fish caught on this or the preceding day; some trout, and the rest in size and taste between the mullet and a herring." On his return southward, stopping at Ounalaska, he reports "plenty of fish, at first mostly salmon, both fresh and dried; some of the salmon in high perfection; also salmon, trout, and once a halibut that weighed 254 lbs.;" and in describing the habits of the islanders he reports that "they dry large quantities of fish in summer, which they lay up in small huts for winter's use." Such is the testimony of Captain Cook.

No experience on the coast is more instructive than that of Portlock, and from his Report I compile a succinct diary. July 20, 1786, at Graham's Harbour, Cook's Inlet: "The Russian Chief brought me as a present a quantity of fine salmon, sufficient to serve both ships for one day." July 21: "In several hauls caught about thirty salmon and a few flat-fish;" also, further, "the Russian Settlement had on one side a small lake of fresh water, on which plenty of fine salmon were caught." July 22: "The boat returned deeply loaded with fine salmon." July 28, latitude 60° 9': "Two small canoes came off; they had nothing to barter but a few dried salmon." July 30: "Plenty of excellent fresh salmon obtained for beads and buttons." August 3: "Plenty of fine salmon." August 9, at Cook's Inlet: "The greatest abundance of fine salmon." August 13: "Hereabouts would be most desirable situation for carrying on a whale fishery, the whales being on the coast and close in shore in vast numbers, and there being convenient and excellent harbours quite handy for the business." After these entries the English navigator left the coast for the Sandwich Islands.

Returning during the next year, Portlock continued to record his observations, which I abstract in brief. May 21, 1787, Port Etches, latitude 60° 21': "The harbour affords very fine crabs and muscles." June 4: "A few Indians came alongside, bringing some halibut and cod." June 20: "Plenty of flounders, crabs also plenty and fine. Several fishing alongside for flounders caught cod and halibut." June 22: "Sent the canoe out some distance in the bay, and it soon returned with a fine load of cod and halibut. This induced me to send her out frequently with a fishing party, and they caught considerably more than was sufficient for daily consumption." June 30: "In hauling the seine caught a large quantity of herrings and some salmon; the herrings, though small, were very good, and two hogsheads of them were salted for sea store." July 7: "We daily caught large quantities of salmon, but, the unsettled state of the weather not permitting us to cure them on board, sent the boatswain with a party on shore to build a house to smoke them in." July 11: "The seine was frequently hauled, and not less than 2,000 salmon caught at each haul. The weather, however, preventing us from curing them as well as could have been wished, we kept only a sufficient quantity for present use and let the rest escape. The salmon were now in such numbers along the shores that any quantity whatever might be caught with the greatest ease." All this testimony of the English navigator is singularly explicit, while it is in complete harmony with that of the Russian visitors and of Cook, who preceded.

The Report of Meares is similar, although less minute. Speaking of the natives generally, he says "they live entirely upon fish, but of all others they prefer the whale." Then, again, going into more detail, he says, "vast quantities of fish are to be found, both on the coast and in the sounds or harbours. Among these there are the halibut, herring, sardine, silver beam, salmon, trout, cod, all of which we have seen in the possession of the natives, or have been caught by ourselves." The herrings he describes as taken in such numbers "that a whole village has not been able to cleanse them." At Nootka the salmon was of a very delicate flavour, and "the cod taken by the natives of the best quality." French testimony is not wanting, although it is less precise. The early navigator, who was on the coast in 1779, remarks that "the fish most abundant is the salmon." La Pérouse, who was there in 1787, mentions a large fish weighing sometimes more than 100 lbs., and several other fish, but he preferred "the salmon and trout, which the Indians sold in larger numbers than could be consumed." A similar report was made by Marchant, the other French navigator, who finds the sea and rivers abounding in "excellent fish," particularly salmon and trout.

Afterwards came the Russian navigator Billings in 1792; and here we have a similar report, only different in form. Describing the natives of Ounalaska, the book in which this visit is recorded says "they *dry salmon, cod, and halibut* for a winter supply." At Kodiak, it says, "whales are in amazing numbers about the straits of the islands and in the vicinity of Kodiak." Then, again, the reporter, who was the naturalist Sauer, says, "I observed the same species of *salmon* here as at Okhotsk, and saw crabs." Then, again, "the *halibuts* in these seas are extremely large, some weighing 17 poods, or 612 lbs. avoirdupois. The liver of this fish, as also of *cod*, the natives deem unhealthy and never eat, but extract the oil from them." Then, again, returning to Ounalaska, the reporter says "the other fish are *halibut, cod, two or three species of salmon*, and sometimes one very common in Kamtchatka between 4 and 5 feet long."

From Lisiansky, another Russian navigator, who was on the coast in 1804. I take two passages. The first relates to the fish of Sitka. "For some time," he says, "we had been able to catch no fish but the *halibut*. Those of the species which we caught were fine, some weighing 18 stone, and were of an excellent flavour. This fish abounds here from March to November, when it retires from the coast till the winter is at an end." The other passage relates to the subsistence of the inhabitants during the winter. "They live," he says, "on *dried salmon*, train oil, and the spawn of fish, especially that of *herrings*, of which they always lay in a good stock."

Langsdorf, who was there at the same time, is more full and explicit. Of Ounalaska he says "the principal food consists of fish, sea-dogs, and the flesh of whales. Among the fish the most common and most abundant are *several sorts of salmon, cod, herrings, and holybutt.* The holybutts, which are the sort held in the highest esteem, are sometimes of an enormous size, weighing even several hundred pounds." Then, again, of Kodiak he says, "the most common fish, those which *fresh and dry* constitute a principal article of food, are *herrings, cod, holybutt,* and *several sorts of salmon*; the latter are taken in *prodigious numbers* by means of nets or dams." Of Sitka he says, "we have several sorts of *salmon, holybutt,* whitings, *cod and herrings*." A goodly variety.

Lütke, also a Russian, tells us that he found fish the standing dish at Sitka, from the humblest servant to the Governor. and he mentions *salmon, herrings, cod,* and turbot. Of salmon there are no less than four kinds, which were eaten fresh when possible, but after June they were sent to the fortress salted. The herrings appeared in February and March. The cod and turbot were caught in the straits during winter. Lütke also reports "fresh cod" at Kodiak.

I close this abstract of foreign testimony by two English authorities often quoted. Sir Edward Belcher, while on this coast in 1837, records that "fish, *halibut,* and *salmon* of two kinds were abundant and moderate, of which the crews purchased and cured great quantities." Sir George Simpson, who was at Sitka in 1841, says, "*halibut, cod, herrings,* flounders, and many other sorts of fish are always to be had for the taking in unlimited quantities. Salmon have been known literally to embarrass the movements of a canoe. About 100,000 of this fish, equivalent to 1,500 barrels, are annually salted for the use of the establishment." Nothing could be stronger as statement, and when we consider the character of its author, nothing could be stronger as authority.

Cumulative upon all this accumulation of testimony is that of recent visitors. Nobody visits this coast without testifying. The fish are so demonstrative in their abundance that all remark it. Officers of the United States' navy report the same fish substantially which Cook reported as far north as the Frozen Ocean. Scientific explorers, prompted by the Smithsonian Institution, report cod in Behring Straits, on the limits of the Arctic Circle. One of these reports that while anchored near Ounimak in 1865 the ship, with a couple of lines, caught "a great many fine cod, most of them between 2 and 3 feet in length." He supposes that there is no place on the coast where they are not numerous. A citizen of Massachusetts, who has recently returned from a prolonged residence on this coast, writes me from Boston, under date of the 8th March, 1867, that "the whale and cod fisheries of the North Pacific are destined to form a very important element in the wealth of California and Washington Territory, and that already numbers of fishermen are engaged there, and more are intending to leave." From all this testimony there can be but one conclusion with regard, at least, to certain kinds of fish.

Salmon exist in unequalled numbers, so that this fish, so aristocratic elsewhere, becomes common enough. Not merely the prize of epicures, it is the food of all. Not merely the pastime of gentle natures, like Isaac Walton or Humphrey Davy, who employ in its pursuit an elegant leisure, its capture is the daily reward of the humblest. On Vancouver's Island it is the constant ration given out by the Hudson Bay Company to the men in their service. At Sitka ships are supplied with it gratuitously by the natives. By the side of the incalculable multitudes swarming out of the Arctic waters, haunting this extended coast, and peopling its rivers, so that at a single haul Portlock took not less than 2,000, how small an allowance are the 200,000 which the salmon fisheries of England annually supply.

Herring seem to be not less multitudinous than the salmon. Their name, derived from the German *heer,* signifying an army, is amply verified. As on the coast of Norway they move in such hosts at times that a boat makes its way with difficulty through the compact mass. I do not speak at a venture, for I have received this incident from a scientific gentleman who witnessed it on the coast. This fish, less aristocratic than the salmon, is a universal food; but here it would seem to be enough for all.

The *halibut,* which is so often mentioned for its size and abundance, is less generally known than the others. It is common in the fisheries of Norway, Iceland, and Greenland. In our country its reputation is local. Even at the seaport of Norfolk, in Virginia, it does not appear to have been known before 1843, when its arrival was announced as that of a distinguished stranger: "Our market yesterday morning was enriched with a delicacy from the northern waters, the halibut, a strange fish in these parts, known only to epicures and naturalists." The larger fish are sometimes coarse and far from delicate, but they furnish a substantial meal, while the smaller halibut is much liked.

The *cod* is perhaps the most generally diffused and abundant of all, for it swims in all the waters of this coast from the Frozen Ocean to the southern limit, and in some places it is in immense numbers. It is a popular fish, and when cured or salted is an excellent food in all parts of the world. Palatable, digestible, and nutritious, the cod, as compared with other fish, is as beef compared with other meats, so that its incalculable multitudes seem to be according to a wise economy of Nature. A female cod is estimated to contain 3,400,000 eggs. Talk of multiplication a hundredfold! Here it is to infinity. Imagine these million eggs grown into fish, and then the process of reproduction repeated, and you have numbers which, like astronomical distances, are beyond human conception. But here the ravenous powers of other fish are more destructive than any efforts of the fisherman.

Behind all these is the *whale*, whose corporal dimensions fitly represent the space which he occupies in the fisheries of the world, hardly diminished by petroleum or gas. On this extended coast and in all these seas he is at home. Here is his retreat and playground. This is especially the case with the right whale, or, according to whalers, the "*right* whale to catch," with his bountiful supply of oil and bone, who is everywhere throughout this region, appearing at all points, and swarming its waters. At times they are very large. Kotzebue reports them at Ounalaska of fabulous proportions, called by the natives "Aliamak," and so long "that people engaged at the opposite end of the fish must halloo very loud to be able to understand each other." There is another whale known as the "bow-head," which is so much about Kodiak that it is sometimes called the Kodiak whale. The valuable sperm whale, whose head and hunch are so productive in spermaceti, belongs to a milder sea, but he sometimes strays to the Aleutians. The narwhal, with his two long tusks of ivory, out of which was made the famous throne of the early Danish Kings, belongs to the Frozen Ocean ; but he, too, strays into the straits below. As no sea is now *mare clausum*, all these may be pursued by a ship under any flag, except directly on the coast and within its territorial limit. And yet it seems as if the possession of this coast as a commercial base must necessarily give to its people peculiar advantages in this pursuit. What is now done under difficulties will be done then with facilities, such at least as neighbourhood supplied to the natives even with their small craft.

In our country the whale fishery has been a great and prosperous commerce, counted by millions. It has yielded very considerable gains, and sometimes large fortunes. The town of New Bedford, one of the most beautiful in the world, has been enriched by this fishery, and yet you cannot fail to remark the impediments which the business has been compelled to overcome. The ship has been fitted on the Atlantic coast for a voyage of two or three years, and all the crew have entered into a partnership with regard to the oil. Traversing two oceans, separated by a stormy cape, it reaches its distant destination at last in these northern seas, and commences its tardy work, interrupted by occasional rest and opportunity to refit at the Sandwich Islands. This now will be changed, as the ship sallies forth from friendly harbours near the game which is its mighty chase.

From the whale fishery I turn to another branch of inquiry. Undoubtedly there are infinite numbers of fish on this coast ; but in order to determine whether they can constitute a permanent and profitable fishery, there are at least three different considerations which must not be disregarded : (1) the existence of banks or soundings ; (2) proper climatic conditions for catching and curing the fish ; (3) a market.

1. The *necessity of banks or soundings* is according to reason. Fish are not caught in the deep ocean. It is their nature to seek the bottom, where they are found in some way by the fisherman, armed with trawl, seine, or hook. As among the ancient Romans private luxury provided tanks and ponds for the preservation of fish, so Nature provides banks, which are only *immense fish preserves*. Soundings attest their existence in a margin along the coast ; but it becomes important to know if they actually exist to much extent away from the coast. On this point our information is already considerable, if not decisive.

The Sea and Straits of Behring as far as the Frozen Ocean have been surveyed by a naval expedition of the United States under Commander John Rogers. From one of his charts now before me it appears that, beginning at the Frozen Ocean and descending through Behring Straits and Behring Sea, embracing Kotzebue Sound, Norton Bay, and Bristol Bay, to the Peninsula of Alaska, a distance of more than 12 degrees, there are constant uninterrupted soundings from 20 to 50 fathoms, thus presenting an immense extent proper in this respect for fishery. The famous Dogger Bank, between England and Holland, teeming with cod and constituting an inexhaustible fishing ground, has 90 fathoms of water. South of Alaska another chart shows soundings along the coast, with a considerable extent of bank in the neighbourhood of the Shumagins and Kodiak, being precisely where all the evidence shows the existence of cod. These banks, north and south of Alaska, taken together, according to the indications of the two charts, have an extent unsurpassed by any other in the world.

There is another illustration full of instruction. It is a Map of the World, in the new work of "Murray on Mammals," "showing approximately the 100-fathom line of soundings," prepared from information furnished by the Hydrographic Department of the British Admiralty. Here are all the soundings of the world. At a glance you discern the remarkable line on the Pacific coast, beginning at 40 degrees of latitude and widening constantly in a north-westerly direction; then with a gentle concave to the coast, stretching from Sitka to the Aleutians, which it envelops with a wide margin, and then embracing and covering Behring Straits to the Frozen Ocean; the whole space, as indicated on the map, seeming like an immense unbroken sea-meadow adjoining the land, and constituting plainly the largest extent of soundings known in the world, larger even than those of Newfoundland added to those of Great Britain. This map, which has been prepared by a scientific authority, simply in the interest of science, is an unimpeachable and disinterested witness.

Actual experience is better authority still. I learn that the people of California have already found cod-banks in these seas, and not deterred by distance have begun to gather a harvest. In 1866 no less than seventeen vessels left San Francisco for cod fishery on the Asiatic coast. This was a long voyage, requiring eighty days in going and returning. On the way better grounds were discovered among the Aleutians with a better fish; and then, again, other fishing grounds, better in every way, were discovered south of Alaska, in the neighbourhood of the Shumagins, with an excellent harbour at hand. Here one vessel began its work on the 14th May, and, notwithstanding stormy weather, finished it on the 24th July, having taken 52,000 fish. The largest catch in a single day was 2,300. The average weight of the fish dried was 3 lbs. Old fishermen compared the fish in taking and quality with that of Newfoundland. Large profits are anticipated. While fish from the Atlantic side bring at San Francisco not less than 12 cents a pound, it is supposed that Shumagin fish at only 8 cents a pound will yield a better return than the coasting trade. It remains to be seen if these flattering reports are confirmed by further experience.

From an opposite quarter is other confirmation. Here is a letter which I have just received from Charles Bryant, Esq., at present a Member of the Massachusetts Legislature, but for eighteen years acquainted with these seas, where he was engaged in the whale fishery. After mentioning the timber at certain places as a reason for the acquisition of these possessions, he says:—

"But the chiefest value, and this alone is worth more than the pittance asked for it, consists in its extensive cod and halibut fish grounds. To the eastward of Kodiak or Aleutian Islands are extensive banks or shoals nearly, if not quite, equal in extent to those of Newfoundland, and as well stocked with fish. Also west of the Aleutian Islands, which extend from Alaska south-west half-way to Kamtchatka, and inclosing that part of land laid down as Bristol Bay, and west of it, is an extensive area of sea varying from 40 fathoms in depth to 20, where I have found the supply of codfish and halibut unfailing. These islands furnish good harbours for curing and preparing fish, as well as shelter in storm."

In another letter Mr. Bryant says that the shoals east of the entrance to Cook's Inlet widen as they extend southward to latitude 50°; and that there are also large shoals south of Prince William Sound, and again off Cross Sound and Sitka. The retired ship-master adds that he never examined these shoals to ascertain their exact limits, but only incidentally, in the course of his regular business, that he might know when and where to obtain fish if he wished them. His report goes beyond any charts of soundings which I have seen, although the charts are coincident with it as far as they go. Cook particularly notices soundings in Bristol Bay and in various places along the coast. Other navigators have done the same. Careful surveys have accomplished so much that at this time the bottom of Behring Sea and of Behring Straits as far as the Frozen Ocean, constituting one immense bank, is completely known in its depth and character.

Add to all this the official Report of Mr. Giddings, Acting Surveyor of Washington Territory, made to the Secretary of the Interior in 1866, where he says:—

"Along the coast, between Cape Flattery and Sitka, in the Russian possessions, both cod and halibut are very plenty, and of a much larger size than those taken at the cape or further up the straits and sound. No one who knows these facts doubts that if vessels similar to those used by the bank fishermen from Massachusetts and Maine were fitted out here and were to fish on the *various banks along this coast* it would even now be a most lucrative business. The cod and halibut on this coast, up near Sitka, are fully equal to the largest taken in the eastern waters."

From all this evidence, including maps and personal experience, it is easy to see that the first condition of a considerable fishery is not wanting.

2. *Proper climatic conditions* must exist also. The proverbial hardihood of fishermen has its limits. Elsewhere weather and storm have compelled the abandonment of banks which promised to be profitable. On a portion of this coast there can be no such rigours. South of Alaska and the Aleutians, and also in Bristol Bay, immediately to the north of Alaska, the fishing grounds will compare in temperature with those of Newfoundland or Norway. It is more important to know if the fish when taken can be properly cured.

This is one of the privileges of northern skies. Within the Tropics fish may be taken in abundance, but the constant sun does not allow their preservation. The constant rains of Sitka, with only a few bright days in the year, must prevent the work of curing on any considerable scale. But the navigators make frequent mention of dry or preserved fish on the coast, and it is understood that fish are now cured at Kodiak. It had for a long time been customary on this island to dry seal flesh in the air, which could not be done on the mainland. Thus, the opportunity of curing the fish seems to exist near the very banks where they are taken. But the California fishermen carry their fish home to be cured, in which they imitate the fishermen of Gloucester. As the yearly fishing product of this port is larger than that of any other in North America, perhaps in the world, this example cannot be without weight.

3. The *market* also is of prime necessity. Fish are not caught and cured except for a market. Besides the extended coast, where an immediate demand must always prevail in proportion to an increasing population, there is an existing market in California, which is attested by long voyages to Kamtchatka for fish and by recent attempts to find fishing grounds. San Francisco at one time took from Okhotsk 900 tons of fish, being about one-eighth of the yearly fishing product of Gloucester. Her fishing-vessels last year brought home from the Shumagin banks 1,500 tons of dried fish and 10,000 gallons of cod-liver oil. There is also a growing market in Washington and Oregon, too, unless I am misinformed. But beyond the domestic market, spreading from the coast into the interior, there will be a foreign market of no limited amount. Mexico, Central America, and the States of South America, all Catholic in religion, will require this subsistence, and being southern in climate they must look northward for a supply. The two best customers of our Atlantic fisheries are Haïti and Cuba, two Catholic countries under a southern sun. The fishermen of Massachusetts began at an early day to send their cod to Portugal, Spain, and Italy, all Catholic countries under a southern sun. Our "salt" fish became popular. The Portuguese Minister at London in 1784, in a conference with Mr. Adams on a Commercial Treaty with the United States, mentioned "salt fish" among the objects most needed in his country, and added. "the consumption of this article in Portugal is immense, and he would avow that the American salt fish was preferred to any other on account of its quality." (John Adams' "Writings," vol. viii, p. 339.) Such facts are more than curious.

But more important than the Pacific States of the American Continent are the great Empires of Japan and China, with uncounted populations depending much on fish. In China one-tenth subsist on fish. Notwithstanding the considerable supplies at home, it does not seem impossible for an energetic and commercial people to find a market here of inconceivable magnitude, which will dwarf that original fur trade with China that was once so tempting.

From this survey you can all judge this question of the fisheries, which I only state without assuming to determine. You can judge if well-stocked fishing banks have been found under such conditions of climate and market as to supply a new and important fishery. Already the people of California have anticipated the answer, and their enterprise has arrested attention in Europe. The journal of Peterman, the "Geographische Mittheilungen," for the present year, which is the authentic German record of geographical science, borrows from a San Francisco paper to announce these successful voyages as the beginning of a new commerce. If this be so, as there is reason to believe, these coasts and seas will have a new value. The future only can disclose the form they may take. They may be a Newfoundland, a Norway, a Scotland, or perhaps a New England, with another Gloucester and another New Bedford.

Influence of Fisheries.

An eminent French writer, an enthusiast on fishes, Lacépède, has depicted the influence of fisheries, which he illustrates by the herring, calling it "one of those natural products whose use has decided the destiny of nations." Without adopting these strong words it is easy to see that such fisheries as seem about to be opened on the Pacific must exercise a wonderful influence over the population there, while they give a new spring to commerce and enlarge the national resources. In these aspects it is impossible to exaggerate. Fishermen are not as other men. They have a character of their own, taking its complexion from their life. In ancient Rome they had a peculiar holiday with games, known as "Piscatorii Ludi." The first among us in this pursuit were the Pilgrims, who even before they left Leyden looked to fishing for a support in their new home, on which King James remarked: "So God hath my soul, 'tis an honest trade; 'twas the Apostles' own calling." As soon as they reached Plymouth they began to fish, and not long afterwards appropriated the profits of the fisheries at Cape Cod to found a free school. From this Puritan origin are derived those fisheries which for a while were our chief commerce, and still continue an important element of national wealth. The cod fisheries of the United States are now valued at more than 2,000,000 dollars annually. Even they are inferior to the French fisheries, whose annual product is more than 3,000,000 dollars; and these again are small by the side of the British fisheries, whose annual product is not far from 25,000,000 dollars. Such an interest must be felt far and near, commercially and financially, while it contributes to the comfort of all. How soon it may prevail on the Pacific who can say? But this Treaty is the beginning.

Of course it is difficult to estimate what is so uncertain, or at least is prospective only.

Our own fisheries, now so considerable, were small in the beginning; they were small even when they inspired the eloquence of Burke in that most splendid page never equalled even by himself. But the Continental Congress, in its original instructions to its Commissioners for the negotiation of peace with Great Britain, required as a fundamental condition, next to independence, that these fisheries should be preserved unimpaired. While this proposition was under discussion Elbridge Gerry, who had grown up among the fishermen of Massachusetts, repelled the attacks upon their pursuit in words which are not out of place here. "It is not so much fishing," he said, "as enterprise, industry, employment. It is not so much fish; it is gold, the produce of that avocation. It is the employment of those who would otherwise be idle, the food of those who would otherwise be hungry, the wealth of those who would otherwise be poor." After debate it was resolved by Congress that "the common right of taking fish should in no case be given up." For this principle the eldest Adams contended with ability and constancy until it was fixed in the Treaty, where it stands side by side with the acknowledgment of independence.

In the discussions which ended thus triumphantly, the argument for the fisheries was stated most compactly by Ralph Izard, of South Carolina, in a letter to John Adams, dated at Paris, the 24th September, 1778; and what he said then may be repeated now :—

"Since the advantages of commerce have been well understood, the fisheries have been looked upon by the Naval Powers of Europe as an object of the greatest importance. The French have been increasing their fishery ever since the Treaty of Utrecht which has enabled them to rival Great Britain at sea. The fisheries of Holland were not only the first rise of the Republic, but have been the constant support of all her commerce and navigation. This branch of trade is of such concern to the Dutch that in their public prayers they are said to request the Supreme Being that it would please him to bless the Government, the Lords, the States, and also the fisheries. The fishery of Newfoundland appears to me to be a mine of infinitely greater value than Mexico and Peru. It enriches the proprietors, is worked at less expense, and is the source of naval strength and protection."—(John Adams' Works, vol. vii. p. 45.)

I have grouped these allusions that you may see how the fisheries of that day, though comparatively small, enlisted the energies of our fathers. Tradition confirms this record. The sculptured image of a cod hanging from the ceiling in the hall of the Massachusetts House of Representatives, where it was placed during the last century, constantly recalls this industrial and commercial staple with the great part which it performed. And now it is my duty to remind you that these fisheries, guarded so watchfully and vindicated with such conquering zeal, had a value prospective rather than present, or at least small compared with what it is now. Exact figures, covering the ten years between 1765 and 1775, show that during this period Massachusetts employed annually in the fisheries 665 vessels amounting to 25,620 tons, and only 4,405 men. In contrast with this interest, which seems so small, although at the time considerable, are the present fisheries of our country: and here again we have exact figures. The number of vessels in the cod fishery alone in 1861, just before the blight of the war reached this business, was 2,753 amounting to 137,665 tons, and with 19,271 men, being more than four times as many vessels and men, and more than five times as much tonnage, as for ten years preceding the Revolution was employed annually by Massachusetts, representing at that time the fishing interest of the country.

Small beginnings, therefore, are no discouragement to me, and I turn with confidence to the future. Already the local fisheries on this coast have developed among the generations of natives a singular gift in building and managing their small craft so as to excite the frequent admiration of voyagers. The larger fisheries there will naturally exercise a corresponding influence on the population destined to build and manage the larger craft. The beautiful baidar will give way to the fishing-smack, the clipper, and the steamer. All things will be changed in form and proportion; but the original aptitude for the sea will remain. A practical race of intrepid navigators will swarm the coast, ready for any enterprise of business or patriotism. Commerce will find new arms; the country new defenders; the national flag new hands to bear it aloft.

Summary.

Mr. President, I now conclude this examination. From a review of the origin of the Treaty, and the general considerations with regard to it, we have passed to an examination of these possessions under different heads, in order to arrive at a knowledge of their character and value; and here we have noticed the existing Government, which was found to be nothing but a Fur Company, whose only object is trade; then the population, where a very few Russians and Creoles are a scanty fringe to the aboriginal races; then the climate, a ruling influence, with its thermal current of ocean and its eccentric isothermal line, by which the rigours of that coast are tempered to a mildness unknown in the same latitude on the Atlantic side; then the vegetable products, so far as known, chief among which are forests of pine and fir waiting for the axe; then the mineral products, among which are coal and copper, if not iron, silver, lead, and gold, besides the two great products of New England, "granite and ice;" then the furs, including precious skins of the black fox and sea-otter, which originally tempted the Settlement, and have remained to this day the exclusive object of pursuit; and lastly, the fisheries, which, in waters superabundant with animal life beyond any of the globe, seem to promise a new commerce to the country. All these I have presented plainly and impartially, exhibiting my authorities as I proceeded. I have done little more than hold the scales. If these have inclined on either side it is because reason or testimony on that side was the weightier.

What remains to be done.

As these extensive possessions, constituting a corner of the continent, pass from the Imperial Government of Russia, they will naturally receive a new name. They will be no longer Russian America. How shall they be called? Clearly any name borrowed from classical history or from individual invention will be little better than a misnomer or a nickname unworthy of such an occasion. Even if taken from our own history it will be of doubtful taste. The name should come from the country itself. It should be indigenous, aboriginal, one of the autochthons of the soil. Happily such a name exists, which is as proper in sound as in origin. It appears from the Report of Cook, the illustrious navigator, to whom I have so often referred. that the euphonious name now applied to the peninsula which is the continental link of the Aleutian chain was the sole word used originally by the native islanders "when speaking of the American Continent in general, which they knew perfectly well to be a great land." It only remains that, following these natives, whose places are now ours, we too should call this "great land" Alaska.

Another change must be made without delay. As the Settlements of this coast came *eastward* from Russia, bringing with them the Russian flag Western time, the day is earlier by twenty-four hours with them than with us, so that their Sunday is our Saturday, and the other days of the week are in corresponding discord. This must be rectified according to the national meridian, so that there shall be the same Sunday for all, and the other days of the week shall be in corresponding harmony. Important changes must follow, of which this is typical. All else must be rectified according to the national meridian, so that within the sphere of our common country there shall be everywhere the same generous rule and one prevailing harmony. Of course, the unreformed Julian Calendar, received from Russia, will give place to ours ; old style yielding to new style.

An object of immediate practical interest will be the survey of the extended and indented coast by our own officers, bringing it all within the domain of science and assuring to navigation much-needed assistance, while the Republic is honoured by a continuation of national charts, where execution vies with science, and the art of engraving is the beautiful handmaid. Associated with this survey, and scarcely inferior in value, will be the examination of the country by scientific explorers, so that its geological structure may become known, with its various products, vegetable and mineral. But your best work and most important endowment will be the Republican Government, which, looking to a long future, you will organize, with schools free to all and with equal laws, before which every citizen will stand erect in the consciousness of manhood. Here will be a motive power, without which coal itself will be insufficient. Here will be a source of wealth more inexhaustible than any fisheries. Bestow such a Government, and you will bestow what is better than all you can receive, whether quintals of fish, sands of gold, choicest fur, or most beautiful ivory.

No. 7.

LEASE BY THE UNITED STATES TO THE ALASKA COMMERCIAL COMPANY.

THIS Indenture, in duplicate, made this 3rd day of August, A.D. 1870, by and between William A. Richardson, Acting Secretary of the Treasury, in pursuance of an Act of Congress, approved the 1st July, 1870, entitled "An Act to prevent the Extermination of Fur-bearing Animals in Alaska," and the Alaska Commercial Company, a Corporation duly established under the laws of the State of California, acting by John F. Miller, its President and Agent, in accordance with a Resolution of said Corporation, duly adopted at a meeting of its Board of Trustees, held the 31st January, 1870;

Witnesseth,—That the said Secretary hereby leases to the said Alaska Commercial Company, without power to transfer, for the term of twenty years, from the 1st day of May, 1870, the right to engage in the business of taking fur seals on the Islands of St. George and St. Paul, within the Territory of Alaska, and to send a vessel or vessels to said islands for the skins of such seals.

And the said Alaska Commercial Company, in consideration of their right under this lease, hereby covenant and agree to pay for each year during said term and in proportion during any part thereof, the sum of 55,000 dollars into the Treasury of the United States, in accordance with the regulations of the Secretary, to be made for this purpose under said Act, which payment shall be secured by deposit of United States' bonds to that amount; and also covenant and agree to pay annually into the Treasury of the United States, under said Rules and Regulations, a revenue tax or duty of 2 dollars upon each fur seal skin taken and shipped by them, in accordance with the provisions of the Act aforesaid; and also the sum of 62½ cents for each fur seal skin taken and shipped, and 55 cents per gallon for each gallon of oil obtained from said seals for sale on said islands and elsewhere, and sold by said Company. And also covenant and agree, in accordance with said Rules and Regulations, to furnish free of charge, the inhabitants of the Islands of St. Paul and St. George annually during said term, 25,000 dried salmon, 60 cords firewood, and a sufficient quantity of salt, and a sufficient number of barrels for preserving the necessary supply of meat.

And the said lessees also hereby covenant and agree during the term aforesaid, to maintain a school on each island, in accordance with said Rules and Regulations, and suitable for the education of the natives of said islands, for a period of not less than eight months in each year.

And the said lessees further covenant and agree not to kill upon said Island of St. Paul more than 75,000 fur seals, and upon the Island of St. George not more than 25,000 fur seals per annum; not to kill any fur seal upon the island aforesaid in any other month except the months of June, July, September and October of each year; not to kill such seals at any time by the use of firearms or other means tending to drive the seals from said islands; not to kill any female seal or any seal less than one year old; not to kill any seal in the waters adjacent to said islands or on the beaches, cliffs or rocks where they haul up from the sea to remain.

And the said lessees further covenant and agree to abide by any restriction or limitation upon the rights to kill seals under this lease, that the Act prescribes or that the Secretary of the Treasury shall judge necessary for the preservation of such seals.

And the said lessees hereby agree that they will not in any way sell, transfer or assign this lease, and that any transfer, sale or assignment of the same shall be void or of no effect.

And the said lessees further covenant and agree to furnish to the several masters of the vessels employed by them, certified copies of this lease, to be presented to the Government revenue officers for the time being in charge of said islands, as the authority of the said lessees for the landing and taking said skins.

And the said lessees further covenant and agree that they or their agents shall not keep, sell, give or dispose of any distilled spirits or spirituous liquors on either of said islands to any of the natives thereof, such person not being a physician furnishing the same for use as medicine.

And the said lessees further covenant and agree that this lease is accepted subject to all needful Rules and Regulations which shall at any time or times hereafter be made by the Secretary of the Treasury for the collection and payment of the rentals herein agreed to be paid by said lessees, for the comfort, maintenance, education and protection of the natives of said islands, and for carrying into effect all the provisions of the Act, aforesaid, and will abide by and conform to said Rules and Regulations.

And the said lessees, accepting this lease with a full knowledge of the provisions of the aforesaid Act of Congress, further covenant and agree that they will fulfil all the provisions, requirements and limitations of said Act, whether herein specifically set out or not.

In witness whereof the parties aforesaid have hereunto set their hands and seals, the day and year above written.

(Signed)   WILLIAM A. RICHARDSON, *Acting Secretary of the Treasury.*

ALASKA COMMERCIAL COMPANY.

(By JNO. F. MILLER, *President.*)

Executed in presence of J. H. SAVILLE.

No. 8.

ARTICLE FROM THE "FORUM," NOVEMBER 1889, BY PROFESSOR JAMES
B. ANGELL, RELATING TO AMERICAN RIGHTS IN BEHRING SEA.

ALASKA is now furnishing us with two international questions of some interest and consequence. The first concerns our right (freely exercised of late under orders of our Treasury Department) to seize foreign vessels engaged in catching fur-bearing seals in Behring Sea many miles away from land, and to send them into port for condemnation and forfeiture. The second concerns the determination of the boundary between Alaska and British America. The former is just now engaging public attention much more than the latter. Possibly the latter may prove both the more important and the more difficult. Naturally enough, some Canadians whose vessels have been seized, and others who wish to annoy the Macdonald Ministry, are using sharp language about the captures. Fortunately the British Government is proceeding with much deliberation and freedom from excitement. If we are reasonable, there is good ground to believe that we can come to an understanding with England and other nations that will secure all the protection we can properly ask for our seals.

What have we been doing to British vessels in Behring Sea? For more than three years armed vessels of our Revenue Marine Service have, in obedience to the commands of the Secretaries of the Treasury, captured British vessels when it was evident that they were catching seals in that sea, even though the vessels were 40, 50, 90 miles, or even farther from shore. These seizures have been made for alleged violation of Section 1956 of the Revised Statutes of the United States, which provides that "no person shall, without the consent of the Secretary of the Treasury, kill any otter, mink, marten, sable, fur-seal, or other fur-bearing animal within the limits of Alaska Territory, or in the waters thereof," under certain penalties.

II. F. French, Acting Secretary of the Treasury, 12th March, 1881, officially interpreted that expression, "in the waters thereof," as including all the waters in Behring Sea within our boundaries. He referred to the description of the western boundary-line of Alaska found in the Treaty of Cession by Russia, which reads as follows:—

"The western limit within which the territories and dominion conveyed are contained passes through a point in Behring Strait on the parallel of 65° 30' north latitude, at its intersection by the meridian which passes midway between the Islands of Krusenstern, or Ignalook, and the Island of Ratmanoff, or Noonarbook, and proceeds due north without limitation into the same Frozen Ocean. The same western limit, beginning at the same initial point, proceeds thence in a course nearly south-west, through Behring Strait and Behring Sea, so as to pass midway between the north-west point of the Island of St. Lawrence and the south-east point of Cape Choukotski, to the meridian of 172° west longitude; thence, from the intersection of that meridian, in a south-westerly direction, so as to pass midway between the Island of Attou and the Copper Island of the Kormandorski couplet or group, in the North Pacific Ocean, to the meridian of 193° west longitude, so as to include in the territory conveyed the whole of the Aleutian Islands east of that meridian."

Mr. French then added:—

"All the waters within that boundary to the western end of the Aleutian Archipelago and chain of islands are considered as comprised within the waters of Alaska Territory. All the penalties prescribed by law against the killing of fur-bearing animals would therefore attach against any violation of law within the limits before described."

Secretary Manning, in 1886, indorsed and adopted this view. Early in 1887 President Cleveland ordered the discontinuance of proceedings against three British sealers which had been seized, the discharge of the vessels, and the release of the persons arrested. But seizures did not cease. Indeed, Secretary Bayard announced to the British Minister that the above action was taken "without conclusion of any questions which may be found to be involved."

At the last Session of Congress an Act was passed (approved the 2nd March, 1889) "to provide for the protection of the salmon fisheries of Alaska." In its third section it provides that "Section 1956 of the Revised Statutes of the United States [quoted in part], above, is hereby declared to include and apply to all the dominions of the United States in the waters of the Behring Sea." It makes it the duty of the President each year to make proclamation accordingly.

On the 22nd March last President Harrison issued his Proclamation, warning "all persons against entering the waters of Behring Sea within the dominion of the United States for the purpose of violating the provisions of said Section 1956, Revised Statutes," and declaring that "all persons found to be or to have been engaged in any violation of the laws of the United States will be arrested and punished as above provided."

Now, whatever may be the nature of our acts of which the British complain, it is obvious that we have not been claiming an exclusive jurisdiction for all purposes over Behring Sea, as in 1821 Russia claimed it for 100 Italian miles from the coast all the way from Behring Strait down to the 51st degree of latitude. The Czar, by his Ukase, excluded foreigners from pursuing "commerce, whaling, fishing, and all other industry" in those waters and on the adjacent lands. Under Mr. French's ruling, followed by Mr. Manning, our revenue-cruizers have been directed to arrest foreign vessels only to prevent them from killing fur-bearing animals. The chief object of the legislation by Congress is to prevent the indiscriminate slaughter and early extinction of the fur-seals, which chiefly resort to the Pribyloff Islands to breed. If sealers are allowed to catch them *ad libitum*, while they are on their way to their breeding place, these animals will soon be exterminated, as they have been elsewhere. Therefore the number that the Alaska Commercial Company, which has the exclusive privilege of taking seals on the Islands of St. Paul and St. George of the Pribyloff group, is allowed by contract with the Government to catch is limited to 100,000 a-year. It is, of course, for the interest of many nations that the race of seals should not be destroyed. It is especially for the interest of Great Britain that the race should be perpetuated, for all the seal-skins procured by us in Behring Sea are sent to London to be dressed and prepared for use.

The question is, whether for this laudable purpose of preserving the fur-bearing seals from extinction, and maintaining our undisputed right to control the taking of these animals on the Pribyloff Islands, we may rightfully board, search, and seize foreign vessels in Behring Sea more than 3 miles away from land. The equal right of all nations to use the high seas for any lawful purpose of commerce, navigation, fishing, or hunting is now so universally recognized; the United States have been so constantly the staunch defender of this right; we have so vigorously opposed all attempts of Great Britain to search our vessels in time of peace; we have claimed so vehemently the right of fishing in Canadian waters sharply up to 3-mile line from shore, that obviously we must show some very plain and cogent reasons to justify our course in Behring Sea. What reasons have been or can be given?

Our Government has given, so far as is known, no other formal statement than that of Acting Secretary French (above quoted in part), to inform either our citizens or foreign Powers of the precise grounds on which the seizure of British sealers is to be justified. No defence of our action by Secretary Bayard, nor up to the time of this writing by Secretary Blaine or Secretary Windom, has been published.

But in our newspapers editorial writers or contributors have suggested lines of defence of our action. The ground they have generally taken as the strongest is that Russia exercised exclusive jurisdiction in Behring Sea, and that by the cession of Alaska she transferred to us the right to exercise the same jurisdiction. Undoubtedly, by the Edict of 1821, the Czar claimed the right to exclude foreign vessels from navigating that sea within 100 miles of the shore for any purpose; but through the pen of John Quincy Adams, Secretary of State, we stoutly and successfully resisted that claim. The first two sections of the Edict read as follows:—

"Section 1. The pursuits of commerce, whaling, and fishing, and of all other industry, on all islands, ports, and gulfs, including the whole of the north-west coast of America, beginning from Behring Strait to the 51st degree of northern latitude; also from the the Aleutian Islands to the eastern coast of Siberia, as well as along the Kurile Islands from Behring Strait to the south cape of the Island of Urup, viz., to 45 50' northern latitude, are exclusively granted to Russian subjects.

"Section 2. It is therefore prohibited to all foreign vessels not only to land on the coasts and islands belonging to Russia, as stated above, but also to approach them within 100 Italian miles. The transgressor's vessel is subject to confiscation along with the whole cargo."

Mr. Adams, replying to the note in which M. Poletica, the Russian Minister at Washington, communicated this Edict, said (25th February, 1822) that the President had seen with surprise this assertion of a territorial claim by Russia down to the 51st degree of latitude on our continent, and added: "To exclude the vessels of our citizens from the shore beyond the ordinary distance to which the territorial jurisdiction extends has excited still greater surprise."

It has been said by some that the controversy between us and Russia did not pertain to Behring Sea, and so that Mr. Adams' contention cannot be pleaded against a claim to jurisdiction by us now over that sea. It is true that the action of Russia in issuing the Edict was chiefly directed against alleged illicit trading by our citizens on the coasts below the Aleutian Islands. There was then little or no trade above them. But the language of the Edict plainly applies to what we call Behring Sea as well as to other parts of the Northern Pacific, although the name Behring Sea was then rarely, if ever, used to designate the waters which we know by that name. Mr. Adams, in sending instructions to Mr. Middleton, our Minister at St. Petersburgh, to guide him in negotiating the Treaty of 1824, wrote (22nd July, 1823) as follows:—

"From the tenour of the Ukase the pretensions of the Imperial Government extend to an exclusive territorial jurisdiction from the 45th degree of north latitude on the Asiatic coast to the latitude of 51° north on the western coast of the American continent;

and they assume the right of interdicting the navigation and the fishery of all other nations to the extent of 100 miles from the whole of that coast. The United States can admit no part of these claims."

And again, in a paper accompanying the above instructions, he said :—

"The right of navigation and of fishing in the Pacific Ocean, even upon the Asiatic coast north of latitude 45°, can as little be interdicted to the United States as that of traffic with the natives of North America."

After reading such language from Mr. Adams, can any one doubt what his answer would have been to a proposition by Russia to concede that the Pacific south of the 55th parallel was an open sea, but that the part north of it formed a closed sea, over which she had exclusive jurisdiction?

It may be worthy of notice that, although the Russians sought to exclude foreigners from within 100 miles of the coast, they did not absolutely base their action on the claim that the North Pacific was a closed sea. Affirming that the conditions might justify such a claim and absolute interdiction of the entrance of foreigners, they chose to set forth as the ground of the Edict the necessity of preventing illicit trade. But Mr. Adams thought it worth while to deny explicitly that they could maintain with any justice the claim that the North Pacific was a closed sea even if they had wished to do so.

The Treaty of 1824 secured to us the right of navigation and fishing "in any part of the great ocean commonly called the Pacific Ocean or South Sea," and (in Article IV) for ten years that of frequenting the interior seas, gulfs, harbours, and creeks upon the coast for the purpose of fishing and trading. At the expiration of the ten years Russia refused to renew this last provision, and it never was formally renewed. But, for nearly fifty years at least, American vessels have been engaged in taking whales in Behring Sea without being disturbed by the Russian Government. Long before the cession of Alaska to us, hundreds of our whaling vessels annually visited the Arctic Ocean and Behring Sea, and brought home rich cargoes. It would seem, therefore, that Russia regarded Behring Sea as a part of the Pacific Ocean, and not as one of the " interior seas," access to which was forbidden by the termination of the IVth Article of the Treaty. H. H. Bancroft, in his "History of Alaska," says that in 1842 the Russian Minister of Foreign Affairs explicitly refused to send cruizers to interfere with our whalemen in that sea on the ground that the Treaty gave us the right of fishing over the whole extent of the Pacific. Whether, therefore, we have regard to Mr. Adams' arguments or to the treatment of our whalers by Russia, it seems that we must find some other justification of our seizures of British sealers than the possession of the right through the cession of Alaska by Russia.

Can we sustain a claim that Behring Sea is a closed sea and so subject to our control? It is, perhaps, impossible to frame a definition of a closed sea which the publicists of all nations will accept. Vattel's closed sea is one "entirely inclosed by the land of a nation, with only a communication with the ocean by a channel, of which that nation may take possession." Hautefeuille substantially adopts this statement, asserting more specifically, however, that the channel must be narrow enough to be defended from the shores. Perels, one of the more eminent of the later German writers, practically accepts Hautefeuille's definition. But so narrow a channel or opening as that indicated by the eminent French writer can hardly be insisted on. Probably most authorities will regard it as a reasonable requirement that the entrance to the sea should be narrow enough to make the naval occupation of it easy or practicable. We, at least, may be expected to prescribe no definition which would make the Gulf of St. Lawrence a closed sea.

Behring Sea is not inclosed wholly by our territory. From the most western island in our possession to the nearest point on the Asiatic shore is more than 300 miles. From our most western island, Attou, to the nearest Russian island, Copper Island, is 183 miles. The sea from east to west measures about 1,100 miles, and from north to south fully 800 miles. The area of the sea must be at least two-thirds as great as that of the Mediterranean, and more than twice that of the North Sea. The Straits of Gibraltar are less than 9 miles wide. The chief entrance to the Gulf of St. Lawrence, which is entirely surrounded by British territory, is only about 50 miles in width. Behring sea is open on the north by the Straits, 36 miles wide, which form a passage-way to the Arctic Ocean. On what grounds and after what modern precedent we could set up a claim to hold this great sea, with its wide approaches, as a *mare clausum*, it is not easy to see.

Our Government has never formally set up the claim that it is a closed sea. Governor Boutwell, when Secretary of the Treasury, in 1872, speaking of intended expeditions of foreign sealers into Behring Sea, said :—

"I do not see that the United States would have the jurisdiction or power to drive off parties going up there for that purpose, unless they made such an attempt within a marine league of the shore."

Congress, guided by the caution of certain Senators, in its Act of the 2nd March, 1889, forbore to use language which might seem to apply the doctrine of *mare clausum* to Behring Sea. The House of Representatives did insert in the Bill a section beginning as follows :—

"Section 1956 of the Revised Statutes of the United States was intended to include and apply, and is hereby declared to include and apply, to all the waters of Behring Sea in Alaska embraced within the boundary-lines mentioned and described in the Treaty with Russia."

The Senate disagreeing with the House on the adoption of this language, a Committee of Conference agreed to the phraseology as it now stands in the Act :—

"Section 1956 of the Revised Statutes of the United States is hereby declared to include and apply to all the dominions of the United States in the waters of Behring Sea."

The President's Proclamation of the 21st March, 1889, merely recites Section 1956 of the Revised Statutes and the 3rd section of the Act of the 2nd March, and gives warning against "violation of the laws of the United States." But obviously neither the Act nor the Proclamation was intended to declare the doctrine of *mare clausum* to be applicable to Behring Sea. They merely affirm that we will exercise our authority in the execution of a certain law wherever our dominion extends in that sea. It is left to be determined, if need be, how far that dominion extends.

An argument for preventing the unrestrained hunting of seals in Behring Sea which our late Minister to Russia, Mr. Lothrop, heard presented by Russians, is of interest. Briefly stated, it is this : The seal fishery is the main resource of the people on the Asiatic shore of that sea for gaining a livelihood. Every people has conceded to it the control of such part of the sea contiguous to its coasts as is essential to the protection of the inhabitants. The common rights to the open sea must be enjoyed in ways compatible with the safety, and certainly with the existence, of the people on its shores. Hence, the Russians should control the seal fishery in their part of the sea.

No doubt the condition of the Siberians on that coast would present a strong case for generous action on the part of foreigners in abstaining from interference with their means of gaining a livelihood. By common consent, out of regard to the hardships of their life, fishermen are not disturbed in their pursuits in time of war. But can the Russian argument, even if it has validity for the Siberians, be used by us ? We have without any scruple for half a century taken whales in the seas adjacent to them. We can hardly assert with much plausibility that the members of the Alaska Commercial Company, which has the monopoly of seal-catching on and near the Pribyloff Islands, can plead, *in formâ pauperis*, for protection on grounds of charity.

It may be argued that, since most of the seals which are taken by the British breed on our soil in the Pribyloff Islands, we have an exclusive claim to them in the sea, or at any rate a right to protect them there from extinction. But some of them breed on Copper Island and Behring Island, both of which belong to Russia. How is it possible to maintain any claim to ownership in seals on the high seas under any principle of law applicable to wild animals ? We can acquire no property rights in animals *feræ naturæ* from their birth on our soil, except for the time that we hold them in our possession. A claim by Canada to the wild ducks hatched in her territory, after the birds have passed her boundary, would seem to be just as valid as ours to seals in the open sea.

I recall only one case which seems to furnish any analogy for the claim that we may regulate seal fishing in the open waters of Behring Sea. The British Government does regulate and control the pearl fisheries in the open sea from 8 to 20 miles west of the northern end of Ceylon. But it is to be presumed that this is done under sufferance of other Powers, because they have had no interest in interfering with the pursuit of the pearl divers. Should they claim the right to seek pearls in those waters, it is not easy to see how Great Britain could oppose any argument except that of long acquiescence by them in her exclusive possession of the pearl grounds ; and it is questionable whether that argument would have much weight.

It may be said that if we have no right to exclude other nations from taking seals in the open waters of Behring Sea, and if the Law and the Treasury Regulations, as they now stand, can be enforced against our own citizens in those same open waters, we are clearly discriminating against our own countrymen. The foreigners may kill seals at times and in places forbidden to us. This is true. It is one of the anomalies and embarrassments of the present situation.

On the whole, we find no good ground on which we can claim as a right the exclusion of foreigners from the open waters of Behring Sea for the purpose of protecting the seals. If we have any good ground, and are determined to stand on it, then we ought to proceed with more vigour in maintaining our policy. To send one little revenue-steamer, carrying a small crew, into Behring Sea, and to dispatch on each of the captured vessels one man, a common seaman, as a prize crew or commanding officer, is simply absurd. Each of the vessels seized, instead of coming within the jurisdiction of a United States' Court, goes to a British port, files its claim for damage with the British authorities, and prepares for another voyage to the same waters in which it was captured. If, however, we have no right to seize foreign vessels in the open waters of Behring Sea, then we ought to lose no time in negotiating with the interested Powers, especially Great Britain, Russia, and Japan, on the best method of preserving the seals from extermination, and of securing to ourselves what we have a right to retain. Those Powers showed, in the correspondence carried on with them by Secretary Bayard, their entire willingness to come to some understanding on the matter. It is so obviously for the interest of the above-named States that the seals should not be exterminated that it cannot be difficult to make some satisfactory adjustment of the question. The limits of this article compel brevity in treating the question of determining the boundary between Alaska and British America. The language of the Treaty of Cession in defining this boundary is copied from the Treaty of 1825 between Russia and Great Britain, Articles III and IV, as follows :—

"Article III. Commencing from the southernmost point of the island called Prince of Wales' Island, which point lies in the parallel of 54° 40′ north latitude, and between the 131st and 133rd degree of west longitude (meridian of Greenwich), the said line shall ascend to the north along the channel called Portland Channel as far as the point of the continent where it strikes the 56th degree of north latitude : and from this last-mentioned point the line of demarcation shall follow the summit of the mountains situated parallel to the coast as far as the point of intersection of the 141st degree of west longitude (of the same meridian) ; and finally, from the said point of intersection. the said meridian line of the 141st degree, in its prolongation as far as the Frozen Ocean, shall form the limit between the Russian and British possessions on the Continent of America to the north-west.

"Article IV. With reference to the line of demarcation laid down in the preceding Article, it is understood :

"First, that the island called Prince of Wales' Island shall belong wholly to Russia. [Now by this cession to the United States.]

"Secondly, that whenever the summit of the mountains that extend in a direction parallel to the coast from the 56th degree of north latitude to the point of intersection of the 141st degree of west longitude shall prove to be at the distance of more than 10 marine leagues from the ocean, the limit between the British possessions and the line of coast which is to belong to Russia, as above mentioned, shall be formed by a line parallel to the winding of the coast, which shall never extend the distance of 10 marine leagues therefrom."

The line thus indicated has never been surveyed. The importance of determining it before long is obvious. If, as is reported, there are valuable mines near the boundary, it is essential to the preservation of the rights of property and of life that the limits of the jurisdiction of the two nations be fixed.

The principal difficulties which have been suggested in determining and marking the boundary are the following : Some of the Canadians have maintained (I am not aware that the British Government has taken such a position) that our maps do not correctly indicate the initial point of the line at Portland Channel. Their contention is probably without good ground. Again, while the Treaty provides that the line " shall follow the summit of the mountains," it is affirmed, and so far as we now know with probable truthfulness, that the mountains do not form a range, but are so scattered here and there that it is impracticable to make a line that shall comply with the Treaty. Furthermore, suppose it were practicable to run a line on the summit, the coast is so irregular and so indented with bays that it may not be easy to agree on a line from which to lay off the 10 marine leagues referred to in the second paragraph of Article IV.

But even if all these obstacles are removed, the actual labour and cost of running the line in this wilderness will be very great. In 1872 our engineering officers estimated that the cost would be 1,500,000 dollars, and the time required for the field work nine years, and for the mapping one more year. If, as seems probable from our scanty information, the line described is an impossible one to run, we shall have to agree on an arbitrary line run from some point in the south of the territory to some point in the neighbourhood of the Chilkat Pass, so as to give us substantially the territory intended to be conveyed by Article IV. But it seems desirable that we should make some preliminary surveys before we take any decisive action. The British, who have had trading and scientific expeditions exploring British Columbia. doubtless know more of the region under consideration than we. They are ready to begin negotiations at once. Congress should not delay action. Our experience has shown us that boundary questions are not speedily settled. After a century of effort, we have at last determined nearly all our boundaries except this between Alaska and British Columbia. If we begin at once, it will be years before we shall have determined and marked this so that the lumberman and the miner on the Alaska mountains will know whether they are amenable to the authority of the United States or to that of Great Britain. It is the part of wisdom to settle this question of boundary while the debatable region is an unoccupied wilderness, rather than to wait until conflicts have arisen and blood has been shed.

(Signed)   JAMES B. ANGELL.

www.ingramcontent.com/pod-product-compliance
Lightning Source LLC
Chambersburg PA
CBHW031438270326
41930CB00007B/765